West

D1187375

IN THE CAUSE OF LIBERTY

Published in Conjunction with
The American Civil War Center at Historic Tredegar

In Can West —

IN THE CAUSE OF
LIBERTY

—————— HOW THE CIVIL WAR ——————
REDEFINED AMERICAN IDEALS

EDITED BY

WILLIAM J. COOPER, JR.

AND

JOHN M. McCARDELL, JR.

JL McCardell

Huntingdon

March 2012

⸭

LOUISIANA STATE UNIVERSITY PRESS

BATON ROUGE

Published with the assistance of the V. Ray Cardozier Fund

Published by Louisiana State University Press
Copyright © 2009 by Louisiana State University Press
All rights reserved
Manufactured in the United States of America
First printing

DESIGNER: Michelle A. Neustrom
TYPEFACE: Adobe Caslon Pro, No. 1 Type
PRINTER AND BINDER: Thomson-Shore, Inc.

LIBRARY OF CONGRESS CATALOGING-IN-PUBLICATION DATA

In the cause of liberty : how the Civil War redefined American ideals /
edited by William J. Cooper, Jr., and John M. McCardell, Jr.
    p. cm.
"Published in conjunction with The American Civil War Center at
Historic Tredegar."
Includes bibliographical references and index.
ISBN 978-0-8071-3444-3 (cloth : alk. paper)
    1. United States—History—Civil War, 1861–1865—Influence.
2. National characteristics, American. 3. Social values—United
States—History. I. Cooper, William J. (William James), 1940– II.
McCardell, John. III. American Civil War Center at Historic Tredegar.
E468.9.I5 2009
973.7—dc22
                                                    2008050906

Contents

Introduction

WILLIAM J. COOPER, JR., AND
JOHN M. McCARDELL, JR.

The Civil War is the central event in American history because it brought about fundamental change. Before the war the institution of racial slavery was legal in fifteen states plus the District of Columbia and exercised a potent influence on the politics and economy of the entire country. Union victory in 1865 meant the end of slavery, a result confirmed by the Thirteenth Amendment, added to the Constitution in that year. The subsequent Fourteenth (1868) and Fifteenth (1870) Amendments redefined citizenship, guaranteeing basic rights to African Americans, including former slaves.

Before 1860 the idea that the United States was a compact of the states, that the states had created the country, was widespread. The legitimacy of the doctrine of secession, that a state had a constitutional right to leave the Union, had considerable intellectual and political standing. Many Americans used the phrase *the United States are,* signaling plurality, rather than the phrase *the United States is,* signaling unity. The outcome of the war ensured that the latter usage would prevail. Since 1865 no one has seriously spoken about the right of secession. No one questions the United States as an indivisible nation.

The essays in this volume address the momentous impact of the war by looking at three Americas: antebellum, wartime, postbellum. Moreover, they recognize the critical role in this transformative era of three sets of Americans—white northerners, white southerners, and African Americans, North and South. These groups responded to this time in different ways, ways that the authors chart and explore.

The essays fall into five different categories. The first, by James McPherson, considers the general import of the war. The next two, by Peter Onuf and Christa Dierksheide and Sean Wilentz, look at central questions affecting all Americans in the prewar years. Then, Richard Carwardine, George C. Rable, and Chandra Manning focus on critical matters relating to the Union, the Confederacy, and African Americans during the war. Following these, Nina Silber, Fitzhugh Brundage, and David Blight discuss how the country dealt with the meaning of the war and its memory for North, South, and African Americans after 1865. In conclusion, John M. McCardell, Jr., suggests the challenges and rewards of using the three perspectives for studying this period and how they relate to the American Civil War Center at Tredegar.

All but one of these essays originated as papers for a symposium sponsored by the American Civil War Center at Tredegar in Richmond, Virginia, in March 2007, and the single exception, Fitzhugh Brundage's, originated as a paper for another Center program. A museum located on the site of the Tredegar Iron Works in Richmond, the Center is unique. It is dedicated to telling the story of the Civil War era and the titanic issues and questions surrounding the war before, during, and after the fighting from three perspectives: Union, or northern; Confederate, or southern; and African American. The Center insists that relating or interrelating all three perspectives simultaneously in the same place is essential for comprehending the magnitude of the war and its impact. In the museum itself the exhibits, the narrative line, and other features do just that.

An integral part of the Center's mission is to encourage and disseminate scholarship on the Civil War era. The symposium that generated this book testifies to that commitment. At this point we would be remiss if we did not acknowledge the enormous contribution of the founding director and first president of the Center, H. Alexander Wise Jr. Alex had a vision for the Center that was inclusive and grounded in sound scholarship and what it could accomplish. His vision became reality.

IN THE CAUSE OF LIBERTY

1

The Civil War and the
Transformation of America

JAMES M. McPHERSON

The tragic irony of the American Civil War is that both sides professed to fight for the heritage of liberty bequeathed to them by the Founding Fathers, who were, in the eyes of the Civil War generation, the "Greatest Generation" of Americans, having founded the nation they inherited with a sacred duty to uphold the principles of 1776. North and South alike wrapped themselves in that mantle of 1776, but the two sides interpreted this heritage in opposite ways, and at first neither side included the slaves in the vision of liberty for which they fought. But the slaves did, and by the time of Lincoln's Gettysburg Address in 1863 the northerners were fighting not merely for the liberty bequeathed to them by the Founders but also for "a new birth of freedom." These multiple and varying meanings of freedom and the ways in which they dissolved and reformed in kaleidoscopic patterns during the war provide the central meaning of the war for the American experience. Therefore we need to examine the three meanings of liberty during the war.

First, the Confederate perspective. When the "Black Republican" Abraham Lincoln won the presidency in 1860 on a platform excluding slavery from the territories, southern whites compared him to George III and declared their independence from "oppressive Yankee rule." "The same spirit of freedom and independence that impelled our Fathers to the separation from the British Government," proclaimed secessionists, would impel the "liberty loving people of the South" to separation from the government of the United States. A Georgia secessionist declared that southerners would be either *"slaves in the Union or freemen out of it."* From "the high and solemn motive of defending and protecting the rights which our fathers bequeathed to us," declared Jefferson Davis, let us "renew such sacrifices as our fathers made to holy cause of constitutional liberty."[1]

Many Confederate soldiers echoed this rhetoric in their letters and diaries. A Texas soldier wrote in 1861 that his forefathers in 1776 had established "Liberty and freedom in this western world" and that he was "now enlisted in 'The Holy Cause of Liberty and Independence' again." An Alabama corporal celebrated the Fourth of July in 1863 by writing that he was fighting for "the same principles which fired the hearts of our ancestors in the revolutionary struggle."[2]

In the minds of most southern soldiers, this struggle for liberty and self-government merged with the most powerful motive of all for fighting: to defend hearth and home from an invading enemy. In 1862 a captain in a Tennessee regiment proclaimed that he was fighting to defend "the invaded soil of our bleeding Country." The South must not "pass under Lincoln rule without the fall of a far greater number of his hireling horde than have yet been slain at the hands of those who are striking for their liberties, homes, firesides, wives and children."[3]

Most northerners ridiculed southerners' professions that they were fighting for the ideals of 1776. That was "a libel upon the whole character and conduct of the men of '76," wrote the antislavery poet and journalist William Cullen Bryant. The Founding Fathers had fought "to establish the rights of man . . . and principles of universal liberty." The South, insisted Bryant, had seceded "not in the interest of general humanity, but of a domestic despotism. . . . Their motto is not liberty, but slavery." Northerners did not deny the right of revolution in principle; the United States had been founded on that right, and northerners as much as southerners were heirs of that legacy. But "the right of revolution," wrote Lincoln in 1861, "is never a legal right. . . . At most, it is but a moral right, when exercised for a morally justifiable cause. When exercised without such a cause revolution is no right, but simply a wicked exercise of physical power." In Lincoln's judgment, secession was just such a wicked exercise. The event that precipitated it was Lincoln's election by a constitutional majority. As northerners saw it, the southern states, having controlled the national government for most of the previous two generations through their domination of the Democratic Party, had decided to leave the Union just because they had lost an election.[4]

For Lincoln and the North it was the Union, not the Confederacy, that represented the ideals of 1776. The republic established by the Founding Fathers as a bulwark of liberty was a fragile experiment in a nineteenth-century world bestrode by kings, queens, emperors, czars, and petty dictators. Throughout history, most republics had eventually been overthrown. Some Americans still alive in 1861 had seen French republics succumb twice to emperors and once to the restoration of the Bourbon monarchy. The hopes of 1848 for the triumph of popular governments in Europe had been crushed by the counterrevolutions that brought a conservative reaction in the Old World. Republican governments in Latin America seemed to come and go with bewildering frequency. The United States in 1861 represented, in Lincoln's words, "the last, best hope" for the survival of republican liberties in the world. Would that hope also collapse? "Our popular government has often been called an experiment," Lincoln told Congress on the Fourth of July 1861. If the Confederacy succeeded in splitting the country in two, it would set a fatal precedent that would destroy the experiment. By invoking this precedent, a minority in the future might secede from the Union whenever it did not like what the majority stood for, until the United States fragmented into a multiple of petty, squabbling autocracies. "The central idea pervading this struggle," said Lincoln, "is the necessity . . . of proving that popular government is not an absurdity. We must settle this question now, whether in a free government the minority have the right to break up the government whenever they choose."[5]

Many Union soldiers echoed Lincoln's statement that secession was "the essence of anarchy." An Indiana lawyer explained to his pacifist wife in April 1861 why he felt compelled to enlist. "It is better to have war for one year than anarchy & revolution for fifty years—if the government should suffer rebels to go on with their work with impunity there would be no end to it & in a short time we would be without any law or order." Union soldiers also invoked the legacy of the Founding Fathers. They believed they had a solemn duty to defend the nation sanctified by the blood and sacrifice of that heroic generation of 1776. "Our fathers made this country," wrote a soldier in the Twelfth Ohio Infantry, "we their children are to save it." A farmer's son who enlisted in the Tenth Wisconsin explained that he had done so because "this second war I consider equally as holy as the first [the Revolution] by which we gained those liberties and privileges" now threatened by "this monstrous rebellion."[6]

Freedom for the slaves was not part of the liberty the North fought for in 1861. That was not because the Lincoln administration supported slavery; quite the contrary. Slavery was "an unqualified evil to the negro, the white man, and the State," said Lincoln on many occasions in words that expressed the sentiments of most northern Republicans. "The monstrous injustice of slavery . . . deprives our republican example of its just influence in the world—enables the enemies of free institutions, with plausibility, to taunt us as hypocrites." Yet in his first inaugural address Lincoln declared that he had "no purpose, directly or indirectly, to interfere with slavery in the States where it exists." He reiterated this pledge in his first message to Congress on 4 July 1861, when the Civil War was nearly three months old.[7]

What explains this apparent inconsistency? The answer lies in the Constitution and in the northern polity of 1861. Lincoln was bound by a constitution that protected slavery in any state where citizens wanted it. The republic of liberty for whose preservation the North was fighting had been a republic in which slavery was legal everywhere in 1776. That was the great American paradox—a land of freedom based on slavery. Even in 1861, four states that remained loyal to the Union were slave states, and the Democratic minority in the free states opposed any move to make this war for the Union a war against slavery.

But as the war went on, the slaves themselves took the first step toward making it a war against slavery. They saw the Union army as an army of liberation before that army itself did. Entering into Union lines by the thousands, they voted with their feet for freedom. As enemy property, they could be confiscated by Union forces as "contraband of war." This stratagem was the thin edge of the wedge that finally shattered that American paradox. By 1863 a series of congressional acts, plus Lincoln's Emancipation Proclamation radically enlarged Union war aims. The North henceforth fought not merely to restore the old Union, not merely to ensure that the nation born in 1776 "shall not perish from the earth," but also to give that nation "a new birth of freedom." The fighting of two hundred thousand black soldiers helped ensure that it would not be a stillbirth.

Northern victory in the Civil War settled two fundamental, festering issues that had been left unresolved by the Revolution of 1776: first, whether this fragile republican experiment called the United States would survive as one nation; and second, whether the house divided would continue to endure half slave and half free. Both of these issues had remained open questions until 1865. Many Americans had doubted the republic's survival; many European conservatives had gleefully predicted its demise. Some Americans had advocated the right of secession and periodically threatened to invoke it, and eleven states did invoke it in 1861. But since 1865 no state or region has seriously threatened secession, not even during the decade of "massive resistance" to desegregation from 1954 to 1964. Before 1865 the United States, boasted "land of liberty," had been the largest slaveholding country in the world. Since 1865 that particular "monstrous injustice" and "hypocrisy" has existed no more.

In the process of preserving the Union of 1776 while purging it of slavery, the Civil War also transformed it. Before 1861 *United States* was a plural noun, as in "The United States have a republican form of government." Since 1865 *United States* has been a singular noun. The North went to war to preserve the Union; it ended by creating a nation. This transformation can be traced in Lincoln's most important wartime addresses. In his first inaugural address the word *Union* occurred twenty times and the word *nation* not once. In Lincoln's first message to Congress, on 3 July 1861, he used *Union* thirty-two times and *nation* only three times. In his famous public letter of 22 August 1862 to Horace Greeley concerning slavery and the war, Lincoln spoke of the Union eight times and the nation not at all. But fifteen months later, in the Gettysburg Address, he did not refer to the Union at all but used the word *nation* five times. And in his second inaugural address, looking back over the trauma of the past four years, Lincoln spoke of one side seeking to dissolve the Union in 1861 and the other side accepting the challenge of war to preserve the nation.

The decentralized antebellum republic, in which the post office was the only agency of national government that touched the average citizen, was transformed by the crucible of war into a centralized polity that taxed people directly and created an internal revenue bureau to collect the taxes, expanded the jurisdiction of federal courts, created a national currency and a federally chartered banking system, drafted men into the army, and created the Freedmen's Bureau, the first national agency for social welfare. Eleven of the first twelve amendments to the Constitution had limited the powers of the national government;

six of the next seven, starting with the Thirteenth Amendment in 1865, radically expanded those powers at the expense of the states. The first three of these postwar amendments transformed 4 million slaves into citizens and voters within five years, the most rapid and fundamental social transformation in American history—even if the nation did backslide on part of this commitment for three generation after 1877.

From 1789 to 1861 a southern slaveholder had been president of the United States two-thirds of the time, and two-thirds of the Speakers of the House and presidents pro tem of the Senate had also been southerners. Twenty of the thirty-five Supreme Court justices during that period had been from the South, which always had a majority on the Court before 1861. After the Civil War, a century passed before another resident of a southern state was elected president. For half a century after the war only one southerner served as Speaker of the House and none as president pro tem of the Senate. Only five of the twenty-six Supreme Court justices appointed during that half-century were southerners. The institutions and ideology of a plantation society and a slave system that had dominated half of the country before 1861 and sought to dominate more went down with a great crash in 1865 and were replaced by the institutions and ideology of free-labor entrepreneurial capitalism. For better or worse, the flames of the Civil War forged the framework of modern America.

The last point requires some elaboration. Before 1865 two socioeconomic and cultural systems had competed for dominance within the body politic of the United States. Although in retrospect the triumph of free-labor capitalism seems to have been inevitable, that was by no means clear for most of the antebellum generation. Not only did the institutions and ideology of the rural, agricultural, plantation South, based on slave labor, dominate the U.S. government during most of that time, but the territory of the slave states also considerably exceeded that of the free states before 1859, and the southern drive for further territorial expansion seemed more aggressive than that of the North. Most of the slave states seceded from the United States in 1861 not only because they feared the potential threat to the long-term survival of slavery posed by Lincoln's election but also because they looked forward to the expansion of a dynamic, independent Confederacy into new territory by the acquisition of Cuba and perhaps more of Mexico and Central America. It is quite possible that if the Confederacy had prevailed in the 1860s, the United States might never have emerged as the world's leading industrial as well as agricultural producer by the end of the nineteenth century. That it did happen is certainly one of the most important legacies of the Civil War, not only for America but for the world.

At the same time, however, the war left the South impoverished, its agricultural economy in shambles, and the freed slaves in a limbo of segregation and second-class citizenship after the failure of Reconstruction in the 1870s to fulfill the promise of civil and political equality embodied in the Fourteenth and Fifteenth Amendments.

Yet all was not lost. Those amendments remained in the Constitution, and the legacy of national unity, a strong national government, and a war for freedom inherited from the triumph of the 1860s was revived again in the civil rights movement of the 1960s, which finally began the momentous process of making good on the promises of a century earlier. Even though many white southerners for generations lamented the cause they had lost in 1865—indeed, mourned the world they had lost, a world they romanticized into a vision of moonlight and magnolias—white as well as black southerners today are probably better off because they lost that war than they would have been if they had won it.

The story of the Civil War and of its legacy is therefore three intertwined stories from three perspectives that initially were separate but increasingly have merged over the past 140 years. There are the northern perspective of a war for national unity; the southern white perspective of a war for home and home rule; and an African American perspective of a war for freedom. By 1863 the first and third of these perspectives merged in a war for Union and freedom. The second perspective has been more complex and clouded, but that complexity makes it all the more important to unravel the story and to understand the values of a rural society and cultural nationalism in the South that were uprooted by the war but have survived in altered form and have done much to enrich as well as to trouble the nation's cultural heritage.

Until the opening of the American Civil War Center at Tredegar in October 2006 no single venue brought these three stories and three legacies together in a meaningful way. This museum has remedied that defect in our understanding of our shared heritage. Richmond, Virginia, is an ideal setting for the Center. The Confederate capital and its largest manufacturing city, Richmond was also the principal target of the Union's largest army, and its defense was the main task of the Confederacy's best army. When the city finally fell after four bloody years, the fall of the Confederacy itself soon followed. One day after the capture of Richmond, President Abraham Lincoln visited the city and was enthusiastically welcomed by its black population, now free. There is no better place to tell the three intertwined stories of the war, to understand how the conflict unfolded as it did and how that unfolding laid the basis for the country we live in today.

2

Slaveholding Nation, Slaveholding Civilization

CHRISTA DIERKSHEIDE AND PETER S. ONUF

On the eve of South Carolina's secession from the Union, Robert Barnwell Rhett predicted what a historian writing in the year 2000 might say about the antebellum South: "Extending their empire across this continent to the Pacific, and down through Mexico to the other side of the great gulf, and over the isles of the sea," Rhett's future historian reported, southerners "established an empire and wrought out a civilization which has never been equaled or surpassed." They "presented to the world the glorious spectacle of a free, prosperous and illustrious people," providentially destined to become the most civilized nation on earth.[1] The foundation of southern greatness was the institution of slavery. As James Henry Hammond told the British abolitionist Thomas Clarkson in 1845, "American slaveholders ... stand in the broadest light of the knowledge, civilization, and improvement of the age."[2]

Proslavery polemicists knew that such claims would provoke a hostile, even incredulous response elsewhere in the "civilized world." Until very recently, southerners themselves generally acknowledged, or at least did not contest, the conventional understanding that slavery was an archaic, unjust institution. Enlightened southerners of the founding generation argued eloquently for ending the slave trade, and a few bold spirits even looked forward to the emancipation and expatriation of the existing slave population. Yet the antislavery consensus was tenuous at best. The comforting notion that European slave traders were responsible for American slavery, as Jefferson claimed in his draft of the Declaration of Independence, could not be reconciled with the

economic realities of plantation societies. Independent Americans did
not constitute a single people with a single destiny. The United States
was instead a fragile union of semi-sovereign states, some heavily reliant on slave labor, that periodically threatened to collapse. When the
end of the Napoleonic Wars promised a new epoch of international
peace, the Union's provisions for collective security seemed less urgent.
Southerners were less apologetic about the consolidation and expansion of slavery: perhaps, they began to argue, it was slavery, and not the
Constitution, that guaranteed America's future prosperity and power.
Slavery was the bedrock, the "cornerstone," of a great nation that would
promote the progress of Christianity and civilization throughout the
world.[3]

Patriotic southerners came to reconcile slavery with Revolutionary
Americans' vaulting faith in the new nation's progressive role in world
history. Between the American Revolution and the Civil War, the idea
of civilization itself proved to be protean, subject to progressive redefinition. In the years leading up to independence, colonists charged that
the British monarch had both reduced them to "slavery" and populated
their shores with enslaved Africans. The king had barbarized his imperial possessions, hindering their moral and political development. The
Revolution would redeem the New World from despotism and corruption and enable Americans to claim their rightful place in the family
of civilized nations. In breaking with Britain, Revolutionary Americans thus would forge closer relations with civilized Europe. "Civilization" was unitary, the shared European legacy of the classical world and
Christendom that enabled modern nations to achieve unprecedented
levels of wealth, refinement, and power.

This monolithic conception of civilization did not survive the great
upheavals of the age that the American Revolution initiated. The "Age
of the Democratic Revolution," to borrow Robert Palmer's title, frac-
tured the old regime, juxtaposing resurgent aristocracy against insurgent democratic forces and giving rise to new national solidarities.[4]
Increasingly, "civilization" was pluralized and nationalized, now manifest in the distinctive history and destiny of particular peoples. When
Americans began to think of the United States as a "great nation" in
the antebellum years, they attributed their ascendancy to a providential combination of nature's bounty and their own genius for progress
and improvement. As they secured their own happiness, they shared

the gifts of Christian civilization with barbarous peoples in their own midst, Indians and black slaves. Antebellum Americans congratulated themselves on taking a leading role in the progress of civilization, even as Europe—civilization's former home—was torn apart by the savage struggles of the Revolutionary age and the ultimate triumph of reactionary forces. Unlike their provincial and Revolutionary predecessors, patriotic Americans of the antebellum decades did not look across the Atlantic for cultural cues. They discovered the sources of national greatness in the "chosen country" that spread out before them, "with room enough for our descendants to the thousandth and thousandth generation."[5] And for visionary, slaveholding southerners like Hammond the key to unlocking the continent's resources was chattel slavery, an institution that a previous generation had presumed or pretended to despise.[6]

THE PROBLEM OF AFRICA IN AMERICA

American colonists had eagerly sought out African slaves to labor in their tobacco, rice, or sugar fields.[7] And yet when Anglo-Americans declared themselves an independent people they minimized their own responsibility for a barbarous and immoral institution that enlightened Europeans now rejected. In their benighted, provincial subjection, colonists had not recognized the evils of slavery. "Nursed and educated in the daily habit of seeing the degraded condition, both bodily and mental, of those unfortunate" slaves, Jefferson recalled, his countrymen never questioned the institution: "the quiet and monotonous course of colonial life . . . disturbed no alarm" and prompted "little reflection on the value of liberty." Yet with the Revolution, the most enlightened Virginians came to recognize slavery as a moral evil and to see that the ultimate success of their republican experiment depended on eliminating the institution.[8]

Ending the transatlantic slave trade was a critical first step in purging survivals of Old World barbarism from the American continent. The trade in human beings that had created a vast enslaved population had been imposed on the colonies by the mother country in its own selfish interest. George III had rebuffed colonists' efforts to regulate the trade. In 1774 citizens of Prince George's County, Virginia, testified that the "African slave trade is injurious to this Colony, obstructs the population of it by freemen, prevents manufacturers and other useful emigrants from Europe from settling amongst us, and occasions an annual increase of the balance of trade against this Colony."[9] And yet, the jurist St. George Tucker recalled, "no exertion to abolish, or even check the progress of, slavery, in Virginia" received "the smallest countenance from the crown."[10] The same year that Prince George's citizens sent their petition across the Atlantic, Jefferson indicted George III in his *Summary View* for preferring the "immediate advantages of a few British corsairs to the lasting interests of the American states, and to the rights of human nature deeply wounded by this infamous practice."[11] By perpetuating the transatlantic slave trade, George III had violated European norms of civility.[12] As Jefferson wrote in his draft of the Declaration, the British monarch had "waged cruel war against human nature itself, violating its most sacred rights of life & liberty in the persons of a distant people who never offended him, captivating & carrying them into slavery in another hemisphere."[13] George III's continued reliance upon the African slave trade was, many patriots believed, symptomatic of Britain's regression away from civilization; it was the fatal flaw that inevitably would retard, even reverse, the empire's progress.

In withdrawing from the British Empire and therefore, they imagined, from the African slave trade, Americans located themselves within a new trajectory of historical development. Scottish Enlightenment thinkers from David Hume to Adam Ferguson and Adam Smith outlined the stages of civilization, from hunter-gatherer to pastoral, to agricultural, and finally commercial. The Scots were both universalist and nationalist, projecting identical stages of development for all peoples, while celebrating Britain's unique achievements. New World provincials questioned the applicability of the Scots' "conjectural history," denying that their own societies were bound to follow the British model and thus remain at a perpetual disadvantage.[14] Even worse, French natural philosophers, including Abbé Raynal and the Comte de Buffon, questioned whether any kind of civilization could be effected in the New World. In Raynal's estimation, "l'Amerique n'ait pas encore produit un bon poëte, un habile mathematicien, un homme de genie dans un seul arte, ou une seule science." Jefferson protested that "this reproach is as unjust as it is unkind," for "America contributes its full share" of "geniuses." Americans were neither "beyond the line" of civility nor yoked to British standards of civilization. The United States instead sought recognition by, and inclusion within, the family of civilized nations.[15]

Leading American patriots insisted that continuing involvement in the foreign slave trade impeded America's development as a nation. In a 1793 speech, the New England grammarian Noah Webster emphasized the degrading effects of slavery and the slave trade on the morals of South Carolinians and Georgians. Because "slavery discourages agriculture and manufactures" even as it subverted the new nation's "moral character," abolition would not be "materially prejudicial" to southerners' interests. The end of the transatlantic trade would instead trigger the emancipation and repatriation of African slaves, the culminating stage of American progress toward civility.[16] Some southerners agreed. Henry Laurens, the South Carolinian slave dealer and former president of the Continental Congress, had once urged the direct importation of slaves from Bance Island to Charles Town, reporting to his English partner Richard Oswald in 1768 "that this will be the best Market for Africans . . . of any in America."[17] Yet on the eve of the Revolution, Laurens withdrew from the trade. "The African Trade is So repugnant to my disposition & my plan for future Life," he wrote in 1774, "that it Seems as if nothing but dire necessity could drive me to it."[18] As Laurens told his son John, he was not "one of those who dare trust in Providence for defence & security of their own Liberty while they enslave . . . thousands who are as well intitled to freedom as themselves."[19] Ending the importation of slaves was a crucial stage in American development; in time, Laurens believed, slavery itself would be expunged from the continent.

Enlightened patriots argued that the slave trade had to be reversed and recast as legitimate commerce. Advocates of abolishing the slave trade also supported the colonization of Africans outside the boundaries of the Union. What was once a barbaric traffic *in* Africans would now become free commerce *with* Africans, thus enabling Americans to fulfill their destiny as a "commercial people" and advance to the highest stage of moral development. In 1791 the New England minister James Dana implored Americans "to banish *all* slavish principles, and assert our liberty as men, citizens and Christians."[20] America might be redeemed when that "inhumane commerce" was replaced by a virtuous, reciprocally beneficial trade with Africa. Another clergyman, James Swan, promised that such trade would "be a means of peopling, and of cultivating" Africa so that it would yield "as great abundance as the *East-Indies.*" Legitimate commerce would "introduce the christian religion" among the Africans, thus "bringing about the more civilized arts and sciences." By civilizing the "captives" of Africa, Anglo-Americans would themselves be redeemed from the sin and barbarism of the slave trade.[21] The theologian Samuel Hopkins agreed that abolition would render Americans "happy . . . as a people and a nation" and "unite" them "from motives of justice and benevolence." An end to the slave trade and the beginning of free commerce would "produce a temporal good and prosperity" and "atone for the evils of the Slave-Trade and slavery."[22]

Enlightened southern slaveowners agreed that the trade had to be ended and Africans sent back to their homeland. Ferdinando Fairfax suggested the "propriety, and even necessity of removing" African slaves "to a distance from this country." Fairfax believed that sending former American slaves to Africa would, "from their industry, and by commercial intercourse, make us ample amends for our expenses, and be enabled to live without our protection." "After some time," he predicted, these former slaves would "become an independent nation."[23] The jurist St. George Tucker pinned his hopes on slaves' colonization beyond the "limits" of the Union: "We might reasonably hope, that time would . . . remove from us a race of men, whom we wish not to incorporate with us." And in 1803 the Virginia slaveowner and agriculturist John Taylor mused that "if England and America would erect and foster a settlement of free negroes in some fertile part of Africa," slavery and the slave trade "might then be gradually re-exported, and philanthropy gratified by a slow re-animation of the virtue, religion, and liberty of the negroes."[24]

Abolishing the "foreign" slave trade and expelling Africans from the Union would eliminate dangerous influences that jeopardized Americans' security as well as their claims to civility. No Revolutionary patriot seriously contemplated large-scale emancipation on American soil. As the South Carolina planter Francis Kinloch told Jefferson after reading his *Notes,* "It is not easy to get rid of old prejudices, and the word 'emancipation' operates like an apparition upon a South Carolina planter."[25] Kinloch agreed with Jefferson that race war was inevitable if former slaves were not expelled from American soil. According to Jefferson's chilling prediction, emancipation without expatriation would lead to the "extermination of the one or the other race." Of course, this genocidal bloodbath would destroy the new nation's hopes for a place among the ranks of civilized nations. Doing nothing about slavery and the slave trade would have equally demoralizing effects, relegating the United States to a permanent state of semibarbarism beyond the pale of European civilization. It was therefore incumbent on enlightened statesman to end the slave trade and replace slave labor with free; by declaring repatriated Africans "a free and independant people" and sponsoring their progress toward civilization, Americans would demonstrate that they were capable of attaining the highest level of civilized development.[26]

TO "AMELIORATE THE CONDITION OF MAN"

Just after his election to the presidency in 1800, Jefferson declared that "our revolution & its consequences, will ameliorate the condition of man over a great portion of the globe." The "revolution of 1800" had secured "a just and solid republican government" as a "standing monument & example for the aim & imitation of the people of other countries." The "people of other countries" that Jefferson had in mind were the inhabitants of war-ravaged Europe, where corrupt and despotic regimes now held sway, even in postrevolutionary France. Jefferson's "satisfaction" with the "benevolent effects of our efforts" called into question the conventional provincial assumption of Europe's cultural superiority.[27]

Before the Imperial Crisis, most Anglo-Americans believed that the success of Britain's empire lay in its extension of liberty at home and abroad. According to the agriculturalist Arthur Young, only 33.5 million people out of an estimated global population of 775.3 million were *not* "the miserable slaves of despotic tyrants . . . and of these few so large a portion as 12,500,000 are subjects of the British empire."[28] But when Jefferson and his fellow revolutionaries broke with Britain, they challenged Young's premises. At the time of Jefferson's inauguration, Britain remained under George III's tyrannical thumb and France, the new nation's "sister republic," had fallen prey to Napoleon's despotic impulses. The "mass of mankind" were inspired by the American example; only America, a lonely beacon in a warring world cast into darkness, could now aspire to promote the political progress of mankind.

"What a satisfaction have we in the contemplation of the benevolent effects of our efforts," Jefferson exulted, particularly when "compared with those of the leaders on the other side, who have discountenanced all advances in science as dangerous innovations, have endeavored to render philosophy and republicanism terms of reproach, to persuade us that man cannot be governed but by the rod."[29]

Jefferson's idea that America might "ameliorate the condition of man" was a progressive vision of *national* civilization. The end of the transatlantic slave trade was in sight—a promise redeemed in Jefferson's second term—and though slavery itself had proven to be a dynamic and expansive institution, Jefferson and his enlightened contemporaries believed that it too could be rendered less violent, less barbaric, and less immoral. The amelioration theme was a staple of revolutionary rhetoric in Virginia. Until the "time will come . . . to abolish this lamentable Evil," Patrick Henry declared in 1773, we must do "every thing we can do . . . to improve it." We must "transmit to our descendants together with our Slaves, a pity for their unhappy Lot, & an abhorrence for Slavery." "Let us treat the unhappy victims with lenity," Henry enjoined his countrymen, for "it is the furthest advance we can make toward Justice."[30] Jefferson struck the same ameliorative note when he advised his young neighbor Edward Coles to "endeavor, with those whom fortune has thrown on our hands, to feed and clothe them well, protect them from ill usage, require such reasonable labor only as is performed voluntarily by freemen, & be led by no repugnancies to abdicate them, and our duties to them."[31] Neither Henry nor Jefferson ever imagined that slavery would become an enduring feature of their republican landscape. To the contrary, they believed that improving slavery—domesticating its violent edges, assuaging the threat of war between the races, and improving slaves' material and moral condition—would hasten its end.[32]

The amelioration of slavery would constitute progress between the abolition of the transatlantic slave trade and the ultimate extinction of the institution in America. As Laurens wrote in 1785, "When we shall be wise enough to stop the importation" of African slaves, "such happy families will become more general and time will work manumission or a state equal to it."[33] Even in South Carolina, where slaves often outnumbered whites ten to one and provided the labor force that buttressed a lucrative rice trade with Europe, some slaveowners looked toward the ultimate end of slavery, recognizing that their claims to civility could no longer be linked to human bondage. Ralph Izard predicted that the ownership of eighty slaves would not enable his son "to maintain a Family in the stile of a gentleman." Izard believed "that the time is at no very great distance when the property in Negroes will be rendered of no value. The enthusiasm of a considerable part of this Country, as well as Europe, on this Subject, can not fail of producing a convulsion which will be severely felt by the Southern States."[34] Of course, it was Izard's understanding—as it was Laurens's and Jefferson's—that slavery and the progress of American civilization were incompatible. In short, the ultimate success of the new nation's republican experiment was predicated on the gradual removal of the slave trade, slavery, and slaves from the American landscape.

Laurens, Jefferson, Henry, and Izard agreed that improving the condition of slaves after the end of the slave trade would prepare the way for a final emancipation. Yet by the early nineteenth century the logic of amelioration pointed in the opposite direction for a growing number of slaveowners. If the institution could be improved, why should it be abolished? Perhaps as planters improved the lives of their slaves, they also improved themselves. Here was an alternative narrative of progress, moving forward from the barbarism of British colonial slavery but not culminating in emancipation. At the turn of the century, the South Carolina planter William Moultrie was pleased to see the "treatment of the slaves in the country altered so much, for their ease, & happ[i]ness; they are now treated with tenderness, & humanity." Such a benevolent scene seemed far removed from the colonial period, when slaves had received "30, 40, or 50 lashes for not doing what was called their task … when perhaps it was impossible for them to do it."[35] Not only did this humane and benevolent version of slavery seem like an improvement over its colonial antecedent but it compared favorably with the brutal treatment of "free" labor in Europe. As Jefferson told his friend the English refugee radical Thomas Cooper in 1814, slaves "are better fed in these States, warmer clothed, and labor less than the journeyman or day-laborers of England." Enslaved men and women "have the comfort, too, of numerous families, in the midst of whom they live without want, or fear of it; a solace which few of the laborers of England possess."[36] The impoverishment of the European laboring classes was a direct result of European despotism, just as the comfort and security of American slaves was a direct result of the republican revolution.

Jefferson insisted to Cooper that "I am not advocating slavery" or "justifying the wrongs we have committed on a foreign people."[37] Yet Jefferson was describing enslaved Africans as "foreigners" at the same time that many slaveowners—including Jefferson himself—were beginning to identify their slaves as loyal domestic servants, as extensions of their own "family." The assumption of Jefferson and other patriots in the post-Revolutionary years had been that African slaves did not, and could not, belong in America. Because slaves were a "captive nation" who had no "amor patriae," they "should be colonized to such a place as circumstances of the time should render most proper." But the place presented a problem. Jefferson conceded that the "ten thousand recollections" of blacks were not of Africa but of the "injuries they have sustained," both of body and mind, at the hands of white American masters. Here lay the ultimate paradox for Jefferson and other advocates of emancipation and repatriation: the stability of the Union was predicated upon the removal of a foreign "people" to their own African homeland, and yet, the "degrading" condition of enslavement had also severed bondsmen from any ties to that homeland. Indeed, Jefferson and his contemporaries saw *slave* and *African* as having distinct meanings: *African* referred to an identity, while *slave* merely referred to a condition. But slavery had erased, or at least muted, Africans' sense of themselves as Africans; it had obfuscated their true history. It therefore was hard to argue that slaves desperately longed to become a "free and independent people" outside of America.[38] To be sure, by the early nineteenth century, few slaveowners saw the necessity of repatriation or pictured slaves as a "foreign" threat. Only insurrectionary slaves, from Gabriel Prosser to Denmark Vesey to Nat Turner, represented fanatical aberrations in what they deemed to be a thoroughly domesticated, loyal, and happy slave population.[39]

In a post-Revolutionary world, slaveowners' emerging identification of their bondsmen as loyal, Christian slaves was a far cry from the Founders' definition of enslaved Africans as foreign threats. Yet Jefferson was not alone in his continuing commitment to an Enlightenment vision of progress culminating in the end of slavery.[40] Slavery would end one day, as long as enlightened masters continued to ameliorate the condition of their slaves.

Yet if many slaveowners could congratulate themselves on their progress as benevolent masters, they recognized that the prospects for emancipation were receding into an increasingly distant future. The slave population had skyrocketed, as one Virginian told James Monroe, thereby threatening to force whites to be "dammed up in a land of slaves."[41] A large population of slaves might unleash what Jefferson had called the "wolf" from slaveowners' tenuous grip. Diffusionists thus promoted the westward spread of slavery and slaves, arguing that a more equal ratio of blacks to whites would make the institution more humane and therefore more easily abolished. During congressional debates following the Treaty of San Lorenzo in 1798, the Virginia representative William Giles argued that "if slaves of the Southern States were permitted to go into the Western country, by lessening the number in those states, and spreading them over a large surface of the country, there would be a great probability in ameliorating their condition, which could never be done whilst they were crowded together as they now are."[42] Jefferson employed similar logic at the height of the Missouri crisis. Insincere Federalists seemed to spin the expansion of slavery as having "a semblance of being Moral," arguing that the containment of slavery was the only way to "halt the progression of the evil." Yet, for Jefferson, "moral the question is certainly not." Indeed, as he told Albert Gallatin, "if there were any morality in the question it is on the other side." Through diffusion, slaves' "happiness will be increased, & the burthen of their future liberation lightened by bringing a greater number of shoulders under it."[43]

Jefferson and other anti-restrictionists firmly believed that diffusion was in keeping with their broader goals of amelioration within the Union. Because they so stringently adhered to the notion that all modern nations were built upon free-labor regimes, neither Jefferson nor Madison could admit that the diffusion of slavery also meant its perpetuation. It took an astute European critic, the Marquis de Lafayette, to point out that diffusion might in fact guarantee slavery's entrenchment, not its abrupt end. "Are you Sure, My dear Friend, that Extending the principle of Slavery to the New Raised States is a Method to facilitate the Means of Getting Rid of it?" he asked Jefferson. "I would have thought," he mused, "that By Spreading the prejudices, Habits, and Calculations of planters over a larger Surface You Rather Encrease the difficulties of final liberation."[44] Lafayette's devastating rejoinder showed just how ludicrous Jefferson's beliefs in the "humanity" and progress of diffusion really were.

But Jefferson never renounced his faith in the ultimate triumph of freedom, even though "the revolution in public opinion which this cause requires, is not to be expected in a day, or perhaps in an age."[45] In the meantime, he comforted himself with the thought that the living conditions of slaves were being progressively ameliorated. After abolishing the transatlantic slave trade in 1808, Americans pursued a humane and benevolent policy by diffusing slaves across the continent; at some point in the future they would abolish the institution altogether. For most slaveowners, there was no question that the institution of slavery was improving by the first few decades of the nineteenth century.[46] What remained controversial was the ultimate end of that improvement. If Jefferson could still tell himself that amelioration pointed toward emancipation, more and more of his fellow planters focused on the institution's transformation. Perhaps the amelioration of slavery, not its ultimate replacement by free labor, was the best guarantee of national greatness.

GREAT NATIONS AND NATIONAL SLAVERY

The United States would emerge as one of the great nations on earth. Or so suggested leading European social critics and geopolitical thinkers, including Destutt de Tracy, Friedrich List, and Alexis de Tocqueville.[47] The age of revolutions had demolished Enlightenment hopes for the continuing progress of European civilization. No longer the gatekeepers of civilization and modernity, European states languished under the despotism and corruption of tyrannical kings who exploited their people and waged senseless wars.[48] As Jefferson had observed in 1782, "The spirit in which she [Great Britain] wages war is the only sample before our eyes, and that does not seem the legitimate offspring either of science or of civilization."[49] Yet the United States seemed different. It would become a great, civilized nation, a polity that derived its power from a sovereign people, expanded to the natural limits of the market, and trumpeted its own particular message of benevolence and Christianity to savage peoples.

With the dissolution of the mythic unity of Europe and its attendant claim to civility, contemporaries began to question whether the international-states system produced civilization or whether great, dominant nations had a providential, "manifest destiny" to promote mankind's progress. By the antebellum period, Americans claimed that their "more perfect union" had delivered the peace, protection, and "happiness" that no other nation in the international order had ever achieved. Civilization did not bring about nationhood; instead, nationhood, the fulfillment of a great people's destiny, spread civilization across the continent and throughout the world. As Americans celebrated the extraordinary development and expansion of their national economy, patriotic southerners began to argue—and economic historians would agree—that the institution of slavery was the foundation of national greatness.[50]

Beginning in the 1830s, the American "great nation" touted its status as the most advanced civilization on the globe. Americans compared the precocious growth of their nation and civilization with that of Britain, once considered the freest, most powerful and civilized empire in the world. Yet American critics insisted that Britain's moment was passing. First, the miserably impoverished state of English factory workers showed that only a tiny proportion of the national population benefited from Britain's domination of world trade.[51] Second, the experiment with emancipation in the West Indies in 1833 proved to be an utter failure; violent slaves, ruined sugar plantations, and destitute planters became the catastrophic outcome of the "freedom" experiment crafted by British reformers. With the British West Indian sugar empire on the wane, Americans predicted that their burgeoning cotton empire, "King Cotton," would assume the dominant position in world trade.[52] Indeed, American civilization, predicated upon the institution of slavery, seemed to achieve a moderate revolutionary end that eluded terror-stricken France and the chaotic post-emancipation British Empire. As the Charleston resident Hugh Swinton Legaré wrote to his sister in 1832, Europe's "everlasting revolutions" carried with them "fearful and unforseen results—the confusion of all distinctions, the contempt of all authority, the savage rudeness and ferocity of jacobinism." He concluded that "no nation in the world can live perpetually in the midst of civil broils and military adventures without degenerating into a horde of Tartars." But the United States, free of such "broils" because of slavery, had achieved the peace and "union" that had so long eluded European nations.[53]

Antebellum southerners saw themselves as the true inheritors of the Revolutionary spirit. But they did not slavishly hew to the Founders' hopelessly naïve political principles. The South Carolina jurist William Harper dismissed the "well-sounding, but unmeaning verbiage of natural equality and inalienable rights" of the Declaration of Independence. Taking "equality" literally, he said, would mean "that our lives are to be put in jeopardy, our property destroyed, and our political institutions overturned or endangered."[54] Only a strictly hierarchical social system predicated upon slavery could guarantee order. Slavery thus safeguarded the federal union that the Founders cherished; it was the "band" of amity that unified a confederacy of sovereign states. The William and Mary professor and political economist Thomas Dew dismissed the notion that slavery's perpetuation would result in race war and disunion. Slaveholders, Dew suggested, were not tyrants; rather, they were paternalistic stewards of their bondsmen. Masters, he wrote, were "characterized by noble and elevated sentiments, by humane and virtuous feelings"; they were "kind and indulgent to their slaves." Indeed, Dew went so far as to suggest that slaveholding "characterizes the true patriot."[55]

The "true patriot" looked to God and to the Bible, not to the Constitution, as the ultimate source of morality and protection. "Happiness," not constitutional liberty, seized true patriots' imaginations. As Harper wrote, "the Creator has sufficiently revealed to us that happiness is the great end of existence" and "the sole object of all animated and sentient beings."[56] Liberty and equality were meaningless abstractions, not "borne in fact." Rather than trumpeting the equality of mankind, southerners suggested that the entire union shared "equally" in the benefits of slavery. The "whole of the United States," Harper maintained, "receiv[ed] in no unequal degree the benefit" of slavery.[57] Thus, the benefits of slavery undermined the Founders' sentiment "that it was desirable to get rid of Slavery." "After a close examination of the subject in all its bearings," James Henry Hammond wrote, southerners had concluded "that in holding slaves we violate no law of God" and "inflict no injustice on any of his creatures."[58] Hammond was instead preoccupied with the moral and religious principles that slavery seemed to protect. The law of nations, in Hammond's formulation, was now moot; only the law of God mattered in determining America's providential status as a great nation.

America seemed like a great nation because of its peculiar—and humane—system of slavery. Indeed, American greatness was predicated on slavery. In comparison with English wage "slaves," Hammond asserted, American slaves' "lives and persons are protected by law, all their sufferings alleviated by the kindest and most interested care, and their domestic affections cherished and maintained." American slavery guaranteed that "there is not a happier, more contented race on the face of this earth." Indeed, the "tendency" of America's domestic institution "is rather to humanize than to brutalize."[59] Thus, in their own perverse formulation, southerners thought American slavery became more humane as slaves became more commoditized, more controlled, more "domesticated." Yet such a humane version of slavery, Hammond asserted, was necessary if the United States was going to fulfill its destiny as a great nation. "Our country is boundless in extent" and "dotted here and there with villages and fields, it is . . . covered with immense forests and swamps of almost unknown size."[60] Only slavery could bring order and civilization to such a place.

And bring civilization it did. Southerners viewed slavery as the institution that guaranteed the progress of nations. Indeed, benevolent slavery was the surest sign of a civilized nation. As Harper argued, "Slavery is an essential process in emerging from savage life." Without it, he wrote, "there can be no accumulation of property, no providence of the future, no tastes for comfort or elegancies, which are the characteristics and essentials of civilization."[61] Slavery granted Americans their own peculiar sense of refinement and moral greatness. Southerners believed it was slavery, not natural rights or the Constitution, that made them a "chosen people." American slavery had brought all whites "to one common level" as "nearly can be expected or even desired in this world," Dew maintained. The "menial and low offices being all performed by the blacks," he wrote, "there is at once taken away the greatest cause of distinction and separation of the ranks of society."[62] As the great homogenizing element in society, slavery created and sustained a white democracy. And at the same time that slavery elevated whites, it also elevated blacks. For if white Americans were the most civilized people on earth, then the American slave was "civilized" at least "comparatively," since he "imbibed the principles, the sentiments, and feelings of the white."[63] Thus, America had achieved the status of a modern great nation because its dynamic and peculiar institution of slavery both created white civilization and sustained its progress.

* * *

During the period of the American founding, patriots construed slavery, whether their own or that of African laborers, to be a reminder of the barbarism foisted upon them under British colonialism and mercantilism. The neocolonial regime, or "empire of liberty," was, in contrast, supposed to ensure American progress away from such barbarism, toward civility and America's emergence as a free and commercial "people." And it was supposed to be the Constitution that made Americans into a sovereign and unified "people."

Yet the Founders had laid the template for the emergence of an antebellum nation that would supersede both European standards of progress and civility and the need for the Constitution itself as the foundation of American claims to union and legitimate nationhood. But antebellum Americans, particularly those in the slaveholding states, recognized the Founders' ideas only as principles that demanded their "improvement." Slaveholding Americans were both "modern" and "enlightened" enough to understand what the Founders had not: slavery was not a barbaric institution but rather the best guarantor of national civilization and "happiness." And the Constitution did not hold the Union together, ensure the emergence of a white democratic order, or render America a distinct "people." No, they agreed, slavery did that.

3

Why Did Southerners Secede?

SEAN WILENTZ

In November 1860, talk of revolution dominated the nation. Those on the proslavery side thought the revolution was just beginning; those on the antislavery side, that it had already been won, but for all of these Americans the election of Abraham Lincoln marked a radical break with the past. "The revolution of 1860 has commenced," the implacably prosecession *Charleston Mercury* declared when the national tally was announced. "On every lip is the stern cry la liberta!" The Massachusetts Republican congressman Charles Francis Adams wrote in his diary that there was now "scarcely a shadow of a doubt that the great revolution has actually taken place, and that the country has once and for all thrown off the domination of the Slaveholders!" Adams's son Henry, recently returned from Europe, found his hometown of Quincy gripped by a mood he later called "lurid beyond description," recalling that "although no one believed in civil war, the air reeked of it."[1]

Not every American, including the man whose election had precipitated the crisis, was so certain. When launching his presidential campaign at the Cooper Institute in New York nine months earlier, Lincoln had proclaimed that his was the truly conservative cause, in line with the spirit and intentions of the nation's founders. Even as the disunionist clamor built during the days and weeks after his victory, Lincoln was convinced that the secessionists remained a radical minority, and he was hopeful that they would fail in what he called their "hot haste to get out of the Union," just as their predecessors, the South Carolina nullifiers, had failed to unite the southern states in 1832–33. "We are not enemies but friends," he said in his inaugural address on 4 March 1861. "We must not be enemies." Yet by then, even as Lincoln spoke that midday, invoking "the better angels of our nature," seven southern states had already left the Union to form the Confederate States of America, in a phalanx that stretched unbroken from South Carolina to Texas. Over the next three months, four more states would join the Confederacy.[2]

Ever since, Americans have argued about why the southerners seceded from the Union. Defenders of the Confederacy, as well as anti-Lincoln, pro-small-government libertarians, contend that secession, whatever its origins, had little or nothing to do with slavery. Supposedly, the real issue for the South was the tariff, or internal improvements, or state rights, or manly honor—anything other than slavery. Supposedly, Lincoln—a racist to his core, his critics claim—also cared little or nothing about slavery. He only exploited the issue during the war, they say, in order to advance his real goal, which was to impose a Leviathan state that would crush individual freedom and the sovereign rights of state governments. And supposedly, Lincoln's political descendants, chiefly Franklin Delano Roosevelt, built on his example to construct a tyrannical federal government that today defies the states' rights theories embodied in the U.S. Constitution.[3]

The weight of the evidence obliterates these claims. No matter how much Lincoln failed to live up to modern standards of racial egalitarianism, he was a liberal on race by the American standards of his day. He was also deeply—and after 1854, fiercely—antislavery. From 1854, when Congress repealed the Missouri Compromise of 1820–21, through the campaign of 1860, he repeatedly proclaimed that he wished to halt slavery's perpetuation. Stopping slavery's spread, Lincoln and other Republicans believed, would place the institution on what Lincoln called, beginning in 1857, "the course of ultimate extinction": eventually eradicating slavery nationwide while adhering, he believed, to the letter as well as the spirit of the U.S. Constitution.

To be sure, in his famous speech on slavery in Peoria, Illinois, in 1854, in which he emphasized his opposition to extending slavery, Lincoln also proclaimed that "much as I hate slavery, I would assent to the extension of it rather than see the Union dissolved."[4] Until the day he died, he would always say that above all else he sought to preserve the Union, the best democratic hope on earth. Yet as the sectional division deepened after 1854, Lincoln stopped explicitly prizing the Union above halting slavery's expansion or saying that he would reject the second if it meant securing the first. The Supreme Court's notorious decision in *Dred Scott v. Sanford* in 1857 convinced him that a conspiratorial southern Slave Power, in league with its northern doughface Democratic allies, was forcing the nation to decide whether it would be all slave or all free, a decision, he believed to his marrow, that would have to favor nationalizing freedom if the Founders' ideals were to survive. Thereafter, Unionism and the territorial restriction of slavery commingled in Lincoln's mind, making it impossible to draw a sharp distinction between his broad antislavery views and his vow to sustain the nation.[5]

As a candidate in 1860, Lincoln adamantly supported the declaration of his party's platform that "the normal condition of all the territory of the United States is that of freedom." As president, he rejected any compromise that would halt secession if it meant abjuring what he believed people had elected him to do, that is, safeguard the Union and work for the exclusion of slavery from the territories and any newly admitted states. Although abolition never became an expressed Union war aim, the war against secession was predicated on the democratic legitimacy both of Lincoln's election in 1860 and of the anti-extension principles he and his party espoused.[6]

Southerners duly seceded in 1860 and 1861 for the very reason that the secessionists themselves said they did: because Lincoln's election to the presidency (or, in some cases, his early actions after taking office) posed, in their by no means irrational view, a direct threat to slavery's long-term and even short-term future. Although other political, economic, and psychological factors came into play, this was the historical bottom line.

Had any of the presidential nominees running against Lincoln been elected, there would have been no secession in 1860–61. Lincoln's victory, however, virtually assured the secession of the lower South, and his deeds after becoming president virtually assured the secession of much of the upper South, despite his own intentions to halt disunion. The issue at hand for the secessionists was neither the tariff nor internal improvements. Nor did it proceed from some abstract theory of states' rights contained in the Constitution, although resentment of the federal government certainly helped to galvanize disunionist opinion. Like

all states' rights arguments, the secessionists' acquired political meaning only within the context of specific political conflicts. By 1860, as
everyone at the time recognized, those conflicts were supremely over
slavery's expansion, and not disembodied disagreements over constitutional interpretation.

The story of southern secession does have its historical complexities
and ironies. Contrary to northern myths of the hot-blooded South,
secession was not solely a southern preoccupation during the new republic's early decades. Nor were white southerners, even in those states
most reliant on slavery, perfectly united over secession as the most desirable political course at the end of the 1850s. Even in 1860–61 it took
a good deal of persuading by the prosecession slaveholders, followed
by Lincoln's ascendancy and then the new president's decision to resist
secession with military force, to convince some white southerners to go
along; and others never would. Nor were all proslavery southerners also
in favor of secession.

Yet by 1860 most white southerners, and certainly most slaveholders, all across the region, rejected any proposed political solution to the
sectional crisis that failed to grant positive federal protection of slavery in at least a portion of the nation's newly obtained territories. And
only a minority of southern whites, even in the upper South, denied
as a matter of principle the basic right of individual states to secede,
a position that in 1860–61 marked a great shift from the nationalism
forcefully promulgated by the Tennessee democrat and slaveholder
President Andrew Jackson thirty years earlier. Lincoln refused to yield
an inch on either proposition. He said he would stick by his pledge
to do everything he could as president to halt slavery's spread; and he
declared, echoing Jackson, that secession was anarchy. Given all that,
Lincoln's election to the White House was bound to trigger the chain
reaction that ended in southern secession.

The great secession winter of 1860–61 was not the first time in the
republic's relatively brief history that the specter of disunion had appeared, cloaked in the rhetorical garb of states' rights, which is perhaps
one reason why some Americans could not quite believe it when secession actually did occur. Tensions about whether the Constitution
formed a compact of sovereign states or a national government with
sovereignty distinct from the states dated back nearly to the Consti-

tution's framing in 1787. In his draft for the Kentucky Resolutions to decry the Alien and Sedition Acts in 1798, Thomas Jefferson wrote as if state legislatures could nullify state laws, a view his collaborator James Madison, often called the father of the Constitution, did not share and omitted from the Virginia Resolutions. Six years later, disunionist talk had a decidedly Yankee accent, as New England Federalists recoiled at the idea that the Louisiana Purchase might keep the Jacobin Jeffersonians permanently in power. "There is no time to be lost, lest [Federalism] should be overwhelmed, and become unable to attempt its own relief," the alarmist Timothy Pickering wrote. "Its last refuge is New England; and immediate exertion, perhaps, its only hope."[7]

Aaron Burr, a less than reliable plotter, dashed these New England secessionist designs before whipping up his own strange, ultimately foiled conspiracy to form a breakaway empire in the West. Yet northern and particularly New England resistance to the War of 1812 led several governors to refuse to commit their state militias to the nation's cause. At the Hartford Convention in 1814 moderate Federalists proclaimed New England's duty to assert its authority over unconstitutional infringements on its sovereignty and left open the possibility of secession if the federal government did not accede to their demands, including removal of the Constitution's three-fifths clause regarding slavery and representation. The signing of the Treaty of Ghent and the news of Andrew Jackson's improbable victory at New Orleans made a dead letter of the convention's resolutions, leaving the three Massachusetts commissioners sent to Washington to deliver New England's complaints wandering the capital's streets dazed and confused.[8]

The Hartford Convention's failure killed what was left of Federalism as a national political force and all but extinguished disunionism as a political temptation in New England and the lower North. Thereafter, insistence on states' rights and, increasingly, on the rights of states to secede was the preserve of southerners, spearheaded by South Carolinians. Vice President John C. Calhoun's secretly drafted pamphlet *Exposition and Protest*, of 1828, justified state nullification of federal laws deemed unconstitutional as an alternative to secession but held out secession as a final resort. Push came to shove in Charleston in 1832, when a special state convention declared the federal tariff passed that year (which cotton planters thought favored northern manufacturers and oppressed the South) null and void in the state of South Carolina and vowed to form a separate, independent government if the federal government tried to interfere.

Unlike the Kentucky and Virginia resolutions, the South Carolinians' complaints focused not on national freedom of expression under the Bill of Rights but on protecting the proclaimed rights of the states in a specific section to strike down national laws and resist alleged oppression by the majority. The complaints had been building for some years, provoked by controversies over Indian removal as well as tariff rates and the funding of road and canal projects. Yet by the time the nullifiers rose up in 1832—following a string of disturbing events, including the abolitionist William Lloyd Garrison's founding of the *Liberator* in Boston, followed by the slave Nat Turner's failed rebellion in Virginia—their leaders acknowledged that slavery lay at the root of the matter. The struggle, Calhoun admitted very early on, involved a deeper alienation of the slaveholding South, whose "peculiar domestick institution" placed it in "opposite relation to the majority of the Union." As the young intransigent Robert Barnwell Rhett (who would become one of the foremost secessionists in 1860) proclaimed, not just the antislavery North but "the whole world are in arms against your institutions. . . . Let Gentlemen be not deceived. It is not the Tariff—not Internal Improvement— . . . which constitutes the great evil against which we are contending."⁹

Yet even as southern malcontents became closely identified with radical states' rights and secession, the region also produced some of the firmest denunciations of nullification and disunion. Above all, President Jackson, in his proclamation denouncing the South Carolina nullifiers, declared the idea of absolute state sovereignty an absurdity, "produced by metaphysical subtlety, in pursuit of an impracticable theory." The Constitution, Jackson insisted, "forms a *government*, not a *league*."¹⁰ Other southern Unionists could be just as blunt as Jackson and even more colorful. In eastern Tennessee, one of Jackson's old army comrades, John Wyly, claimed that inside of two weeks Old Hickory could amass troops in sufficient number at the state border that they could "piss enough . . . to float the whole nullifying crew of South Carolina into the Atlantic." Although some state legislatures, as well as numerous individual southerners, expressed opposition to the tariff and sympathy with South Carolina in its showdown with President Jackson, no other legislature formally endorsed nullification. Thereafter, loyalty to the Union remained a substantial force among white southerners in every class and subregion until the secession crisis of 1860–61. When asked about what was transpiring in and around Charleston in 1861, the veteran South Carolinian Unionist James Petigru reputedly expressed mock pity for his state, saying that it was "too small to be a sovereign nation and too large for an insane asylum."[11]

In sum, neither states' rights nor secession was monopolized by any one party or geographical section in the early republic; and when those issues did become more closely linked to the South, they divided the southern citizenry. President-elect Lincoln, himself the son of a border slave state, may have fallen into wishful, even delusional thinking, but he had sound reasons to believe that secession would fail before it got off the ground. Why was he wrong? How did southern secession— a process that took five full months to complete—come about? And why did the eleven seceding states decide that their ideal of American democracy and liberty (or "liberta," as the *Charleston Mercury* put it) necessitated the creation of a new slaveholders' republic?

Secession was the result of human choice and action, not intangible, irrevocable historical forces. For more than a decade the nerves of Americans, North and South, had been rubbed raw by a series of spectacular political and social upheavals dating back to the Mexican War and the adoption by the House of Representatives of the antislavery Wilmot Proviso. Above all, the civil war in Kansas Territory after 1854, quite apart from its more emotional and demagogic repercussions, demonstrated the futility of finding an orderly, democratic solution to the issue of slavery's expansion. Every instrument designed to impose such a solution—the Lecompton constitution, the Supreme Court's ruling in the *Dred Scott* case, the principle of popular sovereignty as defined and then redefined by Stephen A. Douglas—raised many more new and troublesome questions than it answered.

There were those in both sections who deliberately aggravated the situation. The antislavery terrorist John Brown's raid on Harpers Ferry did not improve proslavery southerners' view of decorous Yankee intentions. Indeed, charges that Brown, already notorious for his remorseless violence amid the fighting in Kansas Territory, had conspired with leading Republicans (including, some said wildly, Abraham Lincoln) to ignite a mammoth slave rebellion made a Republican presidential victory in 1860 all the more unacceptable to agitated southerners. At the heart of southern politics, a hardy and coordinated band of disunionists led by Robert Barnwell Rhett and William Lowndes Yancey did their utmost to worsen sectional mistrust by agitating to reopen the African slave trade and enact a federal code to protect slavery in the territories; they also disrupted the national Democratic Party, the last great cross-sectional political institution remaining, apart from the federal government itself. Yet important as these inflammatory and manipulative figures were as catalysts, they cannot fully explain southern secession or why it occurred when it did.

The election of Lincoln was far more important as the triggering event. It is easy to forget how contingent Lincoln's election actually was. Had the Republicans passed over the moderate westerner Lincoln and nominated the preconvention odds-on favorite, William Henry Seward, Ohio, Illinois, and Indiana (where Lincoln won only razor-thin majorities) might have swung to the Democrat Douglas, thereby throwing the election into the House of Representatives, where the Republicans would almost certainly have lost under the one-state, one-vote rule. Had that happened, secession would have been off the table. A shift of just over twenty-five thousand votes in New York from Lincoln to Douglas, out of a total of more than two-thirds of a million votes cast, would have produced the same result.

By the same token, had the candidate and later president Lincoln listened to some of his advisers (including, ironically, Seward) and made mollifying gestures to the South, antisecession forces in a few southern states might have been emboldened. But although Lincoln always made clear that he intended no interference with slavery where it already existed and that he would enforce the Fugitive Slave Law, he refused to budge on the essential question of trying to prohibit slavery's expansion. On those grounds, proslavery southerners could only see Lincoln as a man of his word who intended to put slavery on the road to destruction, which was reason enough for many white southerners to secede straightaway.

Here lay secession's greatest paradox. The secessionists' decision finally to leave the Union came in the aftermath of a democratic, national election—democratic, that is, within the limits of national democracy as of 1860. By doing so, they affirmed what antislavery northerners considered the slave South's fundamental contempt for democracy, preferring what Lincoln in his inaugural address called "the essence of anarchy" over "the judgment of this great tribunal, the American people." When applied to secessionists who truly disdained political equality for white men as well as for blacks as, in one South Carolinian's words, "the most pernicious humbug of the age," the charges had merit. But for most white southerners, slavery was essential to the only democracy they could imagine: a democratic slavery that, as enshrined in their state constitutions, secured equality among white men. "Nowhere in this broad Union but in the slaveholding states," Albert Gallatin Brown, of Mississippi, proclaimed, "is there a living breathing, exemplification of the beautiful sentiment, that all men are equal." (Brown hastened to add that he meant, of course, white men.) And as if to prove all this, the secessionists proceeded in what they considered a perfectly democratic manner, conducting free and open elections for delegates to special state conventions that would decide whether to leave the Union or stay.[12]

These elections showed that southern white opinion about secession was not monolithic. Even in the Deep South, where prosecession passions ran deepest and disunion proceeded most swiftly, men who had family backgrounds in the upper South or border states or who had connections to northern commerce tended to be far less favorable toward secession than the large plantation owners were. Strong pockets of opposition, ranging from outright Unionism to disagreement with the fire-eaters' precipitate secessionism, existed in eastern Mississippi, northern Alabama, eastern Tennessee, and other southern subregions where the rural yeomanry was concentrated.[13]

Inside the secession conventions, delegates from yeoman-dominated, nonslaveholding areas showed defiance toward those fire-eaters who wanted to secede immediately. One of these delegates, Nicholas J. Davis, of Madison County, Alabama, arose in his state's secession convention and accused the secessionists of acting like British Tories, out "to coerce an unwilling people." Some critics charged that there was less democracy to the secession process than met the eye. One outraged dissenter wrote that the prosecessionists were disregarding any idea of democratic deliberation and "trying the experiment of getting along without the people." In Louisiana (where the results in the del-

egate elections were suppressed for months) as well as in Mobile and
Autauga counties in Alabama, suspiciously high totals for hard-line
secessionist delegates raised suspicions of foul play.[14]

Yet if extreme secessionists almost certainly tampered with the bal-
loting, it appears not to have affected the prosecession outcome. And
the idea that secession was some sort of coup d'état by the fire-eaters,
who undemocratically pulled an unwilling white citizenry out of the
Union, does not stand up to serious scrutiny. Even in normal times,
slaveholders held disproportionate power as elected officials, especially
in the Deep South. That also held true in the secession conventions,
where slaveholder delegates not only were more numerous propor-
tionally than their actual number in the population but struck a more
militant posture than nonslaveholders. More important, the hard reality of Lincoln's victory changed many Dixie skeptics, slaveholders and
nonslaveholders alike, into ardent secessionists. All across the Deep
South, one moderate Georgia newspaper observed, "the hopelessness
of preserving the Union has made disunionists, since the election, of
thousands of Conservative and Union men."[15]

By 1860 the Dixie slaveholders, after decades of practice in party
politics, were also highly adept at appealing to the material interests
as well as the emotions of the nonslaveholding majority, thereby mut-
ing the political and class divisions between planters and yeomen. The
premier southern journalist J. D. B. DeBow advanced the economic argument in 1861, describing the well-being of slaveholders and nonslaveholders as "in the present sectional controversy identical." Although the
great majority of southern whites owned no slaves, DeBow explained,
the yeomen profited from slavery by selling goods and services to the
planters. From those profits, he continued, they could reasonably expect
that one day they or their children would become slaveholders. In any
event, DeBow concluded, the end of slavery would mean a *degrading
equality*" between the races—an appeal to white solidarity and white
male supremacy under slavery that ran even deeper than arguments
about economic upward mobility into the slaveholders' ranks. And
where racism and attachment to the institution of slavery did not fully
win over the yeomen, slaveholders harped on local pride, organizing
irregular militia groups like the minuteman companies of South Carolina, which intended to prevent Lincoln's inauguration or, barring that,

to ward off any military aggression against the South by the Yankee Black Republican government.[16]

The debates over secession in the state conventions of the cotton South were mainly about means, not ends. The major fault line in these assemblies was never between Unionists and disunionists but between two groups of disunionists: the conditional secessionists (sometimes called, a bit confusingly, "cooperationists"), who wanted to slow the process down; and the immediate secessionists, who did not. Few of the conditional secessionists believed that secession was avoidable, and virtually none thought it was illegitimate. Some persistent Unionists refused to assent even when secession came—the residents of one Alabama county burned William Lowndes Yancey in effigy—but the vast majority signed on anyway, out of either localist loyalty or determination to resist Yankee interference.[17]

To be sure, the dynamics of secession in the upper South, the border states, and the mountainous areas were different from those in the cotton South. Indeed, Unionists in Maryland, Kentucky, Missouri, Virginia, North Carolina, Tennessee, and Arkansas mounted successful, explicitly antisecession counteroffensives during the early months of 1861. And while the first three states would never formally secede, the last four would do so only after the firing on Fort Sumter and Lincoln's order to raise troops to suppress the uprising aroused pro-Confederate sympathies (with western Virginia refusing to go along with the rest of Virginia in leaving the Union). Until the final denouement, this southern opposition to secession encouraged northerners like Lincoln and even emboldened some to believe that yeoman farmers and ambivalent slaveholders might overthrow the southern slaveholders' democracy.

But there were sharp limits to the southern antisecession drives. Some portions of the upper South—the Southside counties of Virginia, for example, and the plantation districts of North Carolina—were seething with secessionist discontent. Elsewhere, gentlemen slaveholders, mainly old Whigs, regarded secession not as a necessity to preserve slavery but as suicidal, handing the northern Black Republicans exactly the pretext they needed to abolish slavery not only in the territories but in the states where it already existed. Even with Lincoln as president for four years, they reasoned, slavery was far safer inside the Union (as it had been for generations) than it would be outside the Union. This was the less-than-unconditional Unionism favored by such lively voices as the ardently proslavery East Tennessee editor Rev. William G. Brownlow, who scorned the "fire eating, Union-dissolving, political charlatanism" of the prosecessionists no less than he did the menacing words of antislavery northerners.[18]

Finally, if the upper South antisecession slaveholders were willing to negotiate about compromises that would ban slavery's further extension into northern territories, where it would not flourish, they were hardly willing to bend as much as Lincoln demanded. All but the most flexible wanted to provide what one Virginian called "explicit *protection of slavery*" in the form of a federal code to cover existing and future territories south of the 36°30 Missouri Compromise line, possibly including Cuba, a prospect Lincoln would never entertain. If the upper South antisecessionists obstructed the spread of disunionism, their allegiance to the Union extended only so far as it would preserve, protect, defend, and extend the slaveholders' democracy.[19]

Given this swirl of motives, political strategies, and even basic philosophies about democracy, it is important not to simplify the impulses behind secession. Yet these different impulses did converge by the spring of 1861 in defense of a republican polity based on slavery and an insistence on preserving the slaveholders' liberty against northern despotism. Decades later, during and after Reconstruction, in what has turned out to be one of the most consequential acts of falsification in American history, secessionist leaders denied this elementary fact, which was easily recognizable to any literate newspaper-reading American at the time. Jefferson Davis and Alexander Stephens asserted that, as Davis put it, "the existence of African servitude was in no wise the cause of the conflict, but only an incident."[20]

But secessionists talked very differently in 1860 and 1861. There were, of course, some southerners, especially in the ex-Unionist minority, who claimed to support secession for reasons that had little or nothing to do with slavery. "I care nothing for the 'Peculiar institution,'" one wrote, "but I cant stand the idea of being domineered over by a set of Hypocritical scoundrels such as Sumner, Seward, Wilson, Hale, etc. etc." But for those who made secession happen, slavery and the northern attacks on slavery's extension lay at the heart of everything. All across the emerging Confederacy, secessionists described their cause as a defense of what the Texas convention called "a commonwealth holding, main-taining, and protecting the institution known as negro slavery—the servitude of the African race to the white race within her limits." Even the more moderate heads in the South agreed: the fight over the exten-sion of slavery, one cooperationist Alabama delegate asserted, was "the Iliad of all our woes." The ordinance of secession that Virginia finally approved in mid-April for public ratification charged that the federal government had perverted its powers in order to pursue its "oppression of the Southern slaveholding states."[21]

It is this enormous body of evidence that a few modern pro-Confederate writers, with the patina of scholarship, have tried to ignore or rationalize out of existence. One such study freely admits that there was what the author calls "a flood of verbiage from Southern leaders and writers" who maintained "vociferously" that protecting slavery was the motive for secession. But with a wave of the hand, the author dismisses that flood as an illusion, something that "just does not make sense," because Lincoln came to office in 1861 pledged not to interfere with slavery where it then existed. That Lincoln also came to office pledged to hasten slavery's eventual demise by forbidding its spread into the territories is conveniently overlooked.[22]

Southerners were writing ominously of Lincoln as soon as the 1860 campaign got under way. "The triumph of the party of which Mr. Lin-coln is the representative and leader," one Kentucky editor wrote in the spring, prompted thoughts from "which the mind shrinks appalled." (Lincoln and his party, the editor affirmed, were "warring upon the in-stitution of slavery.") After the election, southern opinion divided over whether Lincoln's victory would bring immediate attacks on slavery and over whether to secede immediately or await some overt hostile act by the new president. But whether they believed, as one New Orleans paper put it, that Lincoln was actually "a thorough radical Abolition-ist, without exception or qualification," or that he was merely a subtler proponent of antislavery doctrine, there was general agreement that his election posed a clear and present danger to the South's peculiar insti-tution. "A party founded on the single sentiment, the exclusive feeling of hatred to African slavery, is now the controlling party in the Con-federacy," the *Richmond Semi-weekly Examiner* observed, summing up the election returns in a typical editorial. "The Government is in the hands of the avowed enemies of one section. It is to be directed in hostility to the property of that section." As one southern antisecessionist editor bluntly asserted, "The ostensible reason for secession, indeed, the only reason given, is the election of Lincoln."[23]

The war that crushed secession wound up crushing slavery as well, throughout the country, forevermore. The border-state pro-Unionists proved prescient in this sense: slavery ended up being much more vulnerable outside the Union than inside, although nobody could have predicted the peculiar political path, let alone the mass carnage, that led to emancipation. In what Lincoln called, at Gettysburg, "a rebirth" of freedom, one version of democracy prevailed over another, as did one version of the nation—one nation indivisible.[24] The tensions over state' rights have, however, continued, an inevitable product of the federal system of checks and balances, which the Framers believed to be essential for stability and freedom. These tensions will remain for as long as the American republic endures.

It is important to distinguish, though, between these continuing tensions and any fixed states' rights theory or model of American politics enshrined by the framers of the Constitution or anyone else. In political practice, there has been no such coherent constitutional theory or model, despite pretensions to the contrary by spokesmen from every section of the Union. Since the Civil War, as from the 1830s through the 1850s, states' rights have been linked mainly to struggles over racial justice and to southern white resistance to the federal government. Whether uttered by Theodore Bilbo, Strom Thurmond, Ronald Reagan, or Trent Lott, "states' rights" has been a slogan masquerading as a theory—or, as in Calhoun's day, in Andrew Jackson's phrase, "metaphysical subtlety, in pursuit of an impracticable theory." Believing that the nullification battle or southern secession, or, for that matter, the New Englanders' Hartford Convention in 1814, was essentially about states' rights is like believing that the battles over federal and state jurisdiction in the 2000 election were essentially about rival theories of constitutional interpretation.

So it was during the great secession winter. States' rights—like the tariff, or the territorial question, or the Fugitive Slave Law—was one of the points under the existing constitutional framework where the essentially moral as well as political conflicts over slavery could be faced.

Lincoln's election, in full compliance with the Constitution, directly threatened the future of southern slavery, meaning that the Constitution, for decades the slaveholders' friend, was now their enemy. As a direct result of Lincoln's election and of his actions upon taking office, eleven southern states seceded—and the war came.

4

"A party man who did not believe in any man who was not"

Abraham Lincoln, the Republican Party, and the Union

RICHARD CARWARDINE

Mr. Lincoln . . . [was] a politician and partisan . . . first of all and always. . . . In prosecuting the war for the Union, in the steps taken for the emancipation of the slaves, Mr. Lincoln appeared to follow rather than to lead the Republican party. But his own views were more advanced usually than those of his party, and he waited patiently and confidently for the healthy movements of public sentiment which he well knew were in the right direction. No man was ever more firmly or consistently the representative of a party than was Mr. Lincoln, and his acknowledged greatness is due, first to the wisdom and justice of the principles and measures of the political party that he represented, and, secondly, to his fidelity . . . to . . . the party with which he was identified.

—GEORGE S. BOUTWELL

Within five years of his nomination for the presidency Abraham Lincoln lay dead. So, too, did the Union that he had won office to serve. When Republican Party leaders had met to select a candidate in Chicago in May 1860, few doubted that the southern slaveholders' system of labor and race relations was deeply entrenched, constitutionally protected, and territorially ambitious. Adopting Lincoln as the nominee most likely to put them in power, the Republicans endorsed a platform promising to quarantine slavery as a moral and political evil, promote a dynamic capitalism, and expand economic opportunity for free labor, while also respecting the rights of the slave states to sovereignty over their domestic affairs. By May 1865, however, as Union troops mopped up the Confederate stragglers, the South's peculiar institution lay in tatters, destined for abolition through the Thirteenth Amendment, which, having recently been passed in both houses of Congress, awaited only a two-thirds vote of the states. Further, the war erased from the mainstream political agenda the issue of the voluntary deportation of African Americans, whose service for the Union and astonishing courage in arms gave them a compelling claim to full citizenship. But the larger agenda of economic and civil rights of free men and women in postwar society would prove highly contested. Emancipation would not mean full equality for blacks, but nor would it mean their unquestioned subordination. What was indubitable, however, was that the war had resolved the antebellum debate over the perpetuity of the Union. That states had rights was certain, but it was equally certain that those rights fell short of the freedom unilaterally to withdraw from the federal republic.

It is a truism that wars release forces that assume a momentum beyond the control of individual participants and that civil wars in particular have the potential for revolutionary change. The struggle for the American Union was no exception: the nation's sociopolitical transformation and the redefinition of its ideals went well beyond what most Americans expected, or even imagined, during the early days of the crisis. But if there is no simple answer to the question who bears primary responsibility for the wartime transfiguring of the nation? it is not difficult to identify the key contributors.

First, we may reflect on the irony of the consequences that southern secessionists visited upon themselves. Whether defined as a revolution or a counterrevolution, secession created conditions of political instability far more hazardous to planters' interests than did the trigger for separation itself, the presidential victory of a Republican Party that overwhelmingly acknowledged the protections accorded to the slave states by the U.S. Constitution. In this respect, Georgia's Alexander H. Stephens was responsibly prescient when he warned against a course that must lead to war: "Revolutions are much easier started than controlled, and the men who begin them, even for the best purposes and objects, seldom end them. . . . The wise and the good who attempt to control them will themselves most likely become the victims."[1] There is no more compelling or poignant counterfactual question than this: what extra life would slavery have enjoyed had the leaders of the Old South acquiesced in the Republicans' control of the presidency?

In either rallying to the regimental flag or providing the moral and material support for those in arms, the overwhelming majority of northerners, in concert with loyalists in the border slave states, initially believed themselves to be working to maintain the old Union, no more and no less. That bedrock of patriotism and the federal forces that gave it loyal, self-sacrificial expression in the field were necessary ingredients in the transfiguration of the Union's purpose into something more elevated still, but they do not in themselves explain it. For that we must turn, in no small part, to the subjects of the wartime revolution: the thousands of runaway slaves who poured across Union lines and forced upon the federal authorities the issue of freedom; the free blacks who joined with the fugitives to provide one in every ten of Union men in arms; and the bondsmen and bondswomen on southern farms whose increasing assertiveness weakened slavery from within.

The single most influential agency in determining and securing the nation's transformation, however, was the administration of Abraham Lincoln. In some respects the president was stating the obvious when he told Albert Hodges that the emancipationist movements of the war had not been of his making: "I claim not to have controlled events, but confess plainly that events have controlled me." But there was disingenuousness in this statement, too, for essential to the story of the wartime redefinition of American ideals were Lincoln's profound grasp of what he called the "friction and abrasion" of war and the opportunities he saw for advancing the principles of the Founders' prospectus for the nation.[2] The following analysis pursues two particular questions: How, if at all, did the war redefine the president's own understanding of the nation's purposes and ideals? And how did he harness the political and ideological energy of the party of his administration—the Republican-Union Party—in reconstructing the nation and renewing its meaning?

LINCOLN'S VISION OF NATIONAL PURPOSE

That Lincoln's political career divides into three distinct phases—Whig, Republican, and Union-saving president—must not obscure its continuities. The fundamentals of Lincoln's social and moral project remained constant over time: the building of an enterprising, commercially prosperous nation in which, under the equal operation of republican laws, each and every citizen would enjoy the right and means to rise within a fluid and expanding society. How this took political shape varied as the context changed. The immediate issues confronting Lincoln the Illinois Whig during the 1830s and 1840s were different from those the Republican Lincoln faced after the passage of the Kansas-Nebraska Act in 1854, while the task confronting the newly elected President Lincoln as the Union splintered was different still. But the essential elements of his vision for the nation were unchanging.[3]

As an aspiring Whig, Lincoln backed a program designed to speed the transition from a subsistence to a market economy and encourage poor farmers and mechanics to aspire, through enterprise and self-discipline, to better themselves as he had done. The logic of Lincoln's economic thought dictated a social and moral order at odds with southern slavery. During Lincoln's years of state-level politics, slavery remained on the edge of his field of vision. But the main elements of his opposition to the South's peculiar institution were already in place before he stepped into the national arena as a U.S. congressman in 1847. "I am naturally anti-slavery," Lincoln later wrote. "If slavery is not wrong, nothing is wrong. I can not remember when I did not so think, and feel." His argument drew especially on the doctrines of natural rights and human equality set out in the nation's founding texts. All men, black and white, he insisted, should be free to enjoy the fruits of their own work. Free labor offered the prospect of "improvement in condition" and kept the social order fluid. By the 1850s a fast-developing industrial sector had spawned a burgeoning wage-earning class, but Lincoln, confident in the boundlessness of America, had no fear of a permanent proletariat; he saw no insuperable barriers to the social progress of any free, enterprising, and conscientious working man. Slavery, however, the enemy of this kind of economic meritocracy, stifled individual enterprise in both planters and slaves and sustained a fundamental inequality: depriving human beings of the just rewards of their labor.[4]

Stephen Douglas's repeal of the Missouri Compromise in 1854 opened the western territories up to slavery's expansion. Historically in a position of defensiveness, slavery might now swamp the nation. Addressing audiences increasingly open to the idea of a slave power conspiracy—the conviction that slaveholders and their northern doughface allies intended to use their control of the federal government to extend slavery across the country—Lincoln spoke with a new moral urgency. In addition to engaging in a Union-threatening piece of political perfidy, he argued, Douglas had reversed the settled policy of the republic at a stroke. The principle of popular sovereignty, he insisted, assumed a moral neutrality toward slavery, leaving it to local communities to decide the issue for themselves, with reference only to their material self-interest. Douglas's claim that the repeal of the Nebraska Act had established the sacred right of self-government ran aground on the rocks of African American manhood: "If the negro is a *man*, why then my ancient faith teaches me that 'all men are created equal'; and that there can be no moral right in connection with one man's making a slave of another." Describing Jefferson's Declaration of Independence as the "sheet anchor of American republicanism," Lincoln insisted that no man was "good enough to govern another man, *without that other's consent*."[5]

At the crossroads of the Christian Faith of the American Soul

The Declaration of Independence was for Lincoln more than a time-bound expression of political grievance. It was a near-sanctified statement of universal principles, and one that squared with belief in a Maker who had created all men equal and whose relations with mankind were based on the principles of justice. Lincoln found the scriptural basis for the Declaration in the book of Genesis: if mankind were created in the image of God, then "the justice of the Creator" had to be extended equally "to *all* His creatures, to the whole great family of man." As he told an audience at Lewistown, Illinois, the Founders had declared that "nothing stamped with the Divine image . . . was sent into the world to be trodden on, and degraded, and imbruted by its fellows." God's words to Adam, "In the sweat of thy face shalt thou eat bread," provided Lincoln with a text for his theology of labor: the burden of work, the individual's duty to engage in it, and his moral right to enjoy the fruits of his labor. James Gillespie recorded the near-Puritan earnestness with which Lincoln insisted that slavery was "an enormous national crime" for which the country "could not expect to escape punishment." The political nation was a moral being. God punished wicked nations for their sins, just as he punished delinquent individuals.[6]

Lincoln's election in 1860 and the secession of the lower South naturally changed his political priorities, but his underlying vision remained the same. The strands in the rope that bound Lincoln resolutely to the Union included his profound faith in the nation's material potential, but far more often he celebrated the political purpose of the Union's free institutions and their moral magnificence. Thanks to the Declaration of Independence, with its philosophical celebration of equality, and the federal Constitution, the guarantor of freedom, the United States enjoyed a unique and unprecedented liberty. "*Most governments* have been based, practically, on the denial of equal rights of men . . . ; *ours* began, by *affirming* those rights. *They* said, some men are too *ignorant, and vicious,* to share in government. Possibly so, said we; and, by your system, you would always keep them ignorant, and vicious. We proposed to give *all* a chance; and we expected the weak to grow stronger, the ignorant, wiser; and all better, and happier together." Lincoln gave the American Union a special role in history. As a beacon of liberty to all, it was "the world's best hope."[7]

Thus, when the South Carolinians turned their guns on Fort Sumter in April 1861, they raised an issue that embraced, in Lincoln's words, "more than the fate of these United States. It presents to the whole family of man, the question, whether a constitutional republic, or a democracy—a government of the people, by the same people—can or cannot, maintain its territorial integrity, against its own domestic foes. . . . It forces us to ask: 'Is there, in all republics, this inherent and fatal weakness?' 'Must a government, of necessity, be too *strong* for the liberties of its own people, or too *weak* to maintain its own existence?'" In Lincoln's view, the rebellion had to be put down to prove to the world that popular government could be maintained against internal attempts at overthrow, "that those who can fairly carry an election, can also suppress a rebellion."[8]

Here is the key to the vision that sustained Lincoln throughout his presidency: the perpetuation of a Union that was freighted with democratic meaning. "There is nothing that can ever bring me willingly to consent to the destruction of this Union," he told New Yorkers as president-elect, "unless it were to be that thing for which the Union itself was made. I understand a ship to be made for the carrying and preservation of the cargo, and so long as the ship can be saved, with the cargo, it should never be abandoned. . . . So long, then, as it is possible that the prosperity and the liberties of the people can be preserved in the Union, it shall be my purpose at all times to preserve it."[9] The Union vessel was most important for the cargo it carried: liberty and equality, and the meritocratic opportunities they implied. During the war, Lincoln came to see that preservation of the cargo required the preservation of the ship and therefore legitimized the emancipation of the slaves.

Lincoln's other acts relating to slavery have been judged by radicals then as well as commentators since to be sluggish, grudging, partial, and forced upon him by events.[10] They note that he made no mention of slavery when he defined his administration's purpose early in the conflict. Further, during the first year of the war he overturned military proclamations that freed the slaves of rebel masters; he sacked his secretary of war, Simon Cameron, for publicly proposing the arming of black soldiers; and he continued to cherish cautious schemes of compensated emancipation and the colonizing of free blacks in overseas settlements. He was unenthusiastic about the two Confiscation Acts passed by Congress, which punished rebel planters with the loss of their chattel goods. When Horace Greeley, the editor of the influential *New York Tribune*, published his "Prayer of Twenty Million," calling on the president to grasp the nettle of emancipation, Lincoln's reply seemed only to confirm his cautious pragmatism: "My paramount object in this struggle *is* to save the Union, and is *not* either to save or to destroy slavery."[11] The Emancipation Proclamation, when finally issued, on New Year's Day 1863, applied with barely an exception to those areas still in rebel hands, freeing those slaves over whom the federal government exercised no immediate control. It accepted the arming of black Americans not out of principle but only because the Union army desperately needed men. Finally, Lincoln's program of reconstruction of the rebel states appeared to leave the door open to slavery and condoned harsh contracted labor systems among loyal slaveholders that were akin to bondage.

The twofold problem with this assessment is, first, that although it rightly stresses Lincoln's temperamental caution, it neglects the political constraints on his freedom of action imposed by the fragility of the Union coalition; and second, that it fails to honor the evidence of his moral purpose and his intellectual relish in seizing the chance of fusing emancipationist means and ends.

Lincoln's political priority during the early stages of the war was to prevent the remaining tier of slave states in the upper South from leaving the Union: given their rich resources, their loss would have sealed the fate of the Union. Had Lincoln declared the removal of slavery a war aim, Missouri, Maryland, and, most seriously, Kentucky, their loyalty already in the balance, would have been lost. His caution and dalliance with compensated emancipation and colonization schemes have to be seen in this context and against a background of deep-rooted northern racism, particularly within the opposition Democratic Party. That the Emancipation Proclamation did not generally apply to slaveholding areas that had been loyal from the outset or were now controlled by Union troops was a mark, not of Lincoln's cynicism, but of his understanding of the constitutional basis on which he felt able to issue the proclamation, namely, as a measure of military policy that he was free to take as commander in chief to put down the rebellion; by definition it should not apply to those areas no longer in revolt.

But Lincoln paralleled his political realism with regular statements of his willingness and constitutional obligation to use all "indispensable" or "necessary" means to preserve the Union.[12] Means that under normal circumstances might be deemed unconstitutionally irregular might in a crisis become "an indispensable necessity" in the pursuit of lawful ends. Lincoln first used the phrase in his special message of July 1861, when he left the door open for a changing relationship between the federal government and the rebel states. The tide of events during the first half of 1862, and above all the humiliation of McClellan's Peninsular Campaign, led him to decide to override the peacetime guarantees of slave property and declare Confederate slaves the subjects of military emancipation. It is essential to understand, however, that Lincoln's recourse to emancipation was not as exclusively instrumentalist as his letter to Greeley has commonly been taken to imply: the Union that he declared he would or would not employ emancipation to save was an antislavery Union dedicated to the ultimate removal of bondage.[13] Lincoln's course was morally fashioned. The Union ship was only worth saving because of the cargo of freedom that it carried. And his stance over the two years following the Emancipation Proclamation is significant for his determination to follow its logic: in the arming of black troops, in the refusal to renege on the promise to emancipate, in the invocation of "a new birth of freedom" in the majesty of the Gettysburg Address, and in energetic efforts to secure a constitutional amendment to end slavery. On the eve of his death, Lincoln was even proposing that certain categories of freedmen—"the very intelligent, and . . . those who serve our cause as soldiers"—be given the vote.[14]

There is, then, a strong sense in which the wartime Lincoln personally saw himself as not *redefining* American ideals but reasserting original principles and values laid down by the Founders and apply-

ing them—in a new birth of freedom—to many Americans previously
deemed beyond their reach. He presented himself, and the Union administration he led, as a conservative upholder of foundational principles against those who defied them. Insofar as there was a new intellectual imperative propelling Lincoln during the war, it lay not in his
discovery of novel political truths but in a more potent understanding
of the nation's place in the divine economy. His determined fight to
sustain a value-laden Union was joined to an altered religious perspective under the pressure of events.

Lincoln ruminated on the operations of providence throughout his
life. Before the war, however, he regarded providence as a superintend-
ing but mechanistic force that operated predictably according to the
rules of the universe. In wartime, Lincoln's "providence" became an
active and more personal God: judgmental, mysterious, and intrusive.
His search for God's purposes revealed itself at the historic cabinet
meeting in September 1862, when he explained that he had vowed to
take a Union victory at Antietam as "an indication of Divine will, and
that it was his duty to move forward in the cause of emancipation": not
he, but "God had decided this question in favor of the slaves."[15] If this
scrutiny of providence was only implicit in the salvationist rhetoric of
Lincoln's Gettysburg Address, it would reveal itself most remarkably in
the explicit biblicism of his second inaugural address.

LINCOLN AND POLITICAL INCLUSION

Lincoln had a variety of agencies with which to mobilize popular support for his administration and the ideals for which he strove, including
the army, churches, and humanitarian organizations.[16] None, however,
was as central to the task of projecting the administration's purpose as
the machinery of party. But the levers of party presented a dilemma.
Elected on a party platform but almost immediately facing the reality
of a broken Union, Lincoln confronted the imperative of rising above
partisanship and acting inclusively. Yet even in wartime the routine of
elections continued, fought by well-organized party loyalists for whom
victory would bring the prospect of government jobs and a clamor for
political favors. Partisan realities contended with the need for political
ecumenism.[17]

Lincoln's inclusive coalition building is the theme of much of the appreciative historical scholarship on his executive leadership, and it goes some way toward explaining the terms in which he articulated the meaning and purposes of the war.[18] He understood, as he reflected to Hill Lamon after the Federal debacle at Chancellorsville, that "if . . . all united in one common purpose, this infernal rebellion would soon be terminated."[19] It was an approach that earned him the humorously barbed reflection of William Pitt Fessenden, who described the president as a liberal man, "so very liberal, so very generous, so very magnanimous a man, that in endeavoring to keep perfectly straight between those of different political parties in this country, he sometimes leans very much backwards."[20] Lincoln set the tone at the outset by stripping from his first inaugural address—whose target audience was surely the population of the loyal states, especially conservatives—explicit mention of the Republican Party and its national conventions of 1856 and 1860.[21] Both before and after taking office, he courted Democrats by directly and indirectly invoking Andrew Jackson's staunch nationalism as president and his earlier recourse at New Orleans, during the War of 1812, to martial law and de facto suspension of habeas corpus.[22]

Jackson's military precedent provided potent ammunition for Lincoln in his reply during the summer of 1863 to a group of anti-administration Democrats who had spoken out at Albany, New York. The arrest under military order of the fiery Ohio Democrat Clement Vallandigham had prompted them to raise the alarm against a burgeoning military despotism. The president's response to his critics took the form of a public letter in which he rebuked them for choosing "to designate themselves 'democrats' rather than 'American citizens.'" "In this time of national peril" he wrote, "I would have preferred to meet you upon a level one step higher than any party platform; because I am sure that from such more elevated position, we could do better battle for the country we all love, than we possibly can from those lower ones, where from the force of habit, the prejudices of the past, and selfish hopes of the future, we are sure to expend much of our ingenuity and strength, in finding fault with, and aiming blows at each other." Then, wielding the rhetorical stiletto, he paid tribute to those patriotic Democrats who had subordinated party to national interest, notably General Ambrose E. Burnside, under whose Order No. 38 Vallandigham had been arrested, and—here he twisted the blade—"all those democrats who are nobly exposing their lives and shedding their blood on the battle-field."[23] Lincoln had his secretary, John Nicolay, distribute the document (known as the "Corning letter," after the former U.S. congressman who had led the Albany protest) to key figures among the War Democrats.[24]

There was more to this than rhetoric. Lincoln also took practical steps to broaden the administration's political base by encouraging Old Whigs and patriotic Democrats to form a coalitional political force. This was especially necessary in Maryland, Kentucky, and other parts of the border region, where there was no grass-roots Republican Party of any consequence and where the building up of a Union political organization was an essential counterpart of the federal military presence. It was true that initially Lincoln dispensed patronage to the benefit of his Republican cheerleaders with no less appetite that his Jacksonian predecessors had to their own kind. During March 1861 Democrats were swept from appointive office by the hundreds and replaced with Lincoln loyalists. As Lincoln put it, "The administration distributed to it's [sic] party friends as nearly all the civil patronage as any administration ever did."[25]

But the subsequent wartime story was considerably more complex, as Lincoln eschewed party proscription in his military appointments, was inclusive in his choice of cabinet secretaries, and played out a strategy of "recognition politics." "When you assumed the Presidential chair," John Wien Forney told Lincoln late in the war, "you were, I have no doubt, profoundly affected by the sentiment that you could not conduct your administration without consulting the leading patriotic minds of the Democracy, and without recognizing them in certain official positions." Forney praised Lincoln for replacing his initial secretary of war, Simon Cameron, with Edwin M. Stanton: "You could scarcely have acted otherwise than to have put your political friends into your first Cabinet, but it stands to your credit, on the book of History, that on every proper occasion you have yourself taken by the hand Democrats who felt that you were the representative of the Union idea, and who were resolved to stand by you to the end."[26]

Forney, a Pennsylvania Democratic editor who had voted the Douglas ticket in 1860 but welcomed the new administration as "the only emblem of the Union," had good personal reasons to appreciate the Republican president's ecumenism. During the summer of 1861, after Forney was defeated for the clerkship of the House of Representatives, Lincoln had actively and successfully intervened, calling upon

U.S. senators "to insist" (Forney's words) that he be elected secretary of the Senate. Forney faced some heavyweight opposition, but in this case the beneficiary's staunch loyalty deprived Republicans of cause for complaint.[27] However, by no means did all of the administration's non-Republican appointments escape the criticism of querulous party loyalists. Samuel Galloway, a Columbus, Ohio, attorney, complained to the president that much of the patronage in the state was in the hands, not of "tried and ardent friends," but rather of those whose loyalty was suspect: "mercenaries" and "political hermaphrodites" who had "made themselves conspicuous by a depreceation [*sic*] of the most vigorous acts of your policy."[28] But Lincoln persisted in his course. When Josiah Grinnell delivered a complaint against a Democrat employed as a government clerk, the president replied: "Don't ask me to strike so low; I have to do with those whom I despise; for we are at war. Democratic aid we must have if possible, and I conciliate to avoid all friction."[29]

Lincoln's appointments to military command were so determinedly blind to party, and their record in the field so mixed, that staunch Republicans, including those on the Joint Committee on the Conduct of the War, deemed the policy a grave mistake.[30] Contemplating the party's poor showing in the fall 1862 elections, Carl Schurz minced no words in telling Lincoln, in a brace of letters: "The defeat of the Administration is the Administration's own fault. It admitted its professed opponents to its counsels. It placed the Army, now a great power in this Republic, into the hands of its enemy's [*sic*]" instead of committing it to those "who, fully understanding and appreciating the tendency of the great revolution in which we are engaged, intend to . . . sustain you honestly."[31] But Lincoln was unrepentant, noting that the administration, having come into power "very largely in a minority of the popular vote," could not even embark on the war "without assistance outside of it's [*sic*] party. It was mere nonsense to suppose a minority could put down a majority in rebellion. . . . It so happened that very few of our friends had a military education or were of the profession of arms." He reminded Schurz, "I have scarcely appointed a democrat to a command, who was not urged by many republicans and opposed by none." McClellan was first brought forward by the Republican governor of Ohio; delegations of congressional Republicans made recommendations that, Lincoln recalled, invariably included a majority of Democrats.

Neither performance in command nor sacrificial courage was the preserve of party. "In sealing their faith with their blood, Baker, an[d] Lyon, and Bohlen, and Richardson, republicans, did all that men could do; but," Lincoln asked rhetorically, "did they any more than Kearney, and Stevens, and Reno, and Mansfield, none of whom were republicans, and some, at least of whom, have been bitterly, and repeatedly, denounced to me as secession sympathizers?"[32] Soon after these exchanges with Schurz, Lincoln told John Seymour, the brother of New York's Democratic governor, that "he had appointed most of the officers of the army from among Democrats because most of the West Point men were Democrats, and he believed a man educated in military affairs was better fitted for military office than an uneducated man, and because antislavery men, being generally much akin to peace, had never interested themselves in military matters and in getting up companies, as Democrats had."[33]

An inclusive aspiration similarly characterized Lincoln's relationship with the newspaper press, which he deemed an essential tool in maintaining popular patriotism in the face of accumulating sacrifice. Significantly, he did not follow thirty years' custom and practice by formally establishing an "administration organ," despite encouragement to do so from within his party. There was no doubt an element of realism here: both the arrival of large-circulation papers run by powerful, independent editors and the creation of the Government Printing Office in 1860 to take on the swell of public printing limited the viability of an "organ." But beyond this, a formal administration newspaper had partisan connotations that threatened to hinder its ability to engender national unity.

Instead, Lincoln sought to engage support across a broad range of editors, Republican and Democrat, not simply those robustly loyal to the government but also conservative Unionists whose criticisms of the administration had not put them beyond the pale. Loyalists included Unionist ex-Democrats like Forney, known as "Lincoln's dog," whose *Philadelphia Press* became an informal mouthpiece for Lincoln, as did his *Washington Daily Chronicle*, which had been established—at the president's suggestion—to carry a message of backboned Unionism every day to the thirty thousand troops of the Army of the Potomac. Conservative Unionist editors, including those of "legitimist" Democratic sheets that supported the war but criticized its management, were far less amenable to White House appeals, but Lincoln's strategy of inclusion involved overtures to James Gordon Bennett's *New York Herald,* formerly Democratic and now independent, one of the two or three most influential newspapers of the day. It is probable that in 1864, to prevent Bennett from championing McClellan, the Democrats' presidential candidate, Lincoln offered him an ambassadorial post in France. It was enough to moderate Bennet's hostility toward the president and direct his disdain equally at both Lincoln and McClellan.[34]

The presidential reelection year in fact witnessed the inclusive Unionist strategy at its most overt. Rebranded as the Union Party, Republican loyalists at the national convention in Baltimore in June yoked Lincoln with a border-state Democrat, Andrew Johnson, as his vice-presidential running mate. The evidence concerning Lincoln's alleged intervention in support of Johnson is murky, but we may put some trust in the recollection of the governor of Iowa that Lincoln had told him that "it might be deemed advisable to select some prominent Union Democrat in order to encourage that sentiment throughout the country and satisfy southern men that the Republican party was not acting altogether upon strict party lines"; the president had added that "the loyal element in the Democratic party had rendered us great assistance in their unselfish devotion to the Union, and it was but just that they should be recognized."[35] In late October, with the election imminent, Forney wrote contentedly to the president: "It would have been a . . . disastrous thing if the whole Democratic party in the free states were now a unit against you, and in sympathy with the rebels. That it is not so, results . . . from your generous and patriotic conduct. . . . You know . . . that nothing is more difficult than to dissipate the prejudices of party."[36]

Lincoln's courting of Democrats and conservative Unionists necessarily shaped the way he pursued and presented his administration's agenda. He was alert to their antipathy to abolitionism and the animating power of their racial prejudice, but he recognized their profound loyalty to an unbroken nation. He understood that southern rebellion had obliterated their sense of political obligation toward the slaveholder: the tide of events was carrying them into a slave-free Union. The broadening public hostility to slavery affected even those most alienated from the administration: by the summer of 1863 the Peace Democrat—or "Copperhead"—William Cornell Jewett, while bitterly admonishing Lincoln for his constitutional "usurpations," acknowledged that "the only reliable chart of safety" in the aftermath of war was a policy "based upon the Constitution & the Union ... with the word slavery, buried."[37] More significant, however, than those outside the tent, such as Jewett, were the officeholders of Democratic orientation whose nationalism glued them to an administration party even when it was in full emancipationist mode. John Brough, of Ohio, provides an instructive example.

Once a thoroughgoing Jacksonian anti-abolitionist, Brough adopted Lincoln's language in describing the United States as "the last best hope for freemen throughout the world," proved energetic in raising troops, and—to meet Vallandigham's challenge—accepted the Union Party's nomination for state governor in 1863. During the presidential canvass of 1864 he stumped for Lincoln. The chief burden of his song was the self-delusion, even treachery, of the Democrats' peace platform, which he deemed likely only to cement disunion, but he also found time to defend the president's course on slavery. In a speech at Circleville, a copy of which he sent to Lincoln, Brough remarked, to laughter: "There is not a word in this platform about slavery. I think, as [Horace] Greeley says, 'the world moves.' I think Democratic brethren are getting educated. It used to be we could not start the wagon off without loading slavery in the fore end and into the hind end and into the middle." Brough was defensive about Lincoln's notorious "To whom it may concern" letter, in which the president had made Confederates' acceptance of emancipation a condition of peace negotiations. But, the governor continued, "I will go this far: I never will consent ... in the restoration or reconstruction of this Union, that the powers of slavery ... shall ever be conferred on it again. .... I will have no more guarantees for slavery."[38] In holding firm to his emancipationist course during 1863 and 1864, Lincoln—no less than Greeley—understood that the world was moving, even among the conservative members of his broad nationalist coalition.

LINCOLN AND THE RADICALIZING POTENTIAL OF PARTY

Lincoln's call for party to be subordinated to a higher patriotism was echoed by a wider chorus of Union propagandists. Tracts such as Francis Lieber's *No Party Now but All for Our Country,* a production of the Loyal Publication Society, circulated in the hundreds of thousands.[39] But in practice partisanship remained a potent element of wartime politics, given oxygen by regular and frequent elections. Influenced by his thirty years' political experience, Lincoln recognized the indispensable function of a well-organized party, even at a time of national emergency. We need not doubt his reported remark to John Seymour early in 1863 "that he was a party man and did not believe in any man who was not."[40] This is not to say that his "broad church" approach was hypocritical; rather, this strategy had to be played out within the framework, almost as old as the republic, of party loyalties, customs, and antipathies.

Although the war disrupted and refashioned partisan loyalties, the Republican Party, even when branded as the Union organization, did not stop operating as just that—a political party—whatever the antiparty stance that accompanied its rhetoric of patriotism and country.[41] Above all, it gave Lincoln the organizational means and ideological energy by which to sustain his drive toward a rededicated Union. George S. Boutwell, of Massachusetts, the administration's appointee as commissioner of internal revenue before he was elected to the House or of Representatives in 1862, saw with arresting clarity how much of Lincoln's achievement was rooted in his tenacious hold on his party and its principles, how statesmanship could flourish only through command of a party.[42] As the Pennsylvania congressman William D. Kelley put it, Lincoln "thought of himself as the accepted representative of Republican principles, and felt that he had been charged with the duty of securing . . . their triumph, and of giving his countrymen whatever blessings these principles might be capable of producing."[43] The overall record of his presidency served to rebut those Republicans who feared that in embracing Democrats and former Constitutional Unionists within the Union coalition, he invited an ideological sellout.

Lincoln involved himself personally in the wartime management and operations of his party in several areas, only the chief of which may be summarized here: patronage, propaganda, and electoral mobilization. His interventions in each of these areas helped him exert some influence over a party whose internal divisions between radicals, moderates, and conservatives were no longer held in congressional check by the presence of a Democratic majority. Lincoln may have found his party to be a source of trial and tribulation, but he also found in it a means to advance administration policy, step by step, to a position that by April 1865 had put the final nails in the coffin of the prewar Union.

First, patronage. While Lincoln certainly came to see the benefits of filling military posts without regard to the appointees' party, the essential purpose of the president's civil appointments was to provide rewards evenhandedly to a clamant horde of Republican office seekers, to lubricate the party's machinery, to punish disloyalty, to enhance discipline, and to nourish support.[44] Thus, in the uncertain atmosphere during the early months of 1864, with signs of congressional revolt and the prospect of challenges to his renomination, Lincoln had no qualms about using his control over jobs to buttress his position. Loyal federal officeholders saw off the challenge from radical supporters of Salmon P. Chase, while patronage secured for the president trusted and instructed delegations to the Baltimore national convention from the six largest states—New York, Pennsylvania, Ohio, Illinois, Indiana, and Massachusetts.[45]

In subsequent congressional elections Lincoln intervened to warn Republican officeholders, including the postmasters of Philadelphia and Chicago, against using their local patronage to stymie the return to Congress of key administration supporters.[46] And when the Indiana editor David P. Holloway initially refused to back George Washington Julian, recently nominated for reelection, as the party's candidate, Lincoln quickly brought him into line by threatening to strip him of his job as commissioner of patents. "Your nomination," the president told the congressman, "is as binding on Republicans as mine, and you can rest assured that Mr. Holloway shall support you, openly and unconditionally, or lose his head."[47] Party patronage provided the means of internal discipline, a way for Lincoln to keep the balance between radicals and conservatives, and for that reason alone he was ready to push himself to exhaustion in disposing of appointments.

In the area of propaganda, Lincoln was acutely attentive to the persuasive power of the word as part of what would be called today "White House communications." His opportunities for speaking to large gatherings were limited, but he seized every timely occasion to reach the public through the written word. The pen, as Douglas Wilson has pithily put it, was "Lincoln's sword."[48] And it was above all through the machinery of party that his printed addresses and public letters circulated, whether through the legion of party newspapers, whose mastheads collectively embraced every city and locality; through the loyal publication societies, nominally nonpartisan but in reality adjuncts of the Union-Republican Party; or in summary in the speeches of loyalist governors and congressmen. Although Lincoln used the Corning letter to rebuke partisanship, the White House made sure that it was immediately circulated to loyal newspapers and leading Republicans for party use. Acknowledging receipt, the Chicago Tribune Company reassured the White House: "We loose [*sic*] no time in spreading before our readers the President's admirable reply to the Albany Copperhead committee. . . . The argument is a *crusher*."[49] An impressed Greeley published the letter prominently in his *Tribune,* and he issued tens of thousands in pamphlet form.[50] Writing from Utica, New York, to acknowledge receipt of a copy "under Nicolay's frank," Roscoe Conkling congratulated Lincoln, saying that "it makes the best Campaign document we can have in this State."[51] Nicolay himself hastened to reassure the loyal editor of the *Rochester Evening Express* that it was not policy but a regrettable mistake that had placed an advance copy of the president's letter in the hands of a rival, Copperhead journal: "Not only is there no disposition on my part to furnish these disloyal sheets with unusual facilities, but it has been my invariable custom to withhold from them the courtesies usually extended to the Press."[52]

    Political etiquette and the business of war management kept Lincoln himself from openly campaigning. But the reversion to recognizably partisan politics from 1862 on, after widespread political cooperation during the initial months of the war, gave him every incentive to do his part in mobilizing and sustaining the Republican-Union Party at the polls. Naturally, the setback in the fall elections of 1862—a mark of his administration's unpopularity—did nothing to tighten his hold, but during the following year his political leverage over the party increased, the consequence both of the watershed battlefield successes in early July and of the introduction of national conscription, with all that that implied for the political interdependence of state and national administrations.[53] It is significant that Lincoln's celebrated letter to James Conkling was written in lieu of the personal appearance that Illinois Republicans had asked the president to make as part of the state election campaign during the late summer of 1863. Although that letter defined the party as a patriotic home for all "noble men," uncorrupted by "partisan malice," this did not alter the document's function as a campaign weapon designed to achieve a party victory that would have a bearing on his own reelection prospects.[54] During the canvass of 1864, as previously, Lincoln was busy behind the scenes, often through his secretaries, intervening to help Republican-Unionists in congressional and gubernatorial races, seeking to bring harmony to fractious, sometimes dysfunctional state parties (as in Pennsylvania), maintaining contact with national and local organizers, taking steps to facilitate soldiers' voting in the field, and generally keeping his finger on the pulse of the campaign.[55]

The excessive and distorting partisanship of politics in the wartime Union encouraged misinterpretation and extremism, and to the extent that it prompted exaggerated fears of treason and military failure, it depressed morale and made the administration's task all the more difficult.[56] But there were advantages, too, as the competition for popular endorsement in successive elections worked to put a squeeze on both opposition Democrats and internal critics. Lincoln's Union Party, appealing to patriotic duty during the nation's life-and-death struggle, used the rhetorical and emotional intensity of campaigns to present Democrats and other non-Republicans with an opportunity for cathartic release from association with Copperhead disloyalty and treachery. Forney was only the most high-profile of White House loyalists working to this end—and with recognized success—in both state and national elections in Pennsylvania.[57]

Even more intense was the electoral pressure on both radical and conservative Republican critics of Lincoln to toe the administration line. That the Democrats functioned as a well-organized opposition party acted to contain the Republicans' ideological fractiousness. Conservatives like Senator Edgar Cowan, of Pennsylvania, an old Whig turned Republican, were bitter in their hostility to the abolitionist minority, to whom, they complained, Lincoln had afforded a disproportionate influence in party matters. In his scorn for the view that there was "salvation in the negro in some shape" Cowan was closer to the Democrats than to the emancipationist elements in his own party, but the hard fact of a two-party electoral system kept him loyal to the administration, for in reality there was nowhere else for him to go.[58]

Although many radicals were alienated by what they deemed the administration's lethargy, its tardiness in embracing emancipation and black enlistments, its opposition to confiscating rebels' property, and its lack of interest in freedmen's rights, election-campaign kept these critics, too, in line. Many of them directed their attention to replacing Lincoln in 1864, especially after his pocket veto of the Wade-Davis Bill in July, but by then his renomination was a fact. It is commonly recognized that the August and September victories at Mobile Bay and Atlanta hamstrung those who were still working for Lincoln's withdrawal, but no less important in reestablishing unity behind the president was the Democrats' nomination at Chicago of George B. McClellan on an antiwar platform. Henry Wilson's earnest letter to the president, written just a few days after these events, revealed just how electoral imperatives shaped the radicals' response, dwarfing their concerns over the party's leader: "I write to say that our friends are fighting up in New England. The Chicago Convention has arroused [*sic*] them to some extent. . . . They have been very much cast down, and I must say to you they have been finding great fau[l]t with their candidate." Noting a widespread loathing of Montgomery Blair for his vehement hostility to the radicals' program, Wilson continued: "We are to have a terrible contest. . . . If we are beaten our friends will cast the blame wholly on you for they believe they can carry the country easy with another candidate."[59] A similar set of priorities prompted Charles Sumner's comment that, should Lincoln not see "that we shall all be stronger and more united under another candidate," then "our duty is . . . to unite in opposition to the common enemy."[60]

Although the radicals were a thorn in Lincoln's side—John Hay commonly referred to them as the "jacobins"—and sometimes provoked him beyond exasperation and into uncharacteristic anger, his relationship with the progressive wing of his party stood at the center of the wartime reassertion and redefinition of American ideals. Each needed the other in ways that the president understood better than most of his radical critics. Lincoln was not blind to the value of the moral and practical energy that the radicals brought to the party's campaigning, especially after his emancipation edict had given them what the conservative Unionist James C. Welling described as "the compactness of a Macedonian phalanx."[61] After two months on the stump during the fall 1863 canvass, during which he spoke in Illinois, Ohio, and New York to crowds totaling more than two hundred thousand, U.S. Senator Zachariah Chandler reported to Lincoln that, taking "Your Proclamation as Our guiding Star[,] . . . we have carried *every State* . . . save one. Ohio & New York were more radically canvassed than *any State ever was before.* Are not these lessons instructive? Conservatives and Traitors are buried together."[62]

Lincoln understood that crusading zeal of this kind, especially when complemented by the energies of a millennialist, progressive Protestant pulpit, provided the administration and its party with an idealistic nationalism, an antidote to creeping defeatism and war-weariness. When he said that the radicals—"the unhandiest devils in the world to deal with"—faced "Zionwards," he implicitly acknowledged that they and he broadly shared a vision of what the United States should become.[63] Certainly, his values and ideals placed him much closer to the radical-progressive side of his party than to the conservatives, while his temperament, his aversion to self-righteousness, and his gritty political realism kept the distance between them. Moving a step at a time toward and then beyond emancipation, never retreating from a position once taken, Lincoln did not so alienate these vocal elements of the party that they were entirely lost to him. Decent relations with radicals such as Owen Lovejoy, Charles Sumner, and Henry Wilson, for instance, provided their own form of encouragement. Lincoln developed real affection for Lovejoy, who defended him against party insurgents in 1864; the president came to describe his fellow Illinoisan as "my most generous friend."[64]

A few of the radicals acknowledged Lincoln's skill in holding the ring and uniting "men of varying shades of sentiment upon a policy radical enough *to destroy slavery,* conservative enough *to save the nation.*"[65] But many remained reluctant to face up to this reality, and their attempts to replace Lincoln with a better man led him to reflect in exasperation to Carl Schurz that were he to withdraw, "it is much more likely that the factions opposed to me would fall to fighting among themselves and . . . bring on a confusion worse confounded." Hurt by the radicals' charge that a lust for power had made him blind to the common cause, he asked, "Have they thought of that common cause when trying to break me down? I hope they have."[66]

What the radicals got was a party leader in the White House who was electorally much more powerful than they were, whose support could give added weight to congressional and gubernatorial candidacies, and whose strategy of political outreach meant that he was widely seen as above party.[67] Benjamin Brewster reported from Philadelphia early in 1864 that "a large body of the old line Democrats will support you when they would not vote for any other nominee of your party." The key to Lincoln's appeal, he later judged, was that "you are not &

never were a politician. The Providence of Almighty God placed you where you are & He will keep you where you are for the good of your country & to vindicate the cause of public liberty & human rights for the whole race."[68] The perception, however mistaken, that Lincoln was fulfilling less a party political role than a providential one was widely held and goes some way toward explaining why he was more popular than his party. John Forney understood this acutely. Taking the public pulse early in 1864, he reported to Lincoln that "in New York as in Philadelphia, you have the people at your back, and to them the party managers must yield. . . . Day by day it becomes clearer that our noble President sways the hearts of all true men as no man since Washington and Jackson has controlled them."[69]

Jesse Fell, one of Lincoln's Illinois associates, writing to the radical U.S. senator Lyman Trumbull in August 1863, delivered this judgment on the president: "We . . . know that he is both honest and patriotic; that if he don't go forward as *fast* as some of us like, he *never goes backward*."[70] It was an apt appraisal, for this was very much how Lincoln saw himself: when Zachariah Chandler, after the party made gains on progressive platforms in the fall 1863 elections, sought to nerve him against an expected conservative backlash, the president replied, "I hope to 'stand firm' enough to not go backward, and yet not go forward fast enough to wreck the country's cause."[71] Only once, during the grim days of August 1864, did Lincoln come close to faltering in his determination never to retreat from a position once adopted: under the duress of events, he considered an overture to the Confederates that would have sidelined emancipation as a condition of reunion. But the moment came and went without action. Rather it is Lincoln's steadfastness in holding to his values and strategic goals that is striking, and that steadfastness was essential to the emergence of a refashioned Union after four years of war.

Equally important in securing this new order was the president's political strategy. Presenting himself as above conventional partisanship, he drew upon the northern Democrats' deep well of nationalism and their broad dislike of slavery. He thereby fashioned a cross-party alliance that remained just strong enough to provide the political basis for a Union victory. But the nation that emerged in April 1865 did not draw equally upon Republican and Democratic philosophical traditions. Rather, it chiefly breathed the antislavery nationalism of the prewar Republicans. That it did so was a measure of Lincoln's ready deployment of his party's agencies. It testified, too, to his sharing of the ideals, though not the political strategy, articulated most forcefully by the radical and progressive elements of the party that he not only led but mastered.

5

Rebels and Patriots in the Confederate "Revolution"

GEORGE C. RABLE

One of the Rebels was a phrase that often appeared on Confederate cards, envelopes, and other items, usually with a drawing of some kind. Who were these rebels? They included George Washington (dubbed a "Southern Gentleman, and Slaveholder"), Martha Washington, southern white women more generally, and even slaves.[1] *Rebel,* a term of derision repeatedly used by northerners, became a badge of honor once Confederates decided to turn the hateful word into a source of pride. As one obviously struggling poet expressed it:

> Rebels before
> Our fathers of yore
> Rebel's the right name
> Washington bore
> Why then be ours the same.[2]

Yet the word still rankled when uttered by Yankees, and many northern newspapers were filled with bitter denunciations of "the rebels." Did northerners not realize that American "independence was won by a rebellion" and "liberty . . . achieved by secession"? asked one Georgia woman. Of course most northerners realized no such thing, and in their mind the "rebellion" had no just cause. Worse still for Confederates, the word *rebel* suggested that the struggle for southern independence might not succeed: the failure of the new southern nation would make Confederates mere "rebels" who would fall under the yoke of Federal tyranny.[3]

The very intensity of the editorials that at first rejected the oppro-brious label and then embraced it suggested not only that word choice mattered—as in this case it surely did—but that even as armies fought in ghastly battles, the bitter debate over naming the war would con-tinue. In July 1861 the editor of the *Richmond Daily Dispatch*, the news-paper in the Confederate capital with the largest circulation, denied that the Confederates had rebelled against the Constitution or the Union (defined as the "creation of the states"). With a bit of sarcastic humor, he added that Confederates were rebelling against "Yankeedom, against Yankee commerce, Yankee manufactures, and Yankee lords and masters," an undeniable fact that surprised and perplexed self-righteous northerners who had tried to place southerners under a moral quaran-tine because of slavery. Just over a month later this same editor added that if epithets had been "missiles of war," the Yankees would long be-fore have conquered the South. Instead, repeated use of the word *rebel* epitomized northerners' "bigoted, pharisaical, self-conceited" attitude toward southerners and failed to recognize that throughout human his-tory those fighting for liberty had often been branded "rebels." Three years later, as the Confederacy tottered toward destruction, the *Dispatch* was not quite sure whether to embrace the term *rebel* with suitable references to George Washington or to spurn it for its implication that southerners were mere subjects who had defied legitimate authority.[4]

Repeatedly, however, Confederate propagandists as well as ordi-nary folk affirmed their loyalty to hallowed traditions, including many associated with the old Union. During the first months of the war, speeches, editorials, and sermons brimmed with "patriotism." In the spring of 1861, patriotism meant not only resisting northern coercion but also sustaining the Confederacy as the last best hope of republican liberty in the world. Ardent southerners missed or ignored the irony of Lincoln and many other northerners' making similar claims, but then, as is often the case, early war enthusiasm produced blinkered views of reality. Civilian and soldier alike appealed to the sacred right of self-determination as enshrined in the Declaration of Independence and the history of the American Revolution. Their crusade was no mere rebellion, yet whether *civil war* or *revolution* fit the case remained a point of contention.[5]

Although conservative southerners had often dismissed Thomas Jefferson's famous affirmation of human equality as vaporous and dangerous theorizing, in his inaugural address as provisional Confederate president, Jefferson Davis explicitly appealed to the Declaration of Independence (and cribbed its language), observing that the "American idea of government rests on the consent of the governed" and that any people had a "right" to "alter or abolish governments at will whenever they become destructive of the ends for which they were established." A little over a year later, in his inaugural address as permanent Confederate president, Davis urged the southern people to prove themselves "worthy of the inheritance bequeathed us by the patriots of the Revolution."[6] Of course Abraham Lincoln invoked similar historical memories, so the battle was joined over who were the true heirs of the Founding Fathers. Yet even during the 1850s, if not before, southern nationalists had claimed to be lineal descendants of revered American patriots. "But if we could do as our fathers did," firebrand William Lowndes Yancey had suggested, "[and] organize Committees of Safety . . . [to] fire the Southern heart . . . by one organized, concerted action, we can precipitate the cotton States into a Revolution."[7]

Indeed Jefferson Davis, other politicians, editors, preachers, and ardent Confederates of all stripes discussed patriotism as if the meaning of the word had hardly changed since the eighteenth century, as if the struggles of the 1860s mirrored those of the 1770s. Simply make the spirit of 1776 the spirit of 1861, and the Confederate nation would emerge triumphant. On the Fourth of July 1861, orators from Virginia to Texas trumpeted a second war of independence whose results would overshadow the American Revolution, and they laid claim to the holiday for freeborn southerners. Everyone, from editors to poets, lauded the heroes from the southern states who had helped win the Revolutionary War as inspiring examples for the current generation. In early 1863, with awkward but telling words, Jefferson Davis praised Virginians: "You have shown yourselves in no respect to be degenerate sons of your fathers."[8]

Or mothers for that matter: Reports of noble women cheerfully sending even their youngest sons off to war could never be complete without comparisons to the female patriots of the American Revolution. Hauling old spinning wheels out from attics or reusing eighteenth-century dresses literally placed young women of the war generation in the roles (and sometimes the clothes) of their Revolutionary grandmothers. The sight of women gathering in churches to sew uniforms and flags evoked memories of a previous century. "Let maids and ma-trons, with universal chorus of their sweet praises, crown the fame of the brave officers and soldiers who have driven back the brutal and worse than barbarian hordes that threatened their peaceful homes," ex-ulted one editor after the Confederate victory at First Manassas. Patri-otic women and patriotic armies would ensure the triumph of southern arms against a numerically superior enemy. In fact, Jefferson Davis and his critics agreed that the patriotism of the soldiers and the people gave Confederates great and likely decisive advantages in the contest.[9]

Calls for stalwart freemen to join the fight for liberty had of course been a constant refrain during the Revolution. According to patriot propaganda, sturdy farmers could grab their muskets and defeat the greatest military power on the face of the earth. Although George Washington and many of his officers had emphasized the need for training and discipline in an increasingly professional army, Ameri-cans preferred to recall the noble yeomen of Lexington and Concord.[10] The need for public virtue and patriotic self-sacrifice seemed obvious enough at the beginning of the Civil War; now all southerners had to do was find their own George Washington. Reading over one of Davis's early messages to Congress, young Sarah Wadley, in Louisiana, concluded that the president had just the right qualities: "Wise, moder-ate, and just in council, cool, brave and gallant in battle; firm, energetic and instant in the performance of his executive duties, truly we have in him a second Washington." False but widely circulated reports that Davis himself had been on the field at Manassas undoubtedly encour-aged such comparisons. Only days before that engagement, Joseph E. Johnston, of all people, had in fact suggested that Davis "should appear in the position Genl. Washington occupied during the revolution." He could leave "civil affairs" to the vice president and join the troops in the field. Davis's inauguration ceremony, held on 22 February 1862 near a statue of Washington on the grounds of the Virginia state capitol, con-veyed an unmistakable meaning.[11]

Transforming Davis into a Washington or making the war against the Yankees analogous to the American Revolution became more than rhetorical flourishes as casualties piled up and discouragement set in. In this second war for independence as in the first, there would of course be "Tories," who had no great love for self-government and less stomach for sacrifice, unscrupulous, calculating sorts whose loyalties were for sale to the highest bidder. In the summer of 1861 it was easy to discuss the Tories of 1776 with some historical detachment or even sympathy, and they made a nice contrast to the more degraded Tories of the current age, who offered aid and comfort to a much less honorable cause than king and country. Given the war fever that had swept across the South, however, there seemed little danger that such dissidents posed much of a threat to the Confederate government. Such proud confidence began to crumble, however, as the war in the western theater went badly, and denunciations of southern "Tories" grew more strident. Indeed, condemnations of their treason belied assertions that there were not enough of them to do much harm. Dismissing southern Unionists contemptuously, while describing the dangers of subjugation in ever harsher language or warning that contemporary Tories would become a byword in future generations, sent a decidedly mixed message.[12]

As a source of historical analogies, however, the American Revolution proved indispensable. References to Valley Forge or other low points in the American Revolution offered hope that the Confederate cause too might triumph over adversity. In August 1863 Governor Zebulon Vance, of North Carolina, remained surprisingly optimistic about the war. He actually took heart in weighing the Confederacy's problems against those of the Revolutionary generation. Not only had the British occupied more southern territory than Federals now held but the Whig-Tory divisions had run much deeper and more dangerous than any fissures that had thus far appeared in the Confederacy. In appealing to Revolutionary traditions, Confederate leaders hoped the southern people would remain true to their heritage even as their underdog armies fought with a tenacity worthy of Washington's tattered legions. One Georgia editor compared the year 1778 to 1864 to prove that despite sagging morale, the soldiers in the field would endure to the end. Invasion and occupation should only redouble a determination to resist the enemy; hardship and misfortune became the true tests of national character. Yet the appearance of phrases such as *sunshine patriots* hinted at a widening gap between determined soldiers and disaffected civilians. Simply avowing over and over that the Confederacy could never be conquered would not make it so.[13]

References to the American Revolution generally carried a warm patriotic glow, but they ignored a troublesome aspect of the historical analogy that revealed a fundamental contradiction in Confederate ideology. Despite all the talk of a "Confederate revolution," that word *revolution* evoked some disturbing images. "Secession is nothing but revolution," Robert E. Lee had written as the Deep South states were leaving the Union. "The framers of our Constitution never exhausted so much labor, wisdom, and forbearance in its formation, and surrounded it with so many guards and securities, if it was intended to be broken by every member of the Confederacy at will. . . . It is idle to talk of secession. Anarchy would have been established, and not a government by Washington, Hamilton, Jefferson, Madison and others patriots of the Revolution." Unlike Lee, the Georgian Susan Cornwall could "see nothing now in Union but danger to our sacred rights," yet she worried about the unintended consequences of disunion: "We are in the midst of a revolution. Who can prophesy its results?"[14]

Opponents of secession typically appealed to fears of uncertainty and upheaval. Doubting that the "hasty legislators at Montgomery" were wiser than the Founding Fathers, a conservative North Carolinian deplored "the wild spirit of the revolution" that has "overthrown the greatest and best government which ever blessed and guided the destinies of man." He used the word *usurpations* to describe the actions of the secession conventions, applying a common eighteenth-century epithet against men claiming to model themselves after the patriots of the American Revolution. In a more sober-minded way, that stout opponent of disunion and future vice president of the new southern nation, Alexander H. Stephens, warned shortly after Lincoln's election: "Revolutions are much easier started than controlled and the men that begin them, even for the best purposes and objects, seldom end them. The American Revolution of 1776 was one of the few exceptions to this remark that the history of the world furnishes."[15]

Whatever one's stance on the constitutional issues involved, supporters and opponents of secession all talked of a southern "revolution," especially after delegates assembled in Montgomery, Alabama, to create the Confederate States of America. Newspapers routinely referred to the progress of the revolution in everything from news snippets to long editorials. Yet from the beginning it seemed a peculiar revolution, because the firebrands did not become the leaders of the new government. "I should not have voted for Mr. Stephens [for Vice President]," Postmaster General John H. Reagan, himself no radical, recalled after the war. "It was the first time I had known of a people embarking in a revolution and selecting as one of their leaders a person known to be opposed to it."[16]

The meaning of revolution became diffuse, and it often seemed that those who talked about a Confederate revolution did not really mean it. Shortly before Davis's inauguration in Richmond, the Georgia politician Howell Cobb extolled a Confederate "constitution characterized by the conservatism which so eminently distinguished 'the Father of his Country.'" Invoking the spirit of 1776 and George Washington made the crusade for southern independence seem less radical and less disruptive. Jefferson Davis had at first denied that a revolution was taking place at all—a statement no doubt designed to ease fears in the Border South and a sentiment echoed by other cautious politicians. Secession had followed strictly constitutional procedures, and as one pamphleteer expressed it, the true "revolutionary sentiment . . . originated with our enemies." Prominent Confederates cast disunion as a careful and legitimate step; one delegate to the Alabama secession convention claimed that it was a "revolution that has been accomplished without anarchy."[17]

In selecting delegates for the secession conventions, voters had used the ballot box to launch a revolution by sovereign states in a perfectly legal and peaceful manner. They had chosen not to foment disorder but rather to "escape" from "anarchy" and "preserve those conservative principles of the fathers of the Republic, which were fast being overwhelmed by popular fanaticism," Cobb proclaimed in his farewell address as president of the Provisional Congress.[18] In many respects of course *conservative revolution* is an oxymoron that hardly explains the problem facing the new Confederacy. "We are not revolutionists—we are resisting revolution," the prominent Presbyterian theologian James Henley Thornwell avowed after the war had been going on for more than a year. The rhetoric, however, had long since become Orwellian. As Virginia was being dragged toward disunion, the *Richmond Examiner* had warned against further kowtowing to northern demands: "Submission is revolution; Secession will be conservatism." Not satisfied with that baffling logic, the editor went on to justify bold steps with a seemingly conservative argument: "To escape revolution in fact we must adopt revolution in form. To stand still is revolution—revolution already inflicted on us by our bitter, fanatical, unrelenting enemies." Here were the multiple meanings of *revolution* in all their glory. The proslavery ideologue George Fitzhugh described the "Revolution of 1861" as a "reactionary" movement to roll back the excesses of both the Protestant Reformation and the American Revolution. He praised southerners for creating a society based on "prescription" rather than "speculation."[19]

Such disembodied abstractions were ironically used to justify a "revolution" whose proponents claimed to spurn philosophical speculation. The fear of innovation became apparent even before the delegates at Montgomery had drafted a constitution. "In all revolutions or remodeling of governments, there are sure to arise many crotchety men, with new fangled notions, and utopian dreams, offering new schemes and reforms in government which they think indispensably necessary for the perfection of the system," a Georgia editor warned. He hoped the convention would be "particularly cautious in receiving suggestions of these tinkering experimenters." An address by the Confederate Congress offered reassurance on that score: "This Government is a child of law instead of sedition, of right instead of violence, of deliberation instead of insurrection. Its early life was attended by no anarchy, no rebellion, no suspension of authority, no social disorders, no lawless disturbances." And to drive the point home: "The utmost conservatism marked every proceeding and public act. . . . We were not remitted to brute force or natural law, or the instincts of reason. The charters of freedom were scrupulously observed."[20]

Many white southerners would have argued that slavery remained essential for that conservative social order. "The special boasts of the slave-holding States of America," declared John Gill Shorter, governor of Alabama, "is that we have as the basis of our conservatism an establishment of domestic labor which gives strength and stability to their government." Shorter offered a soothing picture of people calmly going about their business under the protection of just laws. An Alabama commissioner sent to persuade Kentuckians to join the southern revolution presented a millennial vision of a republic that could "clothe the world with our staple, give wings to her commerce, and supply with bread the starving operative in our lands, and at the same time preserve an institution that has done more to civilize and Christianize the heathen than all human agencies besides—an institution alike beneficial to both races, ameliorating the moral, physical, and intellectual condition of the one and giving wealth and happiness to the other." A prosperous future stretched out before a people freed from economic thralldom to the northern states. Southern society had produced a generation of unselfish statesmen; or as one writer asserted more broadly, "Domestic slavery elevates the characters of all men."[21]

That slavery, according to a leading Presbyterian divine, made the "dominant race" conservative seemed axiomatic when defenders of Confederate orthodoxy railed against unbridled democracy in the northern states. The danger of course remained that the new southern nation might fall under the same malign influences. "We have a surfeit of liberty," a Georgia editor confided to Vice President Stephens. "Parties ruined the old government and will ruin us." To his way of thinking the solution was for the state governments and perhaps the Confederate government to follow the lead of South Carolina and restrict the number of elected offices. In magazine essays that circulated primarily among the intellectual elite, ultraconservatives bemoaned the influence of presidential and congressional elections whose excesses spilled over into business, society, and even the church. A Texas judge deplored a "bastard liberty which is the twin brother of Anarchy," whose advocates would "cloak incipient treason under the garb of liberty of speech."[22]

Those who dared criticize the Confederate government's fighting for its own existence and spread gloomy predictions about the war clearly fell under the ban. The candor of such reactionaries was often breathtaking. "Man is not capable of self-government because he is a fallen creature," the Georgia Episcopalian Stephen Elliott thundered. "Interest, passion, ambition, lust sway him far more than reason or honor." Warnings against the tyranny of the majority even elicited calls for the creation of what one writer termed a "Patrician Republic," which would limit the power of the people and end the reign of demagogues. An article in the *Southern Literary Messenger* described the South as a "social Aristocracy" based on slavery that would defend its values against radical democracy and northern tyranny. An even more tactless Richmond editor suggested that the new Confederacy should "consist exclusively of gentlemen and negroes."[23]

Such a statement might seem to flatter the southern masses by defining all white men as gentlemen, but in fact the antidemocratic animus was plain. Secessionists talked of a united people rising up to resist northern aggression, but in state after state they worked hard to prevent a vote on the question. The secession conventions for the most part refused to submit their handiwork to the people. In Montgomery, the Confederacy's founders, chosen by these same conventions, drafted a national constitution and elected a president without the least deference to the popular will. From Mississippi to Virginia, charges of hypocrisy, double-dealing, and even tyranny arose from defeated cooperationists desperately trying to prevent what many foresaw as a political and likely military disaster. They threw the phrase *consent of the governed* back into the faces of would-be revolutionaries who had used appeals for self-determination to justify disunion and then beat back calls for a referendum on the decisions made by the secession conventions. "These are not the times when we should hearken to the small counsels of small politicians, and give ourselves over to the mandates of cross-road caucuses," declared one Alabama secessionist, whose words dripped with contempt for the messiness of democratic politics.[24]

In Virginia and other states, proposed constitutional changes sought to roll back democratic reforms. One Richmond editor held South Carolina up as the "finest model of Government, equally removed from monarchical and mob rule." He even suggested that "thousands of men who would be disfranchised by the adoption of the old [Virginia] Constitution" would be "ready to sign a petition for its restoration." Not surprisingly, the governor of South Carolina, Francis Pickens, extolled the Confederacy as a bulwark against "consolidated democracy" resting on "conservative principles." Such a republic could never be subjugated, because the "ruling race" would spring to arms while their slaves cultivated the fields. He implied of course that other states should become more like South Carolina and reject the excesses, if not the essence, of American democracy. Ironically, the criticisms of Thomas Jefferson—now deemed a "visionary, theoretical, and fanatical political monomaniac" who had foisted "red Republican" ideas on the United States—proceeded apace in his native Virginia.[25]

In the summer of 1861, former Whigs led by Alexander H. H. Stuart, with tireless editorial support from the *Richmond Whig,* denounced majority rule as a pernicious doctrine that had failed. The *Whig*'s editor, Robert Ridgeway, favored restricting the franchise to taxpayers not only in Virginia but throughout the Confederacy. Reducing the number of elected officials would supposedly promote disinterested statesmanship. The state convention drafted a new constitution that would have made most judgeships appointive positions and left most local officials to be selected by the courts, but despite what many considered halfway measures, a largely indifferent electorate defeated it. Perhaps John M. Daniel, editor of the *Richmond Examiner*, best identified the fatal weakness in these moves to limit democracy: they would deprive poor soldiers of their birthright as freemen. And of course setting class against class could prove fatal to the war effort.[26]

The very idea of class divisions ran counter to Confederate definitions of the good society. On arriving in Montgomery for his inauguration, Jefferson Davis claimed that "we shall have nothing to fear at home, because at home we shall have homogeneity." He described his fellow citizens as "men of one flesh, of one bone, of one interest, one purpose, and of identity in domestic institutions." Slavery might have destroyed the old Union, but it would unify the Confederacy. The words *harmony* and *unity* appeared often in public speeches and documents. "We now present the gratifying spectacle of a united and harmonious people satisfied with our institutions, ardently attached to the government and resolved to maintain it," rejoiced Alabama governor A. B. Moore, who asserted that "all classes" had rallied to the cause. Such brave assertions continued throughout the war. In early 1862 several leading Georgia politicians lauded public unity and urged Confederates to remain "forbearing to one another, frowning upon all factious opposition and censorious criticisms." On 4 July 1863, as Lee's army was retreating from Gettysburg, a Richmond editor was still praising the "great and unprecedented unanimity" that had helped the Confederacy avoid the deep divisions that had weakened the patriot cause during the American Revolution. In 1864 an Atlanta editor marveled at how the "decree of Providence has transfigured us into a oneness such as no people ever exhibited." Heroism and devotion had characterized the behavior not only of countless men in the ranks but of women and children as well, making them all "joint heirs of illustrious renown."[27]

Throughout the war, Confederate apologists claimed that men of all classes had eagerly volunteered to serve the new nation. The customary conservative emphasis on society as a unified organic whole became a central theme of speeches and editorials. In early 1864 an address by the Confederate Congress noted how the southern people "rose en masse to assert their liberty and protect their menaced rights." As for the Confederate army, it was "no hireling soldiery," a phrase referring both to the Hessians of the American Revolution and to the offscourings of northern free-labor society. "All vocations and classes contributed to the swelling numbers. Abandoning luxuries and comforts to which they had been accustomed, they submitted cheerfully to the scanty fare and exactive service of the camps." Significantly, the congressmen went out of their way to praise the wealthy for bearing their fair share of the burden, without putting much emphasis on the many poorer men who fought alongside them. In addition, there appeared a tension between social unity and individual valor: "Our soldiers are not a consolidated mass, an unthinking machine, but an army of intelligent units." Thus the citizen soldier distinguished himself even as Confederates celebrated their supposed social cohesion. All this of course begged several questions, including whether this address bore much relationship to reality. But then politicians could hardly afford to probe the question of social tensions in the Confederate ranks. A Georgia editor even defended the infamous exemption of slaveowners and overseers in the conscription law, saying that slavery elevated the position of all whites and "makes the poor man respectable."[28]

Aside from the Yankee invaders, what truly endangered this idyllic picture of social unity was old-fashioned politics. Even before a shot had been fired, a writer in *DeBow's Review* expressed the hope that the new government would somehow escape the baleful influence of "factionists, village lawyers, pot-house politicians, and party myrmidons." According to Howell Cobb, "the spirit of party" had never infected the deliberations of the Provisional Congress, and denunciations of anything that smacked of organized opposition became routine among both supporters and even most critics of the Davis administration. As the southern nation confronted its first great military crisis during the spring of 1862, the Arkansas editor John Eakin avowed that loyal Confederates longed for "a strong and stable government, free from the fluctuations of popular caprice and the arts of the demagogue. . . . We have lost all taste for political rantings. We are tired of the meetings, and everlasting speechifying and elections. We wish quiet room for honest industry." The longing for a political tranquility that never was and never could be reflected a false dichotomy between corrupt politicians and a virtuous people. Whatever their reservations about the use of the word *revolution* or about the excesses of democracy, ardent Confederates loved to portray the movement for an independent southern nation as a popular uprising of self-sacrificing citizens who were willing to stake their honor, their families, and their lives on a cause that transcended the machinations of small-bore politicians.[29]

At the same time, and even before social cracks and internal conflict became undeniable or at least unavoidable, committed southern nationalists pondered a troublesome future. Ironically, some of their worries reflected a strong faith that the Confederates would win the war but might lose the peace if hordes of northerners suddenly descended on the southern Eden. What made that prospect especially frightening had already been established by the rants of sectional agitators. During the secession crisis, the Mississippian L. Q. C. Lamar had described the North as a land of "heterogenous populations, . . . red Republicanism, infidelity and anti-Christian ideas." By defining the Yankees as essentially a foreign people, such statements reinforced a defensiveness and paranoia that went beyond fears of invasion and military occupation. Once the war began, and anticipating future northern migration, proposals soon appeared that would have limited the franchise to the native born. Thomas R. R. Cobb viewed Yankee immigrants as a potentially "discordant" element bound to spark the same kind of trouble that had destroyed the old Union. With overwhelming numbers and infected by dangerous isms, such undesirables threatened, in the words of one Richmond editor, to "subjugate us at the ballot box."[30]

These alarmist cries produced nothing in the way of legislation, perhaps because loyal Confederates believed they could somehow inoculate the young against such dangerous influences. Southern nationalists had long called for a declaration of cultural and educational independence from the Yankees, and secession marked the beginning of a drive to cast off the malign influence of northern ideas. Now was the time not only to expel Yankee teachers but also to produce textbooks inculcating southern values. To throw aside works "infested with abolitionism," as one writer described northern texts, and replace them with books written by authors of sounder views became the fondest desire of fire-eating intellectuals. Even the preface to an English grammar published in Tennessee celebrated the liberation of southern young people from "Abolition dependencies." Reviewing two readers for elementary students, the *Charleston Mercury* expressed the hope that at last southern schoolchildren would learn true English, as opposed to the Yankees' "corrupt provincial dialect." In calling for books written and published by southerners, whose "peculiar social system" was "obnoxious to the pharisseism of the world," educational reformers offered a millennial vision of proslavery principles drawn from the Bible spreading across the globe. Southerners could vindicate their "social system" and put the lie to those who would brand them an "inferior people," declared Calvin H. Wiley, a leading promoter of public schools in North Carolina. Yet Wiley realized that there would always be those who would "repress the masses" in order to preserve their own power and that educational reform ran up against the antidemocratic forces in Confederate politics.[31]

This was not merely another unresolved tension in official ideology; it was a small though significant indication that for all of the talk of 1776, of a conservative revolution, and of social harmony, the rhetoric of unity could not mask the reality of division. While Jefferson Davis continued to praise the southern people for their unstinting support for the war and their "cheerful endurance of privation," by early 1864 even he had to admit that "discontent, disaffections and disloyalty" had appeared among those who "have enjoyed quiet and safety at home." After this none too subtle jab at North Carolinians and Georgians, Davis called for suspending the writ of habeas corpus, because to "temporize with disloyalty in the midst of war is but to quicken it to the growth of treason." Patriotism now meant a willingness to sacrifice some liberties in the defense of others. In reality, the administration faced critics from all sides, some calling for stronger war measures, others crying out for states' rights, and still others making individual liberty their lodestar. "Too many Revolutions have shipwrecked upon internal division," the fire-eater and acerbic Davis critic Laurence Keitt wrote to his wife. "This Revolution proves that canonized imbecility is but a straw before the wrath of the masses—it seems to be a law of humanity that generation after generation must rescue its liberties from the insidious grasp of a foe without or within." And Confederates faced both types of enemy.[32]

That governments in times of war abused their powers had long been a political truism. That free governments faced continuous threats to liberty echoed from eighteenth-century English and American pamphleteers, and these arguments were obviously familiar to Confederates steeped in the history of the American Revolution. Were the southern people themselves virtuous enough to sustain the new government, or would scheming politicians sabotage the entire experiment? The arguments flew back and forth during the war and beyond. Early on, the always critical Thomas R. R. Cobb considered Montgomery "absolutely tainted with selfish, ambitious schemes for personal aggrandizement." This was hardly a new story, and knowledgeable Confederates could cite many examples from ancient and modern history to prove that corruption had often destroyed governments, but they hoped that their virtuous leaders could avoid such a fate. Conveniently forgetting that George Washington had dispensed rum to thirsty Virginians, one reformer suggested that Confederates must end the practice of plying voters with alcohol; another suggested excluding drunkards, gamblers, and adulterers from public office.[33]

Such proposals might seem wildly irrelevant in the midst of a civil war, but then the discussions of rebellion, patriotism, and revolution often seem curiously removed from more practical political and military questions. Yet political ideologues loved to wrestle with such matters, as did the clergy, who called the southern people to repentance for a host of political sins. As Augustus Baldwin Longstreet pointed out in a fast-day sermon, governments of all types face difficulties, whether from too many rulers or too few, whether from corrupt politicians or their selfish constituents, but only the gospel of Jesus Christ could lead a nation in the proper direction. The first Confederate jeremiads warned against conducting politics as usual. The prominent Presbyterian divine Benjamin Morgan Palmer set the tone for the discussion: "Let us strive to bring back the purer days of the republic when honest men waited like Cincinnatus at his plow, to be called forth for service, and before noisy candidates cried their wares at the hustings like fisherwomen in the market—when a ribald press did not thrust its obtrusive gaze into the sanctities of private life, and the road to office did not lead through the pillory of public abuse and scandal—and when the votes of people expressed their virtuous unbiased will." It remained to be seen, the *Charleston Mercury* observed on the opening day of the Montgomery convention, "whether, with slave institutions, the master race can establish and perpetuate free government."[34]

The editor was hardly arguing that slavery and free government were incompatible, but even the most zealous Confederate sometimes had trouble believing that the triumph of the southern revolution was either preordained or inevitable. In at least one respect the early signs were hardly auspicious. The secrecy of the secession conventions, the Montgomery convention, and the Provisional Congress might be justified because, after all, the Founding Fathers had drafted the sacred Constitution in an often stifling atmosphere, behind guarded doors and closed windows. Yet such proceedings hardly inspired public confidence and instead fostered suspicion. The excuse of preventing information from leaking to the enemy soon wore thin as Congress debated in secret session not only military matters but also financial measures and almost any other important issue. One Texas congressmen who generally supported the Davis administration finally concluded that "in Republican governments, the proceedings of Legislative bodies should always be public." This was all fine in theory, but Confederate practice was far different; at first the exception, secret sessions soon became the rule.[35]

Unfortunately, even the northern Congress met in open session, and the idea of shielding the proceedings of government from the public appeared foolhardy and dangerous. Despite often strong reservations about democracy, Confederate leaders had trouble defending such secrecy, and this played into the hands of administration opponents. "The secret sessions of Congress are becoming a blighting curse to the country," declared Georgia governor Joseph E. Brown—a man hypersensitive about his own prerogatives—in a long blast at the Confederate government. "They are used as a convenient mode of covering up from the people such acts or expressions of their representatives as will not bear investigation in the light of day. Almost every act of usurpation of power, or of bad faith, has been conceived, brought forth and nurtured in secret session." Decrying efforts to suspend habeas corpus, an Alabama editor demanded the names of those congressmen "who, in secret conclave, obsequiously laid the liberties of this country at the feet of the President."[36]

That was precisely the problem as some Confederates saw it: secrecy inevitably led to despotism. Worried that congressional sycophants were in league with Jefferson Davis, the *Charleston Mercury* persistently and obsessively attacked secret sessions. The real threat to liberty came not from a few southern Tories, who were far less dangerous than the Tories of 1776, but from a president who threatened to run roughshod over constitutional safeguards. Congress not only did not check such abuses of power but instead fostered the illegitimate expansion of executive authority. "A free government which begins with secrecy naturally ends in tyranny," the *Mercury* thundered.[37]

Fears of despotism extended far beyond the editorial ravings of Robert Barnwell Rhett Sr. and his equally fiery son. According to the thoughtful Georgia politician Herschel Johnson, who doubted that either Jefferson Davis (a "pure patriot") or his generals harbored any desire for dictatorship, a "tendency to absolutism" occurred in "all revolutions." Ironically, such thinking echoed warnings from the opponents of secession. At the beginning of the war, the North Carolinian Jonathan Worth, who never could support the Confederacy with any enthusiasm, worried that disunion would ultimately mean still more fragmentation and the establishment of "petty monarchies or republics." At the other extreme, a few people floated the idea of getting rid of state governments altogether in the interests of greater efficiency. That proposition must have alarmed states' rights advocates, but with the steady expansion of centralized power—including conscription, impressment, and the suspension of habeas corpus—talk of setting up a monarchy refused to die.[38]

In the midst of a difficult and costly war, such debates were hardly surprising, and calls for more energetic government sounded patriotic. Defining "national autonomy" as more essential to freedom than the right of suffrage, the editor of the *Richmond Enquirer*, which was often seen as the quasi-official organ of the Davis administration, bluntly argued for conferring substantial powers on the Confederate government. Others went further: "If necessary, let us convert our country into one vast camp of instruction for the field of every man able to bear arms, and fix our military establishment upon a permanent basis," General Albert Sidney Johnston recommended. To skeptics and especially to states' rights ideologues, such suggestions pointed to the dangerous, often uncontrolled forces of revolution. "We have no 'National life,'" William Lowndes Yancey lectured his Senate colleagues. "The province of this government, its sole province is to defend Constitutional government—the Constitutional liberties of States and of the people of States." Yancey would later suggest that it had been a mistake to draft a permanent constitution and that it might have been better to have simply created a provisional government for "exercising extraordinary powers upon unlooked for emergencies." As the case stood, however, he rejected the argument that pleas of necessity justified violations of individual liberty. More alarming still, the southern people seemed to be meekly surrendering their freedoms to an ever-encroaching national government. In the fall of 1862 Joe Brown stated, "I fear we have much more to apprehend from military despotism than from subjugation by the enemy." Too many citizens were willing to exchange liberty for security and no longer feared the centralizing tendencies of Congress and the executive branch.[39]

By the middle of the war, the word *dictator* was cropping up in public and private discussions of the Confederacy's increasingly desperate circumstances. "Perhaps a Bonaparte or a Cromwell may yet be in store for us," one South Carolina congressman mused. At the same time, Confederate patriots clung to the image of a southern nation defending true republican liberty in a hostile world. A textbook writer offered the following lesson: "A despotism is a tyrannical, oppressive government. The administration of Abraham Lincoln is a despotism." Yet given the Confederate government's own encroachments on civil liberties and mounting criticism of the Davis administration, such self-righteousness surely seemed ironic. In the spring of 1862, with Union general George B. McClellan's army threatening Richmond, rumors circulated that Davis would either be deposed or be made a dictator. A year later a speaking tour by the president sparked new reports that he planned to assume dictatorial powers. One-man rule had often been necessary during revolutions, one Georgia editor remarked, and of course the Continental Congress's deference to George Washington seemed the most important historical precedent.[40]

The president's increasingly shrill critics would have quickly pointed out that Jefferson Davis was no George Washington. "There are and have been but few Cincinnati in the world ready to return to their plows after the emergencies of a community have passed which had given them dictatorial power," a Charleston lawyer commented as debates over suspending habeas corpus raged. Despots seldom relinquished power, and citizens too often adjusted to the yoke. The mere mention of even a temporary dictatorship greatly alarmed defenders of liberty. "I am utterly opposed to anything looking or tending to a dictatorship in this country," wrote Vice President Stephens, bristling over a suggestion made by Howell Cobb. "No language at my command could give utterance to my inexpressible repugnance at the very suggestion of such a lamentable catastrophe." Benjamin Hill, a Georgia politician and reliable administration supporter, tried to reassure Stephens that whatever the president's mistakes, his "heart is right and . . .

nothing could tempt him to be dictator." Davis's political enemies probably knew this was true, but as late as a month before Lee's surrender,
the issue refused to die. Joe Brown remained wary of the president's
intentions, while critics of the governor branded him and his allies as
"monarchists," "Tories," or worse.[41]

The struggle over who could claim the mantle as true heirs of the
American Revolution not only fueled the propaganda war between
Rebels and Yankees but also became a point of contention among
Confederates. In defending the suspension of habeas corpus, a Georgia
editor blasted demagogues and newspapers for refusing to admit that
the Founding Fathers themselves had given that authority to Congress
under the old Constitution. The *Richmond Enquirer* berated dissenters,
who seemed more fearful of their own government than of the enemy. Even after the elections of 1863 turned out many supporters of the
Davis administration, one pamphleteer predicted that the new Congress would be "more deeply imbued with the true Revolutionary spirit."
Now was the time for politicians to "let those playthings of peacetime,
Constitutions, Habeas Corpus, be forgotten for the stern realities of
public safety and national independence. Better a thousand times our
country without any Constitution than no country at all." This polemi-
cist opposed establishing a dictatorship or monarchy but had no fear
of a "Long Parliament" seizing the reigns of power to bring the war to
a successful conclusion. A leading Alabama Episcopalian claimed that
the war had already taught young men to respect authority and hoped
that the "leveling doctrine of human equality" was fast disappearing
among soldiers, who had learned "the stern reality that some men are
'born to honour.'"[42]

Not surprisingly, friends of the Davis administration defined true
patriotism not only as respect for authority but also as support for the
president. Nine-tenths of the opposition and criticism sprang from
"passion, personal ambition, and party maneuver," Ben Hill informed
the Georgia legislature as he contrasted the brave soldiers to the petty
politicians. In many ways the issue boiled down to the predictable as-
sertion that there was no place for political opposition in the midst of
a life-and-death struggle for national survival. Even if the president
had committed errors, as many of his supporters had to concede in an
increasingly hostile political environment, who could have done any
better? That question bedeviled contemporaries, and historians have

struggled to answer it ever since. Aside from winning a few debating points for Davis's side, this was not exactly a rousing defense. In an editorial sustaining the president, the *Richmond Daily Dispatch* pointed out that if Davis was not the right man for the job, then his presidency reflected poorly on Confederate political leaders and voters, who had supported his election with near unanimity. "It is no time now to discuss points of difference," Howell Cobb confided to his wife toward the end of 1863. "Patriotism and policy demand that the President should be sustained and his hands strengthened in fighting the revolution."[43]

Such appeals had been effective and always would be as long as public support for the war held firm. In a sermon preached before a brigade in Lee's army during the summer of 1863, the Alabama Baptist chaplain John Renfroe summed up the thinking of many: "How the hearts of the true patriot sicken at the slander and abuse that are heaped upon the devoted head of our noble president." But then as Davis's allies were quick to point out, such abuse had also been heaped on the head of the sainted Washington.[44]

Did patriotism and commitment to the southern revolution justify the suppression of dissent and protest? Long and bloody wars always raise such a question, and it seemed especially pressing for beleaguered Confederates. Words and phrases such as *spies, alien enemies, Tories,* and *traitors,* all appearing in a New Orleans newspaper editorial concerning the arrests of suspected Unionists in Richmond, helped justify any action the government chose to take. Early in 1864, Howell Cobb tried to shame fellow Georgians into rekindling their loyalty by pointing to the stark and individual choice to be made: "The man whose patriotism has sunk so low as to want a habeas corpus court to decide whether he is to go into the army or not, does not deserve the liberty which is won by the strong arm of others." Such appeals, however, led the editor of the *Athens Southern Watchman* to invoke a classic image of embattled liberty: "Georgians, behold your Chains!—Freemen of a once proud and happy country, contemplate the last act which rivets your bonds and binds you hand and foot at the mercy of an unlimited military authority." A few bold spirits might counsel resistance, as Robert Toombs did, but that begged the question of both methods and consequences.[45]

The patriotic dreams of unity that had helped spark the Confederate revolution threatened to become nightmares of backbiting, division, and defeat. The politicians received much of the blame, the *Charleston Mercury* offering the usual contrast between the patriot and the placeman. On a broader basis, selfishness, covetousness, and extortion had corrupted public and private morals. At the end of 1863, the ardent southern nationalist Albert Gallatin Brown bewailed the "thousands and tens of thousands who have given up their souls to mammon, and in their eager race for money, have forgotten their country, and left it to its fate." The novelist Augusta J. Evans decried the "great national ulcer—demagogism," which grew out of "universal suffrage . . . an effete theory of utopian origin." Supporters of the Confederate cause and especially friends of the Davis administration still tried to rally citizens for renewed sacrifice, but in February 1865 a call by leading Virginia clergy for all classes to donate food for the starving soldiers bespoke more desperation than hope.[46]

Fervent Confederates had long insisted that all southerners were "rebels" with a stake in the southern revolution, yet they worried that somehow the rich might be arrayed against the poor. To claim that rich and poor alike had joined the call to arms, however true, did not mean that class divisions had disappeared. The loyalty of nonslaveholders could not be taken for granted, and by the war's second year cracks had appeared in the social structure. Was it fair for a poor man with ten children to go off to fight for a man who owned ten slaves, a "Soldier" asked the readers of an Atlanta newspaper. Resentment against draft exemptions and wealthy men who stayed home amassing fortunes festered, despite claims by Confederate politicians that all southern whites shared a common interest in slavery. "The blessings of liberty are dear alike to all," Virginia governor John Letcher maintained. "It is the duty of all to unite their efforts and energies in the struggle to secure them for themselves and their posterity. We are so linked together, so mutually dependent, that any disaster which overtakes one class, operates more or less prejudicially upon the interests of all others in the same community." An organic view of society survived among the Confederate elite, who deplored all efforts to stir up class hatred. In a sermon preached after the execution of twenty-two deserters in North Carolina, John Paris pointed out how despair at home, peace meetings, and claims of a rich man's war and a poor man's fight had all caused these desperate men to abandon their posts.[47]

In August 1864 John Beauchamp Jones, a Confederate War Department clerk, wrote a letter to Jefferson Davis in which he called for "exterminating the speculators" because "there must be no partiality, and especially in favor of the rich." In his view, "the patriotism of 1861 must be revived." The clergy tried to convince their congregations that supporting the powers that be conformed to the Lord's will. Loyal Christians should not undermine public confidence by criticizing civilian or military authorities. "Remember that union and harmony is our only earthly hope," Stephen Elliott declared, even though he conceded that revolutions often began with enthusiasm and then succumbed to depression as the suffering and sacrifices mounted. Ultimately, however, such "disaffection leads to treason." To ease class tensions, to rally God's people to the cause, required an inspiring example of dedication and self-sacrifice. Washington had served that purpose from the beginning of the war, and as Confederate fortunes declined, Jefferson Davis once again turned to what many southerners—and northerners, for that matter—considered a sacred period in history. During a long speech in Columbia, South Carolina, in the fall of 1864, the president urged the southern people to "emulate the glory of our sires." He boldly asserted that "our people are even better than were our honored ancestors. They have fought more and bloodier battles, and there are fewer who are lukewarm in the cause now, than existed in days of the Revolution."[48]

Historians have argued that Davis never became an effective revolutionary leader, and for sure his messages and speeches were neither memorable nor inspiring, but in fact the president never saw himself as a revolutionary leader.[49] Nor did he see the Confederacy's struggle for independence as a revolution. "Ours is not revolution," he told a crowd in Augusta, Georgia, in October 1864. "We are a free and independent people, in States that had the right to make a better Government when they saw fit.... We are not engaged in a Quixotic fight for the rights of man; our struggle is for inherited rights, and who would surrender them?" This was no conservative revolution; indeed, it was no revolution at all. A year earlier, Stephen Elliott had described the Confederate government as "stable as ever, directed by the same clear head and sound judgments which have so well guided our affairs." He had appealed to the Founders and the Constitution as witness against the truly revolutionary Yankees, who "have abandoned God and pursued liberty, equality, and fraternity." To brand northerners as the legitimate heirs of French Jacobins remained an appealing theme to conservatives, who genuinely feared revolution, but such statements had limited popular appeal.[50]

The failure to embrace revolution had cast the Confederate experiment in a peculiar light from the beginning, especially given the singular, if not irregular, nature of secession. After the elections of 1863, Henry St. Paul published a pamphlet in Mobile calling for renewed patriotism, but he struck a decidedly different note from that sounded by Jefferson Davis. "Let the people be frankly in revolution," he advised. "Let a few rulers feel the rough handling of public opinion, and let a few extortioners' shops be mobbed and devastated." Was he calling for a counterrevolution? That term was bruited about from the middle of the war on. Malcontents such as Robert Toombs seemed hell-bent on launching their own revolution against the Confederate administration. By the summer of 1863, calls for a negotiated peace, especially in North Carolina and Georgia, had aroused fears among staunch Confederates that a counterrevolution had begun on the home front. In early 1865 a newspaper reporter discovered that even Charleston, South Carolina, the birthplace of secession, was filled "with prophets of evil, with croakers, with fault-finders, with speculators who, having amassed large fortunes, are anxious to save them, even if the Confederacy should fail." The most fervent disunionists "now hint at another revolution!" And that word *revolution* had come to assume more ominous connotations than even the most fearful conservatives of 1861 might have imagined.[51]

North Carolina's Governor Zebulon Vance had his share of differences with Jefferson Davis and the Confederate government, but in the spring of 1864 he was trying to steer a course between fervent supporters of the administration and the peace advocates led by the editor William W. Holden. Appealing to fear and pointing to the consequences of subjugation, he warned of "insurrection after insurrection, revolution upon revolution, war after war," followed by "torrents of blood" should Confederates give up the fight. Vance would find his middle ground and handily defeat Holden in that summer's gubernatorial election, but he would come no closer than Jefferson Davis or other Confederate leaders, or the dissenters for that matter, to solving the riddles of the Confederate revolution.[52]

From the beginning of the war, "patriots" and "rebels" had avowed their devotion to a Confederate "revolution" without establishing a clear definition of these terms or coming to grips with their implications. A rash decision to secede and an even rasher decision to start a war by supposedly conservative men who often lacked political judgment had led to disaster. Whatever the weakness of a southern nation founded on African slavery and facing serious internal divisions during four years of bloody war, politically and especially militarily, the Confederates had shown impressive staying power. Soldiers and their families stood ready for some time to sacrifice much in the defense of family, home, community, and race despite the often uninspiring appeal of a conservative revolution. The nationalism of these Confederates, however, proved far more visceral than intellectual, more emotional than ideological, more stubborn than consistent. The logic of the Confederate "revolution" proved much less substantial. Confederate politicians and thinkers never managed to sort out the tensions between patriotism, rebellion, and revolution. However stalwart Confederate "patriots" might be, in terms of both political theory and even political practice, the Confederate States of America often was little more than a house of cards held up by equal measures of blind hope, wishful thinking, and willful delusion. As some leaders had feared from the outset, the Confederate experiment in the end turned out to be a failed "rebellion," despite the enduring influence of the "Lost Cause."

6

Wartime Nationalism and Race

Comparing the Visions of Confederate, Black Union, and White Union Soldiers

CHANDRA MANNING

In *Dred Scott v. Sanford* (1857) the U.S. Supreme Court found that a black man could not be a citizen of the United States because of his race. In 1868 the Fourteenth Amendment to the U.S. Constitution guaranteed members of that same race the rights and privileges of U.S. citizenship. The contrast between the *Dred Scott* decision and the Fourteenth Amendment demonstrates that the relationship between race, nation, and nationalism underwent a seismic shift in the intervening years. The Civil War was the earthquake that brought about that shift, though few could have predicted any such transformation when war broke out in 1861.

Confederate soldiers, black Union soldiers, and white Union soldiers brought three distinct understandings of the relationship between race and nationalism to the battlefield with them. Confederate nationalism was tightly interwoven with white southerners' ideas about race. Ordinary white southerners' loyalty to the Confederate States of America, which depended upon their trust that an independent Confederacy would better promote the interests of white southern men and their families, contained an inherent tension between the wartime demands of the Confederacy and the individual needs and priorities of white families. Shared belief in the need to gain independence from a Union that soldiers assumed would impose abolition and endanger white supremacy resolved that tension at least enough to keep Confederate soldiers fighting until the spring of 1865, when the Confederacy's legitimate claim on the loyalties of white southerners unraveled because it could no longer secure the privileges of white supremacy.

Race and Union nationalism among black Union soldiers were equally inextricable, but in different ways. Though at first excluded from the Union army as thoroughly as *Dred Scott* excluded them from U.S. citizenship, African Americans from the very beginning of the war envisioned a new nation free of slavery, in which members of their race would be included in the promises of the American Revolution. Black men fought in the Union army in large measure out of an imaginative form of nationalism that sought to bring into being a nation that lived up to its own ideals by securing what many black soldiers called "the manhood of the race," and so for them too race and nationalism were intertwined throughout the war.

White Union soldiers, in contrast, strove assiduously to separate questions of race and nationalism in the early days of the war, when most focused primarily on the necessity of saving the Union in order to prove to the world that representative self-government based on the ideals articulated in the Declaration of Independence could work. Yet despite white troops' determined efforts to avoid difficult and uncomfortable questions about race, the unexpected severity of the war forced white Union soldiers to face the issue of slavery in 1861 and then to confront questions of racial justice, equality, and civil rights in the latter half of the war. For white Union soldiers, then, race and nationalism *became* interrelated during and because of the war itself. Neither the Confederate, the black Union, or the white Union version of nationalism emerged from the war as the unambiguous winner, but the clash between the three versions profoundly altered the relationship between race, nation, and nationalism in the United States.

If Confederate nationalism means the bonds of allegiance and loyalty that white southerners believed connected them to an independent Confederacy, then the strands from which those connecting bonds were woven contained three specific fibers, all of which grew in the soil of shared white southern racial attitudes. To put the point another way, the Confederate States of America could legitimately claim the loyalties and allegiance of Confederates because, and as long as, the Confederate government did what white southerners believed government was supposed to do: promote white liberty, advance white families' best interests, and protect slavery.

The first fiber, the assumption that the Confederate government would promote white liberty, was predicated on a distinctive liberty available exclusively to whites. The liberty that white southerners believed government ought to promote was not an abstract, universally applicable ideal; rather, it was white southerners' specific right, owned like a possession, to pursue material prosperity for themselves and their families in whatever fashion they chose, with minimal outside interference. In the words of one Virginian, liberty consisted of the "good many comforts and privileges" that his family could acquire and enjoy free from governmental meddling.[1] When class disaffection began to ripple through the ranks of a Confederate Missouri regiment, the *Missouri Army Argus,* a camp paper written by enlisted men in the regiment, answered by calling on this sense of liberty rooted in white men's right to pursue their own interests. "What interest has General Sterling Price or Governor Claiborne Jackson or General or Governor anybody else, in the cause of our common country, that you have not?" asked the *Argus.* "How are they or the officers more interested than you or I? There is not a soldier in the army who is not a free man. . . . Not a soldier who may not become rich or great. . . . One man has as much at stake—as much to gain or lose as another."[2]

The second fiber, the idea that an independent Confederacy would better serve the needs of white families, helped attract the early support of men like Josiah Patterson, who told his young sons that he must "leave you and become a soldier" to ensure that they would grow up under a government that would facilitate their "hopes of becoming great and good men."[3] Thomas Taylor, an Alabama private, threw his lot in with the Confederacy at least in part because he thought it would do a better job than the Union government of looking out for the interests of "our dear wives and little children."[4]

The individualistic and familial concerns that made up the first two fibers from which ties of Confederate nationality were woven benefited Confederate nationalism early in the war.[5] They provided convincing reasons why white southerners, who had always thought of themselves as loyal Americans, should fight against the United States of America. They also provided some elasticity in the early years, since a soldier who grew disillusioned with President Davis or the Confederate Congress was unlikely to grow alienated from the Confederate cause if that cause had more to do with his own and his family's best interests than with a government sitting in Richmond.

Yet fibers composed primarily of individual and familial interests were vulnerable to shrinking or snapping under the pressures generated by the war because the demands of the wartime Confederacy often conflicted with families' needs and individuals' priorities. Measures such as a tax in kind, which obligated families to tithe a portion of their crop to the government, and impressment, which allowed Confederate army officers to commandeer civilians' crops in return for virtually worthless IOUs, directly interfered with the material well-being of white southern families, and that interference strained the commitment many soldiers felt to the Confederacy. The North Carolina private James Zimmerman, for one, told his wife that instead of paying tax in kind or submitting to the impressment of crops needed by the Confederate army, she should tell authorities that "you thought your husband was fighting for our rights and you had a notion that you had a right to what little you had luck to make."[6] One Virginia soldier who was considering desertion from the army summed up the tension inherent in Confederate nationalism when he lamented, "I love my country but I love my family better."[7]

The resilient fiber that retained the strength and suppleness to maintain the bond between the Confederacy and its citizenry even as other fibers frayed was a visceral belief shared by the ordinary white men who made up the rank and file that everyone and everything they cared about depended upon the survival of slavery. The Confederacy might try to take a family's crops, and nobody liked that, but unlike the Union, it would not try to destroy slavery, and that conviction explains why Confederate troops remained committed enough to the idea of a Confederate nation to continue fighting for it for four long years. The belief in the necessity of slavery, in turn, grew from powerful racial attitudes that ran much deeper than cool calculation of material interests, and that is why, at its heart, Confederate nationalism could not be separated from the issue of race.

Slavery was necessary in part because it was part of God's plan for a well-ordered society, and if white southerners wanted to retain God's favor (which would surely be necessary for victory), they needed to remain true to what they saw as a social order ordained by God. Slavery, after all, appears in the Bible, so how could any nation that placed *Deo*

Vindice on its seal hope to triumph if it questioned the Bible? Among northerners' most objectionable qualities, according to an Arkansas soldier, was their insistence on "an antislavery Bible and an antislavery God."[8] By tampering with slavery, which white southerners believed had been ordained by God, northerners tampered with the will of God, but by remaining true to it, white southerners, in contrast, proved that their nation was morally superior and thus worthy of victory.[9]

In addition, Confederates believed that slavery was indispensable because it secured white southern men's identity as men, which is to say that the qualities that defined a southern man as a man depended upon the existence of slavery. The rightful order of society, as white southern men understood it, was one in which adult white males possessed the right and responsibility to govern subordinates, such as women and children. Slavery meant that white men also had the right and responsibility to command African Americans even if they did not own a single slave themselves. In no way did white southern men conflate slaves with family members, but calling into question white men's right to rule over blacks could too easily lead to questioning white men's right to command all other subordinates as well.[10] Destroying slavery, then, would certainly weaken the *authority* over others that helped define white men as men, but even more damaging, it would also destroy white men's abilities to fulfill the chief *duty* that defined them as men, the duty to protect and control white women. Newspapers argued that, as the *Richmond Enquirer* put it, "where the two races approximate equality in numbers, slavery is the only protection of the laboring classes against the evils of amalgamation," which was a delicate way of saying that without slavery, white daughters of honest southern yeomen would be helplessly thrown into sexual relationships with black men.[11]

Soldiers echoed this theme relentlessly throughout the war. When John Calton heard a story about a black man who told Confederate soldiers that he would celebrate his freedom by "Seduc[ing] your Sister," Calton was quick to believe it because the anecdote accorded with his own assumption that emancipation would leave white men powerless to protect white women from predatory black men.[12] A Texas woman named Melinda Street was terrified about the impending birth of her first child while she was alone on the family farm. When she wrote to her husband, John, to tell him that he could best care for her by coming home, John replied that if he and his fellow soldiers failed to defend slavery, they might as well lie "supinely upon our backs" while "we are all bound hand and foot & the fair daughters of the south reduced to a level with the flat-footed thick-liped [*sic*] Negro."[13] The absence of slavery, in sum, would interfere with white men's ability to carry out the very duties that defined them as men.

The absence of slavery would also endanger a particular value that was absolutely central to white southerners' sense of what made a man a man: honor. Honor meant something quite different then than it does today. Similar to reputation, it had to do with what other people thought of a man, which was determined in part by whether a man had attributes such as courage, but most of all it depended upon how authoritatively he exercised power and control over subordinates, which meant women, children, and black Americans, whether or not he was a slaveowner.[14] Honor was not an internal quality that a man possessed regardless of what others thought. Instead, a man's honor depended on what other people said about him, and thus it was very vulnerable to insult and had to be guarded. To many white southerners, outside reproaches about slavery insulted southern honor by questioning one way—and therefore *every* way—in which white men exercised authority over others. Insults like that meant war, in the same way that questioning a white man's character or authority over his wife meant a duel or a fight in the white South.[15] Charles Trueheart, a young Texan, believed that secession was unconstitutional, but he supported an independent Confederacy because he saw it as the only way to protect white southern men's honor from the insults inherent in what he saw as the North's growing opposition to slavery. "There is no other alternative left us," he decided, "unless we . . . humble our heads in the dust at the feet of Black Republican masters, disgraced in our own eyes and before the whole world."[16]

Further, slavery was necessary, according to Confederate soldiers, because, they believed, it upheld white supremacy. Slavery and racial hierarchy so pervaded southern life and culture, in ways far beyond the actual ownership of slaves, that many white southerners simply could not imagine a society in which slavery was completely absent. Abolition would not eliminate the racial hierarchy that slavery enforced, because the elimination of racial hierarchy was impossible. Instead, emancipation would *reverse* the racial hierarchy, resulting in a world where, as one private put it, "the Negro population [was] set free and the white population [was] bound by fetters."[17] The *Richmond Enquirer* echoed this point when it cautioned that emancipation would mean "the substitution of the white by the black race in the southern tier of States."[18]

Over and over, Confederate soldiers proclaimed that they must fight or be made slaves, and they were not using slavery as a dramatic metaphor for abstract political rights when they did so. A group of North Carolina prisoners of war explained that abolishing slavery, as the Union would surely do if it won the war, would mean more than setting enslaved blacks free. It would also mean "[confiscating] the property of our people, both real and person, and [apportioning] it among their soldiers and freedmen (slaves whom they have liberated)." It would mean "[taking] the arms from the whites and [putting] them in the hands of the negros, . . . to extend the right of suffrage to the blacks; while among the whites it is to be restricted." In short, if emancipation happened, "the order of nature would be reversed."[19] Soldiers like these were genuinely afraid that the end of black slavery could only result in white men like themselves being reduced to the powerless, libertyless, and emasculated lives and conditions occupied by black slaves, because in the world as they knew it *somebody* had to occupy society's most degraded positions, and without slavery there was no guarantee that those "somebodies" would be black rather than white.

Finally, and probably most important, slavery was necessary because it prevented the racial violence that soldiers were certain would threaten their loved ones if slavery disappeared. Ivy Duggan, for example, warned that abolition was tantamount to an invasion of white southerners' hearths and homes; it meant "fire, sword, and even poison as instruments in desolating our homes, ruining us and degrading our children."[20] Duggan wrote those words in 1861, when no Union troops were anywhere near his central Georgia home and when neither he nor his comrades could imagine lily-livered Yankees fighting well enough to advance much beyond the Potomac, let alone invade their neighborhoods. Yet if white northerners were unlikely to menace Confederates' home communities, black slaves were already there, and if slavery did not keep them in their place, then no white southerner was safe.

Soldiers' focus on their own families was strong, in short, but the fear of what race war would do to those families could unite white southerners more powerfully than any other force. An elite young South Carolinian recognized the unifying potential of perceived threats to slavery when he urged "the whole South to make common cause against the hordes of abolitionists who are swarming southwards."[21] A German immigrant saloon keeper in the Seventh Texas named Joseph Bruckmuller had almost nothing in common with the gentleman from South Carolina. Bruckmuller certainly did not own any slaves, but that did not stop him from relying on fears of race war to unite white southerners. He urged his fellow "adoption citizens" to stand by "your own countrymen and race" against the "murder and arson, hanging and stealing" that were sure to accompany the "liberation of the half-civilized cannibal."[22]

By 1865 almost everything that Confederate soldiers cared about and thought was worth fighting for was severely threatened or had already been destroyed by the war, and yet they kept fighting. They did so partly, of course, because war generates its own momentum, consisting of things like loyalty to one's fellow soldiers, pride in the military record of one's regiment, and hatred of the enemy. But more important, Confederate soldiers kept fighting because no matter how bad the war was, or how disappointed they were in the Confederacy, the Union was worse because the Union meant abolition. Congressional approval of the proposed Thirteenth Amendment to the U.S. Constitution in fact provided one last boost to Confederate troops' fighting spirit. In February 1865, when soldiers heard of the "amendment of the Constitution abolishing slavery," according to a Confederate chaplain, they once again "awakened to the solemn reality" that anyone willing to consider rejoining the Union would in effect "bow his dishonored head for the yoke which abolitionism stands ready to place upon him." The grim reminder provided by the Thirteenth Amendment, in short, brought Confederates "back again to the point we started at four years ago," eager to battle for an independent Confederate nation.[23]

Finally, in the spring of 1865, the last fiber holding the bonds of Confederate nationalism together was severed from the Confederate nation-state, though it did not disappear entirely. By March 1865 too few white men remained in the ranks of the Confederate army, and if the army collapsed, so would the Confederacy. To address the catastrophic manpower shortage, on 13 March the Confederate Congress passed a bill authorizing the enlistment of up to 25 percent of black male slaves between the ages of eighteen and forty-five. Despite the famous endorsement of high-ranking officers like Robert E. Lee, enlisted soldiers saw black enlistment as the final nullification of Confederate nationalism. "We would have to drill and fight side by side with the stinking things," Private Grant Taylor exclaimed. "To think we have been fighting four years to prevent the slaves from being freed, now to turn round," he said, and make soldiers of them was "outrageous." He concluded: "If we are reduced to that extremity . . . stop the war at once and let us come home for if we are to depend on the slaves for our freedom it is gone anyway."[24]

After the passage of the slave soldiers bill, even the most loyal and committed of all the Confederacy's armies, General Robert E. Lee's Army of Northern Virginia, was so seriously depleted by climbing desertion rates that it simply could not hold Richmond any longer: on 2 April, just three weeks after the bill passed, the army evacuated Richmond, and it surrendered one week later, on 9 April.[25] By elevating blacks to the rank of private in the army, the same rank held by the majority of white soldiers, the Confederate government threatened to erase the differences between white and black and thus the one remaining reason that men like Grant Taylor saw for the existence of a separate Confederate nation. Soldiers like Taylor did not stop believing in the need for a mechanism to enforce white supremacy, and in the Jim Crow era that followed Reconstruction they would find effective mechanisms in violence and legal segregation. They did, however, stop believing that a separate Confederacy could or would guarantee the survival of slavery as that mechanism. Until the very end of the war, then, race and nationalism remained intertwined for Confederate soldiers, and when the bond between white supremacy and a separate Confederate nation unraveled, so did the rank and file's will to fight.

Black Union soldiers envisioned an equally close connection between nationalism and race, but one that operated much differently. From the beginning, black Americans insisted that "this war . . . is virtually nothing more nor less than perpetual slavery against universal freedom."[26] The United States faced dissolution precisely because it reneged on the very founding ideals that gave the nation legitimacy. The only way to repair the nation was to live up to those ideals, and that meant confronting uncomfortable questions of slavery and race. Just weeks after Fort Sumter fell, the black newspaper the *Anglo-African* predicted that "no adjustment of the nation's difficulty is possible until the claims of the black man are first met and satisfied. . . . If you would restore the

Union and maintain the government you so fondly cherish, make way for liberty, universal and complete."[27] The universal and complete liberty that the *Anglo-African* called for, of course, had never existed in the United States, but the belief that it could exist, and that black soldiers could help make it exist, was at the core of black Union soldiers' nationalism.

Black Americans viewed the war as a struggle not just to end slavery but also to redefine the place of African Americans within the American republic, and one way to do that was to reclaim the memory of the American Revolution. When Fort Sumter fell and President Abraham Lincoln called for volunteers to put down the rebellion, a prominent black Philadelphian named Alfred Green held a rally and reminded listeners that black soldiers defending Philadelphia in 1777 had helped secure victory in the American Revolution. Now, the rebellion gave both white and black Americans the opportunity to realize the ideals of the Revolution by overthrowing "the tyrant system of slavery" and bringing "truth, justice, and equality to all men."[28] As Private J. H. Hall, of the Fifty-fourth Massachusetts Regiment, put it more than three years later, black soldiers who had fought in the name of Revolutionary heroes such as "Washington, Madison, [and] Jefferson" deserved "Republican privileges" and the right to be "recognized as citizens."[29] By writing black Americans back into the history of the Revolution, men like Green and Hall laid claim to the promises of freedom and equality that grew from the Revolution.

Black Union troops further envisioned the strengthened and reconstituted American nation as a place that would recognize rather than negate what soldier after soldier called the *manhood of the race,* a phrase that had two meanings.[30] First, it meant the adult male identity, the masculinity, of black men. While the existence of slavery was a necessary component of manhood as white southern men understood it, slavery robbed black men of many important nineteenth-century markers of manhood, including courage and the ability to protect and care for one's family. One tenet of proslavery ideology was that black men's failure to exhibit the qualities of manhood showed that they were savages or children rather than real men, and therefore slavery was the best place for them. Since proslavery ideology had led to secession and rebellion, only the destruction of that ideology could end the rebellion and restore the nation to wholeness. By fighting, black soldiers could help defeat the ideology that had prompted the breakup of the Union and demonstrate possession of manhood's key attribute, courage, at the same time. One black Pennsylvanian fighting in Charleston Harbor "saw men fall around me like hail stones," but he made sure to point out that he and his company "stood fast" despite the danger.[31] Other black Union troops saw serving in the army as a way to reclaim their standing as husbands and fathers, which slavery had denied them. A former Missouri slave, Private Spotswood Rice, wrote to Miss Kitty, the owner of his two daughters, to let her know that he planned to free his children when his regiment marched into her community. His children were "a God given rite of my own" as a man and a father, Rice informed Miss Kitty, and she would "burn in hell" if she tried to deny him that right.[32]

Slavery degraded black women and children as well as black men. The second meaning of the phrase *manhood of the race* was the full humanity of all black Americans; black soldiers fought for a version of the American nation that would recognize and honor all African Americans' claims to basic human dignity. Black soldiers who "fight the battles of their noble country," as a member of the Fifty-fifth Massachusetts saw it, had earned the "onward move of my race" toward full and equal rights within the American nation.[33] Similarly, another black volunteer felt that Union victory would not be complete without "the elevation of a downtrodden and oppressed race."[34]

Black Americans' vision of American nationalism was thoroughly rebuffed at first. Despite Alfred Green's 1861 rally in Philadelphia, blacks were barred from the Union army until mid-1862. Once admitted into the ranks, blacks were relegated to noncombat duties until the summer of 1863, earned lower pay until the summer of 1864, and were prohibited from becoming commissioned officers until almost the end of the war.

Yet despite the early impediments and persistent setbacks, by the time the war ended African American soldiers had made dramatic strides in their ability to reap the benefits and promises of the nation they had helped to regenerate. By the spring of 1865 slavery was dying. Black soldiers served in the armed forces and earned the same pay that white soldiers did. Several northern cities desegregated public accommodations. John Rock, a black lawyer, earned the right to argue before the very Supreme Court that in 1857 would have denied his right to even bring a suit there. Northern states that before the war never would have considered allowing black men to vote prepared to hold referenda on black suffrage. No rational observer in 1861 could possibly have predicted that such dramatic changes would take place in just four short years. Small wonder that men like the black artilleryman David Williamson concluded that "the time has come when liberty is in reach of all men without respect to color" in the newly reconstituted American nation.[35] With such dramatic change in so short a time, he had legitimate expectations? In the spring of 1865 it appeared that black Union soldiers' version of an American nationalism rooted in racial egalitarianism stood a chance of coming to fruition.

The relationship between race and nationalism among white Union soldiers was more ambivalent, and it also underwent the greatest change over the course of the war. In the main, Union soldiers cared about the survival intact of the U.S. government in 1861 not primarily because the Union government served their families' interests or because it could remedy racial injustice, but because its survival mattered for the perpetuation of ideals like liberty, equality, and self-government for all humanity, or at least so white Union soldiers thought.[36] From that point of view, the destruction of the Union would turn the idea of government based on the principles of liberty and equality into an international object of ridicule and crush the whole world's hopes for self-government. As one regimental newspaper posed the question, "Destroy this Union and what can republics hope for?"[37] Similarly, a Kansas infantryman worried that "if we fail now, the hope of human rights is extinguished for ages."[38] Both black and white Union soldiers saw larger, more universal ideological implications in Union nationalism than Confederates did in Confederate nationalism, not because northerners were somehow less selfish than southerners but simply because the relationship between personal interests and the nation worked differently. At the same time, white Union troops differed from black soldiers in that black soldiers directly connected race and nationalism, while white Union soldiers, who by and large took white supremacy for granted at first, did their best to keep the topics of race and nationalism entirely separate from each other.

The war quickly made it impossible for white Union soldiers to continue to ignore race. It rarely took more than a month or two of service in the South to make a white northerner realize, in the not especially enlightened words of the Illinois sergeant E. C. Hubbard, that the Union had gotten broken and now men were killing one another "all for a detestable black man."[39]

The immediate impact of that recognition was to compel Union soldiers like Hubbard to face the question of slavery. In the final four months of 1861 Hubbard grew absolutely certain that the Union could not win the war until it abolished slavery, and he said so repeatedly in letters home to his sister and brothers.[40] He was no aberration. Rather, Hubbard was part of a pattern that took shape from August to December 1861, in which enlisted Union soldiers increasingly insisted that since slavery had started the war, only the destruction of slavery could end the war. And they clearly meant the destruction of the institution of slavery itself, not merely punishment for slaveholders, for, as troops saw it, the problem was not simply that individual slaveholders wielded too much power but rather that the institution of slavery itself was a corrupting influence that subverted national ideals and contaminated everything it touched with "social, intellectual, and moral degradation," as one Midwestern soldier summed it up. Until it was flushed out, the nation's survival would be in danger.[41]

In October, a Wisconsin volunteer explained that "the rebellion is abolitionizing the whole army." "You have no idea of the changes that have taken place in the minds of the soldiers in the last two months." "Men of all parties seem unanimous in the belief that to permanently establish the Union, is to first wipe [out] the institution [of slavery]."[42] A full year ahead of the Emancipation Proclamation, enlisted Union soldiers concluded, in the words of one Missouri private, that since "it was slavery that caused the war," it would take "the eternal overthrow of slavery" to win the war.[43] That analysis continued to serve as a refrain among white Union troops for the duration of the conflict. "As long as we ignore the fact (practically) that Slavery is the basis of this struggle," argued a New York soldier the following year, "so long are we simply heading down a vigorously growing plant that will continually spring up and give new trouble at very short intervals. We must emancipate."[44]

Even as more and more soldiers called for an end to the institution of slavery, white northerners' ideas about actual black people proved more resistant to change. In some instances, emancipation prompted northern whites' assumptions about white supremacy to go from latent to explicit. While the form of Union nationalism most often articulated in 1861 had acknowledged no direct connection, positive or negative, between the apparatus of the nation and racial hierarchy, a number of Democratic candidates in state and local elections held on the heels of the preliminary Emancipation Proclamation in the fall of 1862 ran on the platform, "This is a white man's government." Other white northerners insisted that emancipation would not disturb white supremacy because that supremacy was a natural phenomenon and did not require the support of the state to survive. "This talk about 'putting ourselves *on an equality with niggers,*' is to me, the *boldest nonsense* or rather an *insult* to me as one of the Saxon race," claimed Private Leigh Webber, an ardent supporter of emancipation. As Webber saw things, whites' "natural superiority" made any notion of equality an "absurdity."[45] Much more often, white Union troops simply tried to keep the questions of slavery and race separate, firmly arguing for the need to end the first, while doing their best to continue avoiding the second. As one private put it, "I have a good degree of sympathy for the *slave,* but I like the *Negro* the farther off the better."[46]

Almost certainly, most white Union troops would have been quite happy to continue avoiding complicated questions about the place of race within the American nation, to say nothing of the relationship between their own bigotry and slavery's long and healthy life in the United States, but the progress of the war, and especially the summer of 1863, made it increasingly difficult to do so. The Confederate surrender at Vicksburg and the beginning of the seemingly unbeatable Army of Northern Virginia's retreat south after Gettysburg, both on the Fourth of July 1863, made soldiers feel more certain than ever that, as Quincy Campbell put it, "the hand of *God* is in this struggle."[47] The victories were "too important to not be followed by important results," Campbell reflected, but neither he nor his fellow soldiers responded to Gettysburg and Vicksburg with quite the celebratory "God is on our side" attitude that one might expect. Instead, the ghastly cost of battles like Gettysburg convinced Union troops that, in Campbell's words, "the chastisements of the Almighty are not yet ended." The suffering that accompanied the victories made clear that "the Almighty has taken up the cause of the oppressed and . . . will deny us peace until we 'break every yoke' and sweep every vestige of the cursed institution [of slavery] from our land." By every vestige of slavery, Campbell meant not just the institution of slavery itself but also the widespread racial prejudice of *northerners*, which had led them to go along with slavery for so long and still led them to deny basic rights to black people in their own society.[48]

Campbell by no means spoke for the whole army, but neither was he unique or aberrational in the soul-searching that the summer of 1863 forced him to do. God's plan might guarantee a Union victory in the long run, but in the short run battles like Gettysburg felt more like punishment. The sin that brought the punishment, many decided in the wake of that pivotal summer, must be the sin of slavery, for which both North and South were responsible and for which both must pay. God designed the war as "a curse . . . upon the country for the toleration of that inhuman practice, 'Human Slavery,'" James Jessee reasoned, and "not till the last slave is freed need we expect Peace."[49] Another private saw God at work in similar ways. "Where our nation has failed to act in putting the abomination away from them[,] God has allowed war and carnage to operate."[50]

Emancipation by itself did not seem to go far enough. In fact, the Emancipation Proclamation, abolishing slavery in most parts of the South, at least in theory, had gone into effect on 1 January 1863, and since then the war had gotten worse, not better. Soldiers who asked themselves why came face to face with the uncomfortable possibility that their own prejudices had helped make slavery possible and that they were therefore partly to blame for the war, which meant that God would not grant victory until they had repented of their prejudice. As the Vermont soldier Wilbur Fisk reflected after Gettysburg, through their "wholly wrong, unnatural and unjustifiable" bigotry, northern whites had kept "the souls of the African . . . down" and now must face up to their "fearful responsibility" before an angry God.[51] The only way to repent was to settle for nothing short of what an Ohioan called "the equal freedom of all men in this country *regardless of color.*"[52] "As sure as God is God and right is right, so sure may we look for the war to end . . . in the . . . liberation of this oppressed and down trodden race," prophesied James Jessee. "To doubt this would Be to doubt God."[53] Similarly, Private Constant Hanks insisted that the war would be wasted if it did not place the nation firmly "on the broad firm base of eaqual right" for black Americans.[54]

Before the war, only the furthest fringe of radical abolitionism would have given even passing thought to nationwide prejudice as a source of slavery's longevity, but now the unforeseen course of the war itself forced men who had had absolutely no tolerance for abolitionists before the war to confront precisely that possibility. Certainly, plenty of white Union soldiers avoided drawing that unflattering conclusion; nonetheless, soldiers throughout the ranks began to consider that, in the words of an Ohio soldier, "the North is alike guilty with the South . . . and must suffer alike with her" until some sort of amends were made, on both the personal and the national level.[55]

Important as Gettysburg and Vicksburg were in inspiring white troops to consider northern complicity in the sin of slavery, the performances of black Union troops proved equally central because as black soldiers began to take part in combat at Fort Wagner, Milliken's Bend, and other places, they commanded increased respect from their fellow Union soldiers. A white Illinois private who became a company officer in a regiment of black Louisiana soldiers fought with his men in a battle so intense that only one enlisted man in the whole regiment emerged unharmed. The experience moved the Illinoisan to write a stern letter home advising his loved ones, "I never more wish to hear the expression, 'the niggers won't fight.' Come with me 100 yards from where I sit, and I can show you the wounds that cover the bodies of 16 as brave, loyal and patriotic soldiers as ever drew bead on a Rebel. . . . They fought and died defending the cause that we revere."[56] They deserved to be treated as equals by the country they helped to save.

Racist assumptions yielded less than did opinions on emancipation to the pressures of war among white men in the Union ranks, and some soldiers ended the war just as bigoted as they entered it. Other soldiers began to reevaluate their own racial attitudes but then backslid when they or fellow white soldiers faced difficulties or when the fate of African Americans did not seem so urgently entwined with that of the republic. Hardship and suffering soured the racial attitudes of Sergeant William Stevens. In 1864 the Lincoln administration called off prisoner exchanges, chiefly because the Confederacy refused to exchange black Union soldiers on the same terms as white soldiers. To white Union prisoners of war like William Stevens, this meant that they stayed in prison without hope of exchange. Emaciated and infested by lice, William Stevens blamed black soldiers. "The only reason our Government has for leaving us in such a condition was a miserable quibble, about the 'exchange' Negroes," Stevens complained. He "would not willingly endure this again" even if he knew it would benefit "every Negro in the Confederacy."[57] On the other hand, as the Union army started racking up victories late in the war, a confident Illinois soldier named George Hudson reverted to racist stereotypes to oppose measures like black suffrage. "You must have a better oppinion of the Negro than I to leave our Government to their Protection," Hudson wrote to a family member who had expressed approval of black voting.[58] In short, when the progress of the war went badly, or, ironically, exceptionally smoothly, some white troops reverted to their old prejudices.

Yet despite obvious exceptions and despite regression, as the stubborn war persisted, many soldiers explicitly identified white northerners' tacit assent to a version of American nationalism rooted in white supremacy as part of the problem, which meant that altering the relationship between race and nationalism would have to be part of the solution. As one Pennsylvania soldier determined, the war could never be won, nor could the Union be restored, until the North set about "removing the unreasonable prejudice against the colored race."[59] At the close of the war, men who before 1861 had thought little about slavery, had taken white supremacy for granted, and had despised the very mention of abolitionism now called for practical advances—such as legal equality, equal pay for black soldiers, and sometimes even suffrage—that would concretely change the relationship between the nation and race and that they could not in their wildest dreams have imagined advocating just four short years previously.[60] That the entire Union army was not unanimously in favor of black equality must of course be kept in mind, but that is hardly surprising given the prevalence of racism throughout the antebellum United States. What *is* surprising is that *anyone* changed so much in such a short span of time, let alone men who, as E. C. Hubbard ruefully admitted of himself late in the war, had once considered "a negro a parallel case of a dog."[61] At war's end, it was clear that much had changed, changed utterly, to borrow from William Butler Yeats about a different and later rebellion for independence, though whether a terrible beauty had been born remained to be seen.[62]

When Civil War armies met on the battlefield, three conflicting versions of the relationship between nationalism and race clashed as forcefully as infantry and artillery regiments did. None of the three versions won unequivocally, but none failed to leave its mark. The Confederacy witnessed the military defeat of its version, but confronting the Confederacy's race-grounded form of nationalism forced Union nationalism to reckon with race explicitly, despite the clear preference of most white northerners in 1861 to leave assumptions of white supremacy unexamined and questions about racial justice unasked. African Americans' vision of a nation that could be made whole only by embracing racial equality fell short of full fruition both during and after the war, yet, inspired by that vision, black men took up arms in the defense of the United States. In so doing, they made their own exclusion from constitutional rights and liberties indefensible even in the legislative halls of the very U.S. government that had sanctioned slavery during its entire prewar existence. The tumult that resulted from the clash between these three versions made previously unimaginable legal changes possible.

The Thirteenth Amendment abolished slavery; the Fourteenth Amendment guaranteed the rights of citizenship to black Americans; the Fifteenth Amendment guaranteed suffrage to black men; the Civil Rights Act of 1866 guaranteed black Americans' basic rights, such as access to the legal system and the enjoyment of equal protection of person and property, and it also prohibited either "state law or custom" from abridging those rights. These legal changes showed that the very nation-state that before the war had guaranteed the rights of some Americans to own other Americans based on race was now pledged to secure the political, legal, and civil rights of all Americans regardless of race, at least in theory. That the theory grew increasingly distant from reality in the later decades of the nineteenth century shows that the war failed to fulfill the potential that it created. In that sense, the relationship between race and American nationalism remained, and perhaps remains, unsettled.

7

Emancipation without Slavery

Remembering the Union Victory

NINA SILBER

While history tells us, fairly conclusively I think, that the Union won the Civil War, the evidence seems to be considerably more ambiguous on the question of who won the peace. Perhaps somewhat impulsively, many historians, myself included, have awarded victory in this postwar struggle to the Confederacy. In my book *The Romance of Reunion: Northerners and the South, 1865–1900* (1993) I hoped to shed light on "the crucial historical transformation in which, as some have said, 'the North won the war, but the South won the peace.'" Indeed, by the end of the nineteenth century, novelists, artists, and even academics had helped to establish this apparent southern conquest of American culture. Scholars, increasingly concerned with appearing "scientific" and "objective," balanced their condemnations of slavery and secession by embracing certain aspects of the Confederate memorial tradition when they wrote about the Civil War. Although many attacked the injustice of slavery, historians seldom denounced slaveholders and generally endorsed the notion of black inferiority. And until the mid-twentieth century a majority of historians embraced the Confederate perspective that condemned northern excess in the Reconstruction era and hailed the triumph of the "redeemers."[1]

In addition to a scholarly endorsement of a Confederate-oriented history, Americans have also readily accepted—in literature, film, and popular song—an overwhelmingly romantic view of antebellum southern life. Perhaps nothing signals this sentimental conquest better than the wildly popular story of Rhett, Ashley, Melanie, and Scarlett, but the victory of southern romance was apparent even earlier, particularly in the nationwide popularity of the novels of southern authors like Thomas Dixon and the films of southern-born filmmakers like D. W. Griffith. The endorsement of a seemingly southern style of race relations during the 1890s offered additional proof that despite Lee's surrender to Grant, the culture that shaped and celebrated Lee was in the ascendancy. Even today, American culture seems awash with ongoing proof of a southern victory, suggested by the display of Confederate-flag bumper stickers that adorn cars and trucks, North and South. And certainly it must count for something that, as the journalist Tony Horwitz discovered several years ago, reenactors impersonate Confederate soldiers far more often than they do Union ones.[2]

Yet, despite our sense of this strong Confederate undercurrent pulsing through American life, the notion that the Confederacy won the peace does not fully capture the complexity of the postwar settlement, nor does it allow us to account for the variety of ways we continue to remember the war and the Union victory today. In the first place, we would underestimate the power and influence of northern racism if we accepted the idea that white southerners alone created and maintained Jim Crow in a place of strength and dominance until the latter part of the twentieth century. As the historian C. Vann Woodward observed so many years ago, northerners pioneered in the creation of institutional segregation before it made its formal appearance in the post–Civil War South. Then, in the 1890s, when southern states passed laws mandating segregation and disenfranchising African American men, they had the explicit support of northerners and federal politicians. Henry Billings Brown, the Supreme Court justice who authored the majority opinion upholding segregation in *Plessy v. Ferguson,* hailed from Massachusetts and spent most of his legal career in Michigan. In the historical profession too, northern scholars apparently overextended themselves to accommodate a pro-Confederate interpretation of the Civil War and Reconstruction.

Nor were northerners blindly seduced by southern stories of romance, honor, and chivalry when they looked back and remembered the Civil War and antebellum life from the perspective of the postbellum era. Quite a few northern authors wrote those tales themselves; and northern audiences embraced those stories precisely because they spoke to many of their own postwar concerns and anxieties. In a period when northern women had become more visible and more active, when both foreign and native-born laborers began more stridently to voice their opposition to the chieftains of industrial capitalism, and when a handful of Yankee businessmen had accumulated massive amounts of wealth, many who lived north of the Mason-Dixon line appreciated a story that emphasized submissive women, compliant workers, and simple, rural pleasures. Finally, the need to uphold and endorse a story of national progress and triumph further encouraged northerners just as much as southerners to bury the problem of race and the problem of slavery behind an image of whites-only sectional reunification. As studies of postwar reconciliation have suggested, the impulse to heal and to celebrate national regeneration bore the imprint of Unionists' concerns just as much as Confederates'.[3]

But I would also argue that the Union victory and the northerners who celebrated that victory put their stamp on wartime memories in another important respect. Although many northern whites disavowed the notion that slavery had caused the conflict, and although many of them upheld reconciliation, more so than slavery's abolition, as the war's most important legacy, the language of emancipation nonetheless entered the vocabulary of northerners in new and important ways and shaped the way Americans thought about their postwar world. In the most influential study we have to date regarding the process of postwar reconciliation, the historian David Blight has argued that white north-erners and white southerners gradually learned, in the postwar years, to place greater emphasis on reunification and their common wartime experiences of soldiering and sacrifice than on the antislavery aspects of the Civil War or the fate of black Americans in the postemancipation era. "The memory of slavery, emancipation, and the Fourteenth and Fifteenth Amendments," Blight writes, "never fit well into a developing narrative in which the Old and New South were romanticized and wel-comed back to a new nationalism, and in which devotion alone made everyone right, and no one truly wrong, in the remembered Civil War."[4]

While Blight is certainly correct to observe that Americans had great difficulty in reconciling their history of racial oppression with their narrative of progress and romance, this is not to say that emanci-pation and even slavery never became important motifs in northern ac-counts of the Civil War's legacy. In particular, what I hope to suggest in this essay is that for various reasons and among various constituencies a certain type of emancipation thinking did gain ground in northern circles and at times even blended with the story of American progress. I draw for this study from a variety of historical accounts surveying political and cultural developments between the end of the nineteenth century and the middle years of the twentieth, from women's suffrage and antiprostitution campaigns to the work done against and in support of U.S. imperialism. In assessing these activities, I find that the antislavery message of the Civil War offered a powerful image that many northerners, especially white northerners, clung to in the post–Civil War era. The residents of the states that had constituted the Union and perhaps even some of the residents of the onetime Confederacy used the memory of emancipation, or some variation on that theme, to promote a variety of late-nineteenth- and early-twentieth-century causes, although seldom was it used to promote the cause of the former bondsmen and bondswomen themselves. Indeed, more often than not, this type of emancipation memory tried to appropriate a moral imperative from wartime abolition, while obscuring the real story of the war, emancipation, and the unfulfilled promise of black liberation.

To some extent, the language of emancipation became ubiquitous as northerners celebrated the Union's triumph upon the war's conclusion. True, many celebrated the fact that the Union had been saved; but many also found emancipation to be a particularly inspirational component of the Union victory. Moreover, as some Unionists saw it, emancipation had repercussions far beyond the liberation of the slaves, promoting hopes and desires among those who were neither enslaved nor African American. "The contest with the South which destroyed slavery has caused an immense increase to the popular passions for liberty and equality," suggested the Philadelphia lawyer Sidney George Fisher soon after the war closed. The Illinois congressman Isaac Arnold argued that the Union victory had created the country anew, that the nation was "wholly free." And the preacher J. W. Hough maintained that the Union's dedication to emancipation would reverberate around the world, stirring people as far away as Italy and Hungary, "proclaiming everywhere 'liberty to the captives, and the opening of prison to them that are bound.'"[5]

Comments such as these helped to sustain the postwar depiction of Abraham Lincoln as the Great Emancipator. Indeed, eight of the nine statues built to honor Lincoln from 1866 to 1879 showed the president in the act of issuing the Emancipation Proclamation. Certainly, as the tributes and statues suggested, northerners derived considerable inspiration from wartime emancipation and would use that memory as a benchmark of the war's significance for some time. But as the remarks of Fisher, Arnold, and Hough also suggest, recollections of emancipation could produce a more complicated, and more ambiguous, legacy. For many, emancipation offered the foundation for a new American identity, or maybe it would be more accurate to say that it sealed the commitment to an American identity that had previously been glimpsed but not wholly realized. As many saw it, just by declaring the slaves to be free, Americans signaled their commitment to progress, uplift, and righteousness, qualities that would define Americans' mission at home and around the globe for the next 150 years. Such notions extended a preexisting narrative that had begun with the American Revolution and saw American nationalism as uniquely devoted to principles of freedom, be they religious, civil, or political. With the end of the Civil War, and the end of slavery in particular, many northerners saw the promise of American freedom finally and truly fulfilled. The Massachusetts textile manufacturer Edward Atkinson conveyed some of that sense of upward triumph and national mission realized when he identified the day after Congress approved the Thirteenth Amendment as the beginning of "Year 1 of American Independence."[6]

Others, however, drew on the legacy of emancipation by glancing backward more than forward, feeling less certain that all of the nation's future endeavors would bask in the glow of emancipation's righteousness. In this second version of emancipation memory, the liberation of the slaves served as a reminder of the nation's previous association with bondage, an association that had enmeshed both northerners and southerners in a troubling past defined variously as a time of economic backwardness, social injustice, and racial turmoil. Consequently, as these northerners saw it, the memory of emancipation should foster a pledge from Americans and their government to avoid entangling themselves in questionable labor practices in the future, a demand raised most prominently in turn-of-the-century discussions of global imperialism and expansionism. Last, for some the notion of emancipation spoke not to unfettered progress for the future, nor to warnings about potential entanglements with slavelike conditions abroad, but to a promise that should be extended beyond the circle of black slaves to include a wide range of Americans who suffered under various forms of exploitation. Indeed, depending on how *slavery* was defined, the conditions of many different people could be described as a form of bondage. Thus, in this iteration of emancipation thinking, it became incumbent on Americans and their lawmakers to sever the ongoing bonds of oppression. As articulated by some, including women seeking political rights, reformers decrying the prostitution trade, and workers demanding the right to unionize, the demand for liberation was even more pressing now because so many of those who suffered from new forms of enslavement were white.

Among those who saw a promise for greater freedom for themselves in light of the legacy of slave emancipation were nineteenth-century women. With many having participated directly and actively in the prewar and wartime struggle for abolition, female activists believed they were in a unique position to lay claim to the liberties born of wartime and demand an end to their own form of "enslavement." This female slavery, as they saw it, entailed married women's onerous and persistent legal obligations to husbands and the continued political disenfranchisement of all women. As the suffrage leaders Elizabeth Cady Stanton and Susan B. Anthony argued, the Civil War meant "liberty to all" and "national protection for every citizen under our flag." Female activists, having somewhat tentatively endorsed a call for women's suffrage before the Civil War, now saw the opportunities presented by emancipation and black enfranchisement as critical for the advancement of women of all races. What is more, many of those activists put their faith in the Republicans Party, which, they believed, having led the struggle to end slavery, would now lead in the fight for women's emancipation. The members of the American Woman Suffrage Association believed that the true import of Lincoln's Emancipation Proclamation would be lost if those who had worked toward the emancipation of all humankind worked to "keep women in thralldom." In this respect, women's rights activists, especially in the early postwar years, took an optimistic view of the promises contained in slave emancipation and their ultimate extension to women. The first step had been taken, they argued; now women and their Republican allies must see to it that the next logical step, for women's legal and political freedom, was taken.[7]

In fairly short order, however, the Republican leadership made clear their lack of interest in women's suffrage and their desire to secure the political rights of black men first and foremost. The rupture between the women's rights agenda and the Republican Party platform first became apparent with the passage of the Reconstruction amendments, most notably the Fourteenth and Fifteenth amendments, which not only established the foundation for black men's political rights but also continued to block the extension of those political rights to women.

This turn of events prompted some women's rights activists, especially those allied with Stanton and Anthony, to take a more pessimistic, even sinister view of slave emancipation. Now, some female suffragists maintained, wartime emancipation had an unsavory quality, because it had unfairly bequeathed rights to African Americans while failing to deliver on freedom for white women. Increasingly, these female activists adhered to a white supremacist version of emancipation: that those who were most deserving of emancipation's promises, namely, white people, had been denied those promises, while less-deserving African Americans had benefited. "When in the enfranchisement of the black man they saw another ignorant class of voters placed above their heads," Stanton and Anthony wrote, women "were coolly told that the black man had earned the right to vote, that he had fought and bled and died for his country."

Ultimately, these arguments questioned the moral foundation of slave emancipation. As Stanton and Anthony's wing of the suffrage movement explained: "The rights of the black man, for whom the women had worked and waited, were secured, but under the new amendment, by which his race had been made free, the white women of the United States were more securely held in political slavery." As these women and their allies disputed the politics of Reconstruction and increasingly embraced a position that privileged the demands of white women specifically, they no longer celebrated the liberating potential they had once seen in wartime freedom, nor did they recognize the extent to which former slaves, women and men, had themselves achieved only a partial emancipation. Just as women's rights activists would, after this point, pursue their own independent political path, so they would also look for a different type of political language and a distinct political model for their own liberation, rejecting the framework of Civil War–era emancipation.[8]

With apparently more enthusiasm and less ambiguity than women's rights activists, late-nineteenth-century labor leaders viewed wartime emancipation as a clarion call for freeing laborers everywhere from the compulsions of what they termed *wage slavery*. The fledgling union movement of the 1870s and 1880s celebrated the Thirteenth Amendment as a "glorious labor amendment" that was relevant not only to the South's system of racial slavery but also to the increasingly predominant wage system, which forced a laborer to sell his time and the product he produced. "It must not be supposed that the proclamation of emancipation liberated mankind from slavery," said labor activists. "The most subtle form of slavery—wages slavery—remains to be abolished."

Rejecting the notion that contract freedom offered the wage worker true freedom over how he disposed of his labor and earned his living, labor leaders upheld the mantle of wartime emancipation, seeing in it a pledge to all laborers that they would have greater control over how, and how much, they labored. Occasionally, like some of their counterparts in the women's movement, they argued for the special privileges of white workers who, unlike enslaved black men and women, had failed to reap the benefits of emancipation. "True," argued a member of the Knights of Labor, "the colored people are free, but how many thousands of white slaves are there all over the country?" More often, though, they focused, not on the injustice of denying freedom to white people, but on the injustice of the contract system, which forbade laborers from meeting or organizing collectively. Some went even further and saw the root of enslavement in the wage system itself, as it forced workers to sell their time, and thus their physical beings, to an employer rather than selling the product or commodity they had produced. At the very least, such reformers argued, working people were justified in seeking a limit—most favored eight hours a day—to the amount of time they were forced to work for others.[9]

As the historian Amy Stanley has shown, labor leaders formulated their understanding of emancipation's legacy in sharp distinction to the very different vision adopted by mostly Republican employers and manufacturers and the judicial courts of Gilded Age America. Unlike workers and union activists, who saw in wartime emancipation a pledge to bring freedom to a wider array of citizens, employers interpreted slave emancipation as the decisive moment that ushered the United States from a backward past into a progressive and enlightened future. Thus, the most important thing about wartime emancipation was not the promise of greater freedom to come but the fact that emancipation made it possible for a laborer to own himself and sell his labor in a free and open market. "Until very recently," wrote one late-nineteenth-century political economist, "the great majority of men were in a condition of personal dependence, which, although varying much in different countries and at different times, may be fairly termed personal slavery." The trend toward emancipation in the nineteenth century had, he claimed, converted "the laborer into an independent human being on the same footing exactly as the master" and as someone who could sell his own commodity in the form of his time and his labor. In effect, Gilded Age employers very much celebrated the emancipationist legacy of the Civil War, not because they believed that the fate of the former slaves required the nation's attention or that the United States must reckon with its past of racial atrocities, but because the abolition of slavery lent their own objectives and goals, especially the spread of the wage contract, a moral legitimacy that it might have lacked had there been no Civil War and no Emancipation Proclamation. In celebrating the unmitigated triumph of the labor contract, employers obscured the actual conditions of wartime abolition and, more importantly, the ongoing economic and political oppression experienced by ex-slaves in the South, much of which had in fact resulted from contract inequities.[10]

One of the sharpest invocations of the emancipation legacy came from early-twentieth-century crusaders who decried the deplorable practices of the so-called white slave trade. Drawing on a term that had been widely used by Anglo-Americans in the early nineteenth century as an alternative to *wage slavery*, late-nineteenth-century British reformers gradually began to use the expression *white slavery* to refer to the traffic in prostitution, specifically to a practice in which they claimed that young white women were being kidnapped and forced into an international sex trade. Of course, abolitionists had long drawn connections between prostitution and the enslavement of Africans in the South, highlighting the sexual exploitation of young female slaves as a hallmark of slavery's depravity. But in the United States at the turn of the century the talk was not about the buying and selling of black girls for slaveowners' sexual pleasure but about an illicit network that lured young white women into prostitution. Indeed, scholars have found little evidence of widespread abduction and kidnapping of women, although as increasing numbers of young women began to move to cities in search of work and pleasure, no doubt growing numbers were being compelled to turn to prostitution to earn a living. In any event, the first decade of the twentieth century was marked by a growing outrage against an offense that, despite being hard to substantiate, was often likened to earlier forms of bondage and prompted reformers to draw upon the legacy of nineteenth-century abolitionism and emancipation to establish the urgency of their cause.[11]

Clearly, the very phrase *white slavery*, as antiprostitution reformers used it, was meant to suggest a parallel with an institution that had earned widespread condemnation. Yet, many who campaigned against white slavery developed the analogy to suggest that the current crimes being committed against young white women were far worse than what befell African Americans. The reformers' first objective, explained the crusader Clifford Roe, "was to enlighten about ninety-five per cent of the people; to bring home to them the realization that a vast system of slavery, far more debasing than that of blacks, was flourishing under their very eyes." Indeed, as many developed the argument, the fact that white women were being harmed and coerced into sex seemed to imply depths of depravity not reached even in the days of chattel slavery in the South. Thus, as Roe went on to explain, "the country could not bear the spectacle of black folk enslaved in the south, and the most terrible civil war in all history was the result." But, he observed, in Chicago "women, white of skin and civilized of mind, are kept in slavery under conditions worse than that of the slave quarters before the war." In highlighting the then horrors of the white slave trade, Roe and his fellow reformers thus offered a subtle reworking of Civil War history, not only suggesting that "the country" had been motivated by moral outrage against slavery but also minimizing the brutality of black enslavement, especially the sexual coercion of black female slaves. Much as they styled themselves modern-day abolitionists, Roe and his colleagues distorted the antebellum abolitionist legacy by erasing one of the most fundamental points of an earlier generation's antislavery argument.[12]

Some "white slave" reformers went even further in suggesting relatively good, even happy conditions for southern slaves. White slavery, explained a prominent campaigner, is "far worse than African slavery, for many of the black slaves were happy and many of them were good, even deeply religious; while no woman, though she be deceived and made an innocent victim, can be happy after she has been ruined." Only white women, it seems, could be "ruined," and only white women merited the sympathies of early-twentieth-century Americans for the way they had become innocent victims." Moreover, in a way that was consistent with current trends in American popular culture, white slave reformers lent further credence to the myth of the happy slave, a rhetorical gesture that could even make it possible for white southerners to lend support to the new anti-(white) slavery campaign. Here, in effect, was an emancipationist position that blended with the new conciliatory imperative in American culture, a perspective that erased the real conditions of southern slavery and might even foster a bond among white Americans across sectional lines as they united in a campaign to protect the virtue of "innocent" white females. If nothing else, surely there was some resonance between the desire to protect allegedly innocent white girls from the horrors of white slavery in the urban North and the violent determination of white southerners to shield "their women" from the invented threat of lustful black male rapists.[13]

Even as they sought to claim the high moral posture of Civil War–era emancipation, white slave reformers belittled the gravity of the earlier struggle, suggesting that it had lacked the moral weight of their own. This, in effect, was precisely the point made by one female reformer who spoke at a public event honoring the centennial of Lincoln's birth in Chicago in 1909. "We are celebrating here in Chicago this week," explained Ellen Henrotin, "the birthday of the liberator of slaves. Perhaps a hundred years from today America will be celebrating the birth of some woman wise enough and brave enough and noble enough to be the liberator of women from a slavery far worse than that from which Lincoln freed the negro." Henrotin thus simultaneously drew upon, and blunted, the legacy of Lincoln and Civil War–era emancipation. She also offered a somewhat contradictory message about women's emancipation. On the one hand, her argument helped advance the demands of (white) female activists, who by the early twentieth century had become deeply engaged and heavily invested in social welfare reform. There was no better way, she implied, for women to advance than by assuming the moral mantle of the Civil War era's Great Emancipator and accomplishing the liberation of young white women forced into an even more brutalizing condition of enslavement. Yet, as the white-slavery argument also suggested, young white girls, the innocent victims of sex traders, were no models of female activism: these girls needed rescuing, protecting, and liberating, especially from the dangerous and immoral influences that surrounded them in modern urban America.[14]

While various reform campaigns paid homage, however weakly, to Lincoln and emancipation, some of the most contested invocations of the abolition legacy appeared in debates regarding turn-of-the-century imperialist expansion. As the United States embarked on a more aggressive approach to foreign affairs—made manifest in the 1898 annexation of Hawaii, the wars in Cuba and the Philippines, and then the 1898 acquisition of the Philippines—Americans divided over whether to support or oppose the imperialist agenda. Perhaps not surprisingly, late-nineteenth-century anti-imperialists, many of whom had close personal ties to the antebellum abolitionist movement, frequently spoke the language of antislavery in their arguments against U.S. involvement in colonization. Prominent members of the U.S. Anti-Imperialist League could, and did, point proudly to their abolitionist roots. Others, such as William Lloyd Garrison III and Oswald Garrison Villard, bore the names of their abolitionist forebears. Indeed, at the league's founding meeting, speakers referred to the abolitionist legacy that was now embodied in the turn-of-the-century struggle against imperialism. "A generation has elapsed since the country by a violent effort threw off the disease of slavery," one speaker remarked. Now, anti-imperialists argued, in the threat of overseas expansion, America faced a new, equally dangerous challenge to its people and its institutions.[15]

The link between Civil War–era emancipation and late-nineteenth-century anti-imperialism went beyond rhetoric and surnames. Some in the anti-imperialist camp argued against expansion by suggesting that imperialist entanglement necessarily brought with it an alliance with coercive labor practices that were reminiscent of slavery. Colonization, some labor leaders argued, especially in tropical regions, made the U.S. economy more dependent on conditions of forced labor, especially in light of the supposedly inferior racial stock of the colonized laborers. In Hawaii, the American Federation of Labor leader Samuel Gompers argued, the Chinese, Japanese, Portuguese, and South Sea Island workers who lived there were "practically slave laborers." The annexation of the Hawaiian Islands, he contended, had allowed the United States to legitimize these coercive labor practices and thus come dangerously close to reviving a discredited alliance with enslavement. The real problem with such a policy, argued Gompers, whether applied in Hawaii or in the Philippines, had less to do with the immoral practices perpetuated overseas and more to do with the way such practices degraded the status of labor within the United States. Thus, for Gompers, the cry that "slavery" was practiced on foreign shores provided a means for establishing the superiority of American labor. It also presented an argument less for emancipation than against foreign entanglements in order to protect the superior status, and income, of the American worker.[16]

Gompers's argument was further developed by the prominent anti-imperialist David Starr Jordan, who served as president of Stanford University at the time of the Philippine war. Jordan argued that no colonial power or industrial force had managed to find a way to control the so-called tropical races and make their work profitable without turning to "some form of slavery." Making explicit what Gompers had implied, Jordan stated that these residents of tropical colonies were "slave races," and he believed that contact with such people, as well as with the system of bondage that attached itself to them, must be avoided. Ultimately, in condemning the U.S. acquisition of the Philippine Islands, Jordan called up the spirit of Lincoln and argued, "We cannot run a republic in the West and a slave plantation in the East." Here, we might note, was a particularly troubling version of the emancipation memory: an argument that obscured the true nature of slavery and emancipation by associating dark-skinned peoples with conditions of slavery and obscuring the historical role of whites in practicing and shaping the institution. Again, neither Jordan nor Gompers seemed particularly intent on taking up the struggle against overseas slavery; they were more interested in keeping the United States removed from overseas involvements. Thus, the argument allowed anti-imperialists like Jordan to envision American society as a place where the emancipation legacy had been truly fulfilled—thus ignoring the perpetuation of oppressive racial practices in the Jim Crow, sharecropping South—while the uncivilized "East," where people of inferior racial stock predominated, remained mired in conditions of slavelike backwardness.[17]

Not all anti-imperialists employed the same kind of white supremacist logic. As James McPherson has observed, many of those with links to the abolitionist past attacked imperialist expansion precisely because it allowed white colonizers to promote new forms of racial oppression and enslavement that the colonized peoples were struggling to resist. The United States, argued William Lloyd Garrison Jr., was "attempting to enslave the countrymen of [Filipino rebel leader Emilio] Aguinaldo," who "was fighting in the same cause for which John Brown died." In the case of the Philippines, the discussion regarding slavery and emancipation became even more complicated when Americans learned that a form of slavery persisted on the Sulu Archipelago, which had been brought under U.S. control as part of the terms of an 1899 treaty. Anti-imperialists, most notably the aging former abolitionist Edward Atkinson, seized on this fact and used it to underscore their argument against any and all forms of colonial entanglement. The headline of Atkinson's anti-imperialist journal thus blared the news that slavery had been "reestablished under the jurisdiction of the United States so far as can be done by authority of William McKinley, in carrying on this effort to deprive the people of the Philippine Islands of their liberty."[18]

But while Atkinson used slavery in the Philippines as an argument to discredit U.S. expansionist efforts, the publicizing of bonded labor on the Sulu Archipelago provided the opportunity, explains the historian Michael Salman, for yet another kind of emancipation argument, one that envisioned the United States reprising its role as liberator and freeing oppressed peoples around the world from the backward chains of enslavement. This argument did not originate in this particular U.S. overseas venture or even with U.S. imperialists themselves; rather, it seems to have been a strategy that Americans learned by looking across the Atlantic. Before the United States began to draw on its "antislavery past," British officials saw the power of an emancipationist history and even learned to use it in their international disputes with the slaveholding United States. When, for example, the American settlers in Texas declared their independence from Mexico in 1836, Britain's Lord Palmerston saw an opportunity to link British abolitionist demands to curtail any reinstitution of the slave trade between Texas and the West Indies with Great Britain's interest in blocking U.S. expansionist interests in a southwesterly direction. The British, of course, did not stop the annexation of Texas, but England's empire builders continued to pursue a course of global intervention by adopting a position as international moral arbiter, particularly on matters related to the international slave trade. Emancipation provided, in effect, a humanitarian backdrop for British empire building. After David Livingstone explored Africa in the 1850s and 1860s and reported on the slave trade practices he encountered, British officials stepped up their efforts to expand British missions and other institutions on the African continent. Other European powers followed suit, relying on an image of Africa as a continent overrun with self-imposed slavery that could only be crushed, or reformed, by the enlightened power of abolition-inspired Western imperialism.[19]

Amidst all this, and in singularly dramatic fashion, the United States freed its slaves. It was an act that, among other things, gave Americans an entry point into this emerging imperialist discussion. First, it offered a response to anti-imperialists, who had criticized the new imperialist orientation being adopted at the end of the nineteenth century as a fundamental departure from the American historical tradition. If fin-de-siècle imperialism could be presented as a form of emancipation, then surely it was in keeping with America's historical beliefs. Second, it provided the United States with its own moral platform for claiming an enlightened form of colonial oversight, perhaps even more enlightened than the colonialism practiced by other imperial powers, where the emancipation impulse may not have been as pronounced. As president in the 1870s, Ulysses Grant, himself a participant in the experience of wartime emancipation, unsuccessfully advocated for the annexation of Santo Domingo by arguing that the acquisition would make the United States less dependent on slave-based societies like Brazil and Cuba and thus would contribute to the death of that "hated system of enforced labor."[20]

The analogy between U.S. imperialism and slave liberation was applied far more successfully in the Philippine conflict thirty years later. In justifying the U.S. seizure of the Philippines in July 1898, a correspondent of the secretary of the navy argued that returning the islands to Spanish "misgovernment seems . . . little more consistent with our duty . . . [than] in the War of the Rebellion, the sending back into slavery of the Negroes who came into our lines and even those who fought as soldiers under our own flag." Although most African Americans opposed Philippine annexation, a handful of black leaders, hoping to demonstrate the patriotism of the black community and seeking to rally greater black support for the cause, drew on the emancipation legacy as justification for greater U.S. involvement in the islands. "The natives in these far-away islands in the Pacific," argued a leading black Republican in 1899, "are now being offered the same boon that was offered the American Negro in 1861—the opportunity to become subjects of a great and good government." Moreover, the revelation that forms of slavery were in fact practiced in parts of the Philippines provided further ammunition for an antislavery/pro-imperialist position. Disputing the *anti*-imperialist argument that U.S. colonialism sanctioned enslavement, *pro*-imperialists constructed an image of Filipinos as a backward people who were, as one newspaper proclaimed, "still far removed from that stage of civilization which recognizes evil in the ownership of human beings." Consequently, they justified the United States' continued hold on the islands because of the moral uplift and enlightenment that U.S. oversight would bring. Civil War emancipation, it seemed, had impressed upon Americans an obligation to bring liberty wherever they were in a position to do so. The further implication was that as a predominantly white and Anglo-Saxon nation, Americans were more uniquely suited to the role of liberator than were those nonwhite peoples, like the Moros on the Sulu Archipelago, who had allowed slavery to flourish.[21]

Ultimately, this type of emancipation argument successfully buttressed the imperialist calls for acquisition of the Philippine Islands. In later years, the argument that placed the United States in the position of global emancipator would be employed repeatedly to gain the support of Americans at home and allies abroad for a variety of overseas ventures. In these reprisals of the emancipation argument, however, the slavery that Americans sought to vanquish was generally more metaphorical than actual. Recognizing the moral weight that attached itself to Lincoln's emancipationist image, the British prime minister Lloyd George even turned the United States–as–emancipator argument back to the American people to gain popular approval for American intervention in World War I. "Has there not grown up in this continent [of Europe]," he argued in a special Lincoln Day message in February 1917, "a new form of slavery, a militarist slavery, which has not only been crushing out the freedom of the people under its control, but which in recent years has also been moving toward crushing out freedom and fraternity in Europe as well?" Americans, he implied, must be true to Lincoln and their own abolitionist legacy by pledging themselves to end the new type of slavery that Germany and its allies sought to spread across Europe.[22]

Yet, perhaps because the United States had had its own direct experience with slavery, the slavery analogy would remain troublesome for

Americans bent on pursuing a traditional imperialist course of action in the twentieth century. With American slavery a relatively recent memory, the argument that imperialist intervention represented a new form of emancipation could sound decidedly hollow. Perhaps, too, because the imperialist project involved the participation of not only northerners but also white southerners, those associated most notoriously with slavery and continued racial oppression, the connections made between imperialist practices and U.S. slavery could resonate even more powerfully. And as the oppression of black Americans in the Jim Crow South received greater scrutiny, both domestic and international, it became that much more difficult for American imperialists to claim the moral high ground that an emancipation legacy might have provided.

Not surprisingly, some of the most pointed observations regarding the hypocritical claims of imperialist "emancipators" came from black Americans. Starting with the initial imperialist ventures of the late nineteenth century, African Americans began linking U.S. imperialist actions toward dark-skinned peoples abroad with racist practices at home. A black U.S. soldier in the Philippines observed in 1899 that his fellow white soldiers, in their dealings with the Philippine people, had "begun to establish their diabolical race hatred in all its home rancor ... even endeavoring to propagate the phobia among the Spaniards and Filipinos so as to be sure of the foundation of their supremacy when the civil rule . . . is established." Turning his attention to the U.S. occupation of Haiti in the early twentieth century, the black writer and activist James Weldon Johnson believed that the U.S. attitude toward the black inhabitants of the island was characterized by a particularly virulent strain of racial animosity that had much to do with the personal prejudices of the marines, "a great number [of whom came] from the South." Seeing a palpable link between the slavery of an earlier generation and the imperialist practices of his time, Johnson went on to compare the forced-labor system practiced by U.S. marines against Haitian subjects to "the African slave raids of past centuries."[23]

Like Johnson, other African Americans in the years during and after the Second World War began to investigate the links between twentieth-century colonialism and earlier practices of slavery and racial bondage. As the historian Penny Von Eschen has argued, African Americans gave increasing attention to the idea of an African diaspora and a transnational black community. As a result, they increasingly

identified their own conditions as grounded in the history and conditions of a wide variety of dark-skinned, colonized people, not because of
an essential racial or even cultural link, but because of "a shared history
of the racism spawned by slavery, colonialism, and imperialism." Black
Americans, in other words, rejected the versions of the emancipationist
legacy that had gained currency during the Philippine war: either that
the United States had a unique destiny to fulfill in bringing freedom—
through imperialism—to oppressed peoples abroad or that slavery was
a by-product of colored peoples' backwardness and thus something
American emancipationists must avoid. Rather, black Americans criticized twentieth-century colonialism as a practice that had roots in the
economic exploitation and enslavement of Africans dating from the
fifteenth century. "The age of hate," argued the African American *Chicago Defender,* had begun not with twentieth-century fascists who tar-
geted those deemed racially inferior but with "the slave trade and the
intensification of prejudice which followed the liberation of the slaves."
Increasingly, then, African American anti-imperialists believed that the
true spirit of the emancipation legacy demanded support both for the
colonized in their democratic struggles against colonial powers and for
African Americans in the United States.[24]

Although they were not as consistent or outspoken in condemning U.S. imperialism, some white Americans also criticized imperialist actions by linking them, either directly or indirectly, to U.S. racial
practices. Certainly this had been the thrust of the critique made by
late-nineteenth-century anti-imperialists like William Lloyd Garrison
Jr., who saw parallels between the Filipino people's struggles against
U.S. rule and the antislavery fighters of old. In similar fashion, the anti-
imperialist Edward Clement saw a troubling similarity between the 1898
annexation of Hawaii and the Supreme Court's almost simultaneous
decision to uphold Mississippi's disenfranchisement laws. The Court's
decision, legalizing what Clement called the "practical re-establishment
of slavery," struck him "as if it were a part of the imperializing pro-
gramme." The U.S. occupation of Haiti in the early twentieth century
prompted further reflection on how earlier forms of racial oppression
might echo in contemporary imperialist practices. Like James Weldon
Johnson, an American missionary testifying before Congress in 1918
saw a troubling parallel between slavery and the labor policy imple-
mented by U.S. Marines in Haiti. In his testimony, he reported seeing

numerous Haitians "roped tightly and cruelly together, and driven like slaves." Following these kinds of exposures, the Haitian corvée system, as it was known, was partially dismantled, although U.S. occupation of the West Indian nation continued.[25]

Still, because the United States generally avoided the kind of direct colonial oversight that had been practiced by western European powers, American leaders could, certainly in the years immediately following World War II, uniquely position themselves as the champions of freedom. In this way the language of emancipation once again became a crucial staple of U.S. foreign policy, now doing double duty in the battle against communism and in the fight against European colonialism. Thus, on the one hand, U.S. imperialists and cold warriors portrayed the Soviet Union and its communist allies as slavemongers who sought to impose a system of bondage wherever they could. The U.S. State Department's crucial cold-war document, NSC 68, described the post–World War II struggle with communism as one that pitted "the idea of freedom" against the "idea of slavery under the grim oligarchy of the Kremlin." In the cold-war context, the emancipation legacy demanded that American foreign policy direct its focus toward obliterating the "slavery," political and economic, that came with Soviet totalitarianism.[26]

At the same time, fighting against "slavery" also entailed fighting against the old colonial empires, especially the crumbling regimes of the French and the English, and giving encouragement to the independence movements in emerging third-world nations. Waging this kind of battle, however, posed challenges for American leaders, especially as they often found themselves berated by leaders in South Asia, Latin America, Africa, and the Middle East, who expressed considerable skepticism about America's so-called emancipationist legacy. How, after all, could Americans really see themselves as emancipators in these predominantly nonwhite nations, given their own history of racial slavery and their ongoing system of oppression directed against black Americans?

Eventually those challenges prompted a renewed wave of activism against the injustices of the Jim Crow system, especially on the part of black Americans in the 1950s and 1960s. Eventually, too, those challenges prompted U.S. politicians to address some of the most blatant signs of racial inequality and even to reassess the history they told of U.S. slavery. Finally, the debate regarding the fitness of the United States to be a global leader in a world of newly emerging third-world nations also helped to shape a new language of emancipation that worked its way into American culture. Through the vehicle of Hollywood films, American culture again embraced the story of emancipation, albeit this time in the form of biblical epics like *The Ten Commandments,* which retold the story of the Hebrews' liberation from ancient slavery. In those portrayals, as the scholar Melani McAlister suggests, filmmakers linked the struggles against oppression in the ancient Middle East and the modern-day struggles of Middle Eastern nationalists against the old colonial powers of Europe. Thus, in cold-war rhetoric, public political statements, and motion pictures, antislavery rhetoric in the 1950s gestured not only toward the U.S. struggle against communism but also toward third-world nationalist struggles against the old colonial empire.[27]

Even today, in our post-cold-war, antiterrorist era, a language that depicts the United States as fighting with the same motives and objectives that supposedly animated Americans in the Civil War has resurfaced. Indeed, as recently as the fall of 2006 the image of Civil War emancipation was invoked yet again and applied to the war in Iraq. In an interview with *Essence* magazine, Secretary of State Condoleeza Rice compared those who advocated U.S. withdrawal from Iraq to those nineteenth-century northerners who, as she put it, might have said, "Why don't we get out of this now, take a peace with the South, but leave the South with slaves." Thus, as Rice hoped to suggest, Abraham Lincoln's emancipation tradition lives today in the current policies of George W. Bush, whose goal is to end Iraqis' enslavement, while Islamic fundamentalists and "terrorists" presumably play the part of contemporary slavemongers. But more than this, Rice, as an African American speaking to a largely black audience, also seemed to be claiming the African American community's long-standing tendency to connect the antislavery struggle in the United States with third-world struggles against oppression. Her comments, however, clearly elide the fact that increasing numbers of people around the globe, including in Iraq itself, now cast the United States, perhaps more than any other domestic or foreign force, on the side of oppression. Moreover, Rice errs where so many others before her have erred: in using the emancipation legacy of the Civil War to claim a moral high ground for an agenda, in this case continuing the war in Iraq, that has at best a questionable moral foundation. Much as historians might appreciate the attempts made to bring historical knowledge into present-day conversations, perhaps we also need to be wary of the many, not always clarifying ways in which the legacy of Civil War emancipation has been invoked in the 150 years since it took effect.[28]

8

Redeeming a Failed Revolution

Confederate Memory

W. FITZHUGH BRUNDAGE

Confederate commemoration during the half-century after the Civil War is a reminder of how grief, anxiety, and tragedy can be twisted to serve reprehensible ends. The consequences of the various uses of Confederate memory for the region and its white and black residents as well as for the nation and its delayed achievement of democracy were profound and enduring. It is hardly novel to suggest that white southerners after the Civil War manipulated the memory of their war against the Union to advance a reactionary form of racial sectionalism. There was little scope for nuance or subtlety in the remembered past of the Lost Cause. Even so, various groups of white southerners had divergent interpretations of the region's Confederate history. Even at the close of the nineteenth century, when the Confederate commemoration reached its most intense phase, white southerners harnessed their recalled past to diverging ambitions for themselves and their region.

To make sense of white southern memory, there is no better place to begin than the scale of southern defeat. The slaveholder's republic was not just defeated; it was crushed. Jefferson Davis, its president, was captured in embarrassing circumstances as he fled headlong in disguise in the hinterland of Georgia. Most of its armies were in disarray, incapable of impeding the advance of Union forces. Virtually all of its major cities either were occupied by the Union army or had been reduced to ruins. Its white population was demoralized; the high desertion rate within the Confederate army testified to the inability of Confederate soldiers to reconcile their defense of the insurgent nation with their duty to protect their homes and families.

These manifestations of the collapse of the Confederate nation have been the fodder of historical fiction for generations. Other, less obvious scars of the war were equally important in the long term. To the extent that the physical carnage of the Civil War is acknowledged today, it is usually by reciting the number of war casualties. But to observe that the Civil War was, by orders of magnitude, the bloodiest war in American history does not do justice to its toll of death and human wreckage. No definitive count of Confederate war dead is possible, owing to the paucity of Confederate war records. There are estimates, or, better said, guesses, that the Confederate dead numbered between 250,000 and 300,000. Confederate forces during the war totaled between 750,000 and 1.25 million. Thus, between one in five and one in three Confederate soldiers died during the war.

To begin to grasp the scale of the war's slaughter, it is necessary to linger a moment longer on the Confederate casualties. Considerably more than half of the Confederate dead had been ravaged by disease, sometimes as a consequence of battle wounds, but often the disease was entirely unrelated to combat. And then there were the wounded. The number of wounded Confederate soldiers who survived the war may have equaled the number of Confederate dead. That Mississippi devoted one-fifth of its state budget to wooden limbs in 1866 is one measure of the number of disabled veterans who returned from war. There also were the tens of thousands of captured Confederates who spent time in Union prisoner camps, where the mortality rates often exceeded 20 percent of the inmates. The odds of a soldier in Lee's Army of Northern Virginia surviving the war alive without serious injury and without being captured were probably about one in five.[1]

But even the bodily intact Confederate veterans bore scars of war for the rest of their lives. Mid-nineteenth-century Americans had neither the vocabulary nor the science to diagnose post-traumatic stress disorder. Nevertheless, there is compelling evidence of the lingering effects of psychological trauma on veterans on both sides. A recent study traced the mental-health history of more than fifteen thousand Union veterans. Postwar pension and health records reveal that 44 percent of Union veterans suffered from some form of mental illness. Researchers concluded that there was a strong correlation between traumatic experience during the war and subsequent mental illness, a finding they believed indicated that post-traumatic stress disorder was endemic among Civil War soldiers. Because there are no comparable postwar medical records for Confederate veterans, no analogous study for Confederate soldiers is possible. Even so, given the carnage and hardship that Confederate soldiers endured, there is every reason to assume that post-traumatic stress disorder was as common among Confederate veterans as among Union veterans.[2]

The story of Benjamin Withers as traced by David Silkenat is emblematic of the dark undertow of the war experience. Withers enlisted on 1 February 1862 in Mecklenburg County, North Carolina, at the age of twenty-six, joining the hard-fighting Bethel Regiment. He fought in North Carolina, eastern Virginia, and at Gettysburg, where he saw fifty members of his regiment killed in an hour. Later he fought at Bristoe Station, the Wilderness, Spotsylvania, Cold Harbor, and Petersburg. During the trench warfare around Petersburg he spent weeks ankle-deep in mud, besieged by rats, and sleepless because of almost constant artillery barrage. There, in the closing months of the war a bullet from a Union sharpshooter splintered Withers's right forearm. At a field hospital a Confederate surgeon amputated Withers's right arm at the elbow, leaving a tender stump that caused him pain for the remainder of his life. Although he managed to eke out a living as a painter in North Carolina for sixteen years after Appomattox, he never regained his prewar vitality. When he committed suicide in June 1881 by shooting himself in the head, few of his neighbors were surprised; they concluded that his lingering war wound provided ample explanation for his suicide.[3]

Withers's postwar life is suggestive not just because of his suffering but also because of his decision to end his life violently. Silkenat's study concludes that the phenomenon was rare among whites before the Civil War but that after the war white men, especially wounded or psychologically scarred veterans, committed suicide in unprecedented numbers. Contemporary observers wrung their hands over an apparent epidemic of suicide.

This litany of the war's scars is intended to remind us of the urgent need in the postwar white South to find a salve for ubiquitous human suffering and loss in the region. In addition to regaining a place in the

Union, replacing slavery with a new form of labor, and rebuilding the southern economy, white southerners also confronted the equally vexing challenge of making sense of a catastrophic war that had achieved none of its avowed purposes. It was against this backdrop that the commemoration of the Confederacy took place.

The impulse to commemorate the sacrifice of white southerners was inevitable. But how best to commemorate the war defied simple answer. At least three groups strove to be architects of Confederate memory. Given the conspicuous role of white clerics in defending the institution of slavery and championing the Confederate cause, the need to explain the war's outcome with God's will was inescapable. White ministers had no doubt that God's hand was evident in the South's defeat. Nevertheless, the collapse of the southern nation did not prompt whites to abandon their conviction that God favored them or that God had a transcendent purpose for the Confederacy. The *Southern Advocate*, a Methodist journal, had described the Confederacy as engaged in a "Holy War," and a Georgia Methodist had spoken for many white southerners when he pronounced that "God is on our side." Rather than interpret Appomattox as evidence of God's wrath, white southerners concluded that they were latter-day Israelites of the Old Testament and that God had used the ungodly to chasten his chosen people. They reasserted their submission to the divine order that would eventually deliver them. As Father Abram Ryan, one of the most beloved clerical contributors to the theology of the Lost Cause, wrote in his poem "The Land We Love," "Each link of the chain that enslaves / Shall bind us the closer to thee." The trials that white southerners suffered during the war and its aftermath were reminders of the wickedness that always threatened God's chosen. As the South Carolina Methodist Conference put it, "To be innocent and to be oppressed are the body and soul of Christianity."[4]

Postwar white southern evangelicalism was at the center of late-nineteenth-century Confederate commemoration. Although more tendentious than most of his contemporaries, Robert Lewis Dabney voiced an influential defense of antebellum institutions, secession, white supremacy, and the eventual vindication of the white South. For Dabney and many other white southern evangelicals, the antebellum South had been becoming both more evangelical and more prosperous before the firing on Fort Sumter. At the same time, the institution of slavery had flourished. Therefore, the argument followed, God had ordained slavery in the South to reward Christian slaveholders and to evangelize their slaves. God clearly had providential purposes for slavery; he would not have allowed it to thrive had it not been part of his plan. The attack on slavery had been contrary to God's will. Nor should they doubt the benevolence of Providence or their special destiny. As the Reverend J. L. Gilbert put it in 1869, the war had been a "necessary disciplinary ordeal, chosen by God," to prepare white southern Christians "for their high and holy mission, as custodians of unadulterated evangelicalism and as his honored instruments for the development of a pure Christian civilization throughout this continent and throughout Christendom."[5]

The enduring innovation of southern white clerics was to sacralize the war and the Confederate warriors who fought in it. They provided a bulwark against suggestions that white southerners had been treasonous or immoral. And by emphasizing the providential purpose of the war, they removed from individual white southerners the burden for the defeat of the southern republic.

Confederate veterans were no less keen than white clerics to make sense of the Civil War. Within a few years of Appomattox, local benevolent associations with ties to veterans proliferated across Dixie. Groups such as the Oglethorpe (GA) Light Infantry Association, the Northeast Mississippi Confederate Veteran Association, and the Charleston Light Dragoons Monumental Association were small, closely knit organizations that performed both memorial and charitable work within their immediate communities. By 1869 former Confederate officers in New Orleans who harbored larger ambitions launched the Southern Historical Society. A year later, Confederate veterans eager to memorialize Robert E. Lee founded the Association of the Army of Northern Virginia.[6]

These organizations devoted themselves principally to compiling Confederate records, publishing justifications for the Confederacy, and excusing the South's defeat. Their purpose was to codify the explanation for the war's outcome. They concluded that the Lost Cause had been just, and its generals and soldiers uncommonly brave and tenacious, but that these qualities could not outlast the North's superior industry and numbers. Had the two contending armies been evenly matched in materiel and forces, Confederate victory, they insisted, would have been inevitable and swift. Herein was another vital contribution to the vindication of white southern honor.

Tens of thousands of Confederate veterans, like the amputee Benjamin Withers, needed more than just a salve for their wounded pride. They had ongoing medical needs, and some required financial support because they were unable to support themselves. Like their Union counterparts, Confederate veterans needed social services in a nation that lacked even the rudiments of a social welfare system. But whereas needy Union veterans became a powerful interest group that eventually received federal pensions, Confederate veterans had to rely on the charity of white southerners. When white southerners regained political power across the region during the 1870s, they replicated, at the state level and on a more modest scale, the pensions that the federal government provided to Union soldiers. And voluntary groups across the South, many led by white women, established veterans' homes for the enfeebled and the indigent. Confederate veterans were thus simultaneously the catalyst for and recipients of a nascent system of social welfare in the former Confederacy.[7]

The image of aged and hobbled Confederate veterans as objects of charity is a fairly accurate measure of their place in Confederate commemoration. They were the focus of veneration, but their own ability to control the memory of the Civil War was ephemeral. The United Confederate Veterans (UCV), an organization of affiliated veterans' groups formed in 1889, exerted considerable influence over white memory from 1890 to 1910. At its peak, more than fifteen hundred local "camps" of the organization, comprising as many as eighty thousand veterans, dotted the South, and its official organ, the *Confederate Veteran,* carried its message to an estimated fifty thousand readers. But the life span of the UCV was only as long as that of its members, and its influence diminished rapidly after 1910. The Sons of the Confederacy, a spin-off organization, faltered from its inception. The *Confederate Veteran* survived the withering of the UCV only because the United Daughters of the Confederacy (UDC) adopted the journal as its official organ. Moreover, what Confederate veterans needed and wanted most was the veneration of their society, and this they could not provide themselves. Consequently, those white southerners who had not fought, especially women, had an essential role to play in Confederate commemoration.[8]

Victorian conventions of mourning also assigned to women prominent roles in public remembrance. After Appomattox, white women often transformed their wartime soldiers' aid societies into memorial associations devoted to commemorating the Confederate dead. The Columbus, Georgia, Soldiers' Aid Society, for instance, begat the postbellum Columbus Ladies' Memorial Association. The first task undertaken by this group and many others was the creation of a Confederate cemetery. Beyond seeing to the proper burial of the Confederate dead, white women created rituals of remembrance. The pathos of widows gave rise to Confederate Memorial Day, which allegedly originated in Columbus, Georgia, in 1866, after a soldier's widow circulated an open letter to southern women calling upon them to decorate the humble graves of the Confederate dead at least once a year. The appeal found wide support, and by 1870 local memorial observances had been knit into a regionwide holiday. For countless white women in the late-nineteenth-century South, Confederate Memorial Day was the year's most important public event. They devoted months to recruiting schoolchildren, writing and distributing flyers, meeting with public officials, publishing articles in local newspapers, inviting orators, cleaning up cemeteries, and tending to the minutiae inherent in any public occasion. On the day itself, women performed the central ritual, the decoration of the graves. They also marched along the parade routes and sometimes even spoke to the gathered crowds, at the time still controversial and symbolically powerful poses to take in public.[9]

Men sometimes bankrolled these activities, but women assumed effective leadership. They did so because memorialization and mourning belonged to the realm of sentiment, which white men deemed, and white women accepted, to be "peculiarly fitting to women." Speaking at the 1875 unveiling of the Confederate monument in Augusta, Georgia, the Reverend General C. A. Evans explained that "it was not man's privilege but woman's to raise these monuments throughout the land." With the hierarchical order of the South shaken by war, many elite white women recoiled from the potential social chaos and committed themselves to reestablishing antebellum class and racial hierarchies. The participation of white women in the burgeoning Confederate celebration was a salve for their psychic wounds as well as those of Confederate veterans; women's memorial associations functioned as choruses that reassured white men of their manliness and authority and of feminine deference.[10]

Yet when white women scripted, oversaw, and participated in the memorialization of the Confederate dead, they expanded the boundaries that confined their behavior and authority. Throughout the antebellum period mourning customs had narrowly confined women's conduct and dictated the most minute details of their dress. But at the same time convention had allowed and encouraged women to demonstrate their grief openly. So great were the region's losses during the Civil War that white women necessarily revised the restrictive customs that they themselves otherwise maintained. United in mourning, white women redirected their networks of voluntary associations to perform tasks that government either could not or chose not to perform. Whereas the Union dead were assured a burial in national cemeteries established by the federal government, the Confederate dead often rested in unmarked graves, sometimes far from home. Ladies' memorial associations across the South retrieved the bodies of tens of thousands of fallen Confederates and returned them to Dixie. Once the remains were properly interred, ladies' associations tended the graves, for local and state governments in the South lacked the resources to assume these tasks.[11]

White southern women contributed more than sentiment and fundraising acumen to the campaign to immortalize the Lost Cause. They provided crucial ideological ballast for white supremacy by situating the Civil War in a seemingly ordained historical narrative of white triumph and privilege. In autobiographies, essays on contemporary issues, nostalgic recollections published in the *Confederate Veteran*, and historical novels, white women contributed mightily to the moonlight-and-magnolia imagery of the Old South. Even before academic historians at Johns Hopkins, Columbia, and elsewhere produced their "pro-slavery" historiography, white women rendered idyllic the institution of slavery. Taken together, their writings and other representations of slavery and antebellum life achieved a kind of classic purity. The setting might vary from Revolution to the Civil War, but women populated their accounts with idealized renderings of dashing and honorable white planters, beautiful and refined plantation mistresses, content black mammies, and armies of loyal and innately ignorant slaves.[12]

To these fictional renderings of the Old South, organized southern white women added pageants of nostalgia. When, for instance, members of a Texas UDC chapter contemplated "Slavery Days" fifty years after the Emancipation Proclamation, they did so with unabashed fondness. In addition to performing music evocative of the Old South, such as "Swing Low Sweet Chariot," "My Kentucky Home," "Old Black Joe," and "Uncle Ned," the daughters heard readings from Joel Chandler Harris, a sketch entitled "The Pickanines in the Quarter," and a paean to the "Black Mammy and her White Chillun." Other clubwomen went so far as to appropriate black dialect, dress, and alleged mannerisms to glorify slavery and the social order that it had made possible. Cordelia Powell Odenheimer, of Virginia, won over audiences at fund-raisers by wearing blackface, singing "old darkey hymns," dancing the "Juba," and performing "Old Mammy" monologues. The glorification of the loving and faithful black mammy by white clubwomen was particularly conspicuous, reaching its zenith during the 1920s, when the UDC proposed, and Congress considered, a national monument to black mammies on the Washington Mall.[13]

White southern women also dotted the American landscape with monuments to Confederate heros. As the organized might and political influence of white women's groups waxed at the end of the nineteenth century, their claims on public space expanded as well. In the immediate postwar years women's groups had erected cemetery monuments in keeping with their mission to give public expression and permanence to their mourning. But by the dawn of the twentieth century white women were funding showy statues to Confederate leaders in the most conspicuous civic spaces in the region's cities. The ultimate expression of their ambitions was the grandiose plan to turn Stone Mountain, near Atlanta, Georgia, into a Confederate answer to Mount Rushmore.[14]

By the 1920s, when the prodigious work of carving Stone Mountain began, the consolidation of Confederate commemoration was largely complete. The central tenets of the creed of the Lost Cause were in place, even if they would subsequently be adapted to changing circumstances during the Depression and the cold war. Even more important, by 1920 the white southern memory of the Civil War had been folded into the more capacious national memory of the struggle. By then the ennobling of Robert E. Lee, the superiority of southern valor, and the justice of the southern cause were conceded by many, maybe even most, white Americans.

The commemorative activities of Confederate veterans, white clubwomen, and regional politicians revealed the diverse ambitions of white southerners. While veterans sought confirmation of their honor and masculinity, clubwomen claimed a civic role as defenders of regional heritage, and conservative politicians yoked filiopietism to the Confederate cause to the maintenance of the power of the Democratic Party. These divergent uses of the past often meshed without acrimony—the success of many Confederate veterans' reunions depended on each group playing its self-appointed role—but on occasion competition over resources, publicity, and prestige generated friction among Confederate commemorators.

Yet, most white southerners were united in their search for a redemptive narrative of their failed revolution. That they were so invested in this narrative was hardly surprising. After all, they had sacrificed and squandered so much in its behalf. But that the nation would in time come to embrace the Confederate memory, with its reactionary and racist underpinnings, was in no way inevitable. Any explanation of the power and tenacity of Confederate memory, then, must explain its appeal to and grip on white Americans, and not just its tireless and remarkable effective architects.

9

Traced by Blood

African Americans and the Legacies
of the Civil War

DAVID W. BLIGHT

Of all the words we use in our language to think about and use the past, *legacy* is one of the most common. But what do we mean when we all but unconsciously refer to the legacies of a major event or a social force in history? What indeed is a legacy? It can be another word for historical memory, but it normally carries a current interpretive, political, or social meaning. Legacies take many forms in our minds and hearts. They can be emotional, intellectual, physical, or political. They can be sacred or secular or both wrapped into one. Sometimes we can see a legacy; other times we can only feel it. And often we discuss how legacies of certain events and historical processes are alive in policy debates. How often we hear the phrases *legacies of the Founding Fathers, legacies of Reconstruction, legacies of the Civil War, legacies of the New Deal,* and *legacies of the 1960s,* and wonder just what the speaker or writer means. The truest thing we can say about such legacies is that if they are important enough, they are always unfinished, contested, and malleable. Often a legacy is what is left over in public memory, behavior, and policy after historians have written their scholarship, museums have mounted exhibitions, teachers have taught their classes, and elders at the grassroots level have tried to instruct their young. A legacy is what endures all our filterings of the past, our struggles to forge a *story* we believe we are living. It is where past and present connect and where people try to determine who they are in relation to their history.

No legacies are more important to African Americans, or to Americans generally, than those of slavery, the Civil War, emancipation, and

Reconstruction. Understanding the meaning of that epoch, its trans-formations, horrors, and glories, is central to understanding American history. And no legacy in the nation's collective memory has been more difficult to understand than the emancipation of 4 million slaves in the midst of an all-out war for unconditional surrender between North and South in the 1860s. In our national memory today we much prefer nar-ratives of America as the nation that freed its slaves to the more trou-bling story of America as the nation that sanctioned one of the largest, most enduring slave societies in modern history. And just how do we explain that among all the nations and empires in which slaves were freed by some legal means in the nineteenth century, only in the divided United States did it occur in a bloody, all-encompassing civil war? For a people who have generally wished to see their history as a story of human progress and evolving liberty, these questions have never been easy to answer. Often we have avoided answering them at all. William Faulkner captured this reality in a single statement made by a character in his novel *The Hamlet:* "Only thank God men have done learned how to forget quick what they ain't brave enough to cure."[1] Rooted in hu-man frailty, venality, and even necessity at times, forgetting has always been the twin impulse of remembering as Americans contemplated the meaning of their Civil War.

For African Americans in the late nineteenth century, former slaves as well as their freeborn children, the past was especially acute in their very identity as Americans. If the war and emancipation had made them citizens, as the reinvented Constitution said, what kind of citi-zens could they be? How free were they? How equal before the law, as those resounding words in the Fourteenth Amendment declared to the world? How safe were they in the South, surrounded by embittered, defeated whites, some of whom were their former masters?

From the 1870s to 1900 and beyond, blacks faced endless decisions over just how to compete for a secure place in America's collective memory. Should they embrace or reject the nation that had enslaved them but which they had helped so much to preserve and reinvent? Should they look to their past to shape their new story or merely la-ment its agonies and aggressively move on to the future, never looking back any more than necessary? Should they fight the Lost Cause and Confederate traditions that were taking hold so firmly in the South by the end of Reconstruction or try to ignore them and retreat into group self-development in the emerging racial apartheid of the states of the former Confederacy? Should blacks remind the nation of their enslavement—should they remind themselves—or simply not look backward? Should they eventually see their past in slavery through Booker T. Washington's metaphor of a "school," a stage in their story in which they learned hygiene, modern economic striving, valuable lessons of discipline and faith? Or should they instead employ Frederick Douglass's dominant metaphor of slavery as the "prison" or "tomb" from which they had now been liberated?[2] In a sharecropper's cabin, in a working-class tenement house in a northern city, in a freedmen's school, in the legislative halls of the nation, or in their own novels, autobiographies, and newspapers, how should blacks stake their claim to American memory in the wake of emancipation?

No African American spokesman said or wrote more on this dilemma than the former slave Frederick Douglass, who became the most important black leader, writer, and orator of the nineteenth century. Douglass well knew that the past for his people was both burden and inspiration, something to be cherished and overcome. But he was never on the side of forgetting. "It is not well to forget the past," Douglass warned in one of his many postwar speeches on the subject. "Memory was given to man for some wise purpose. The past is . . . the mirror in which we may discern the dim outlines of the future and by which we may make them more symmetrical." But how was a symmetry to be achieved from a past of such turbulence and a present increasingly characterized by discrimination and violence? According to Douglass, blacks occupied a special place in American historical memory as participants and as custodians. He understood the psychological need of many blacks not to dwell upon the agonies of slavery, but that experience, along with the painful rebirth of emancipation, was so immediate and unforgettable, Douglass believed, because it was a history that could "be traced like that of a wounded man through a crowd by the blood." Douglass urged his fellow blacks to keep their history before the consciousness of American society, to point to the Civil War's most pressing legacies in season and out. "Well may the nation forget," he said in 1888, "it may shut its eyes to the past, and frown on any who do otherwise, but the colored people of this country are bound to keep the past in lively memory till justice shall be done them."[3] In those lines lay the most enduring burden of Civil War memory.

That burden rested most heavily on the younger generation of black leaders in the late nineteenth century as they tried to fashion lives and create institutions in the New South against the backdrop of a dominant white version of memory hostile to their hopes. In 1890 Joseph C. Price, the young president of Livingstone College, in Salisbury, North Carolina, captured the dilemma of Civil War memory for his generation. "The South was more conquered than convinced," declared Price; "it was overpowered rather than persuaded. The Confederacy surrendered its sword at Appomattox, but it did not there surrender its convictions."[4] Price's warning reflected reality all around as the color line sharpened in the South and as Lost Cause advocates, including Confederate veterans and ladies' memorial associations, trumpeted a version of slavery and the war that strongly challenged Douglass's hope for a national memory through which justice might be forged.

The tragic distance between the extremes of black and white memory in the South in the 1890s was vividly demonstrated at the reopening of the White House of the Confederacy, in Richmond, as a museum. On 22 February 1896 the Ladies Memorial Association of Richmond had restored and redecorated the executive mansion Jefferson Davis lived in while he served as president of the Confederacy. The relics were ready; over the doorway of elegant rooms the names of states were emblazoned in gold. Swords, epaulets, field glasses, Bibles, spurs, bits, saddles, blankets, uniforms, letters, and a host of other objects adorned the building. The windows were curtained by Confederate flags; a platform stood in the main room beneath portraits of Jefferson Davis, Andrew "Stonewall" Jackson, and Joseph E. Johnston. On the platform stood a table draped with a tattered Confederate battle flag. Official prayers were delivered, and the Virginia governor, Charles T. O'Ferrall, spoke of the Confederate Lost Cause as a holy heritage. He honored the white southern women for their "courage, fortitude, and strength" during the war as he proclaimed southerners loyal Americans, albeit on thoroughly southern terms.[5]

The principal orator of the day, however, was the former Confederate general Bradley T. Johnson, who delivered an especially unreconstructed brand of Lost Cause ideology. Confirming Joseph Price's warning in brutally explicit terms, Johnson claimed that "the world is surely coming to the conclusion that the cause of the Confederacy was right." With a historical logic that achieved a lasting grip on popular understanding, Johnson boldly declared that the "South did not make war in defense of slavery; slavery was only the incident, the point attacked." And he maintained, astonishingly to our modern ears, that the attack had been by a "free mobocracy of the North" against a "slave democracy of the South." Sometimes big lies need only aggressive spokesmen and pliant, willing audiences to take over a collective imagination, especially when those lies serve deeply felt needs. Here, indeed, was the full-blown myth of the Lost Cause—a glorious, organic civilization destroyed by an avaricious "industrial society" determined to wipe out its cultural foes. Above all, Johnson used this ceremonial occasion to deliver a racial message. In a classic statement of the proslavery argument, touched up for a new age, Johnson defined slavery as "the apprenticeship by which savage races had been educated and trained into civilization by their superiors." Freedom for blacks had been unwarranted and unwanted. "The negro . . . against his will, without his assistance," said Johnson, "has been turned loose in America to do the best he can in the contest with the strongest race that ever lived." Johnson summed up the legacy of the Civil War in a declaration to which many Americans, North and South, had come to at least benignly acquiesce: "The greatest crime of the century," he concluded, "was the emancipation of the Negroes."[6]

Against such convictions and versions of history, African Americans had to wage a high-stakes struggle over the nation's memory. Their struggle would be both internal to their own community and external in the realms of public memory. It would be waged by the famous and not so famous in every hamlet of the country where former slaves passed on their legacies to their children and beyond. And of course the children responded. On 1 January 1909 in Augusta, Georgia, at one of the countless Emancipation Day celebrations that became a strong tradition in black communities, a black Baptist minister, Silas X. Floyd, delivered a speech titled "Abraham Lincoln: Sent of God." The event was sponsored by several churches, fraternal orders, and the local Lincoln League. Floyd was young, charismatic, and a prolific writer of, among other works, a black history for children.

By the early twentieth century the generations among blacks did not always agree or even communicate effectively about the nature and purpose of the past. It could be a contentious, even dangerous topic. But that was exactly the topic Floyd spoke on with a sense of righ-

teous indignation. He admonished those blacks who wished to forget
that "our race was once enslaved in this country." "Did you ever see . . .
a Confederate veteran who desired to forget that he once wore the
gray," asked Floyd, "or who was unwilling to teach his children that he
once proudly marched in battle behind Lee and Gordon, Jackson and
Johnston? Did you ever see a Union solider who was ashamed of the
part which he took in the Great War, or who felt humiliated to tell his
children about it?"[7]

Floyd reminded his audience that they too had a great story to tell:

> And don't you remember that, when the children of Israel un-
> der the leadership of Moses were on the march from Egypt to
> Canaan . . . don't you remember that, after they had safely
> crossed the Red Sea, the Lord commanded them to set up me-
> morial stones by which the event should be remembered? And
> yet some old Negroes wish to forget all about slavery—all about
> the past—and stoutly maintain that we have no right to be cele-
> brating this day that brought freedom to our race . . . may God
> forget my people when they forget this day.[8]

"Don't you remember" were not merely words of nostalgia for African
Americans in the half-century after emancipation. They might lead to
images and remembrance of pride and strength, but they might just as
easily flood the spirit with despair. How could the past become a safe
haven and a source of inspiration rather than a source of nightmares?

These were the questions Floyd sought to boldly conquer. The
youthful minister represented the postfreedom generation challenging
the slavery generation. Often it is the elders who remind the young not
to forget the past, but in this case the challenge was reversed. Floyd
raised some of the central questions confronting blacks as they contemplated their past in an America that was everywhere celebrating
the reconciliation of North and South by honoring the mutual valor of
the white soldiers who wore the blue and the gray. He used this same
military experience to describe the Civil War as the great break in time
when emancipation came after two centuries of bondage in America.
He wanted his people to tell that they too had marched with Grant,
stormed Fort Wagner, and died on battlefields and in prisons and hos-
pitals in order the give the United States a new birth. Floyd wanted his
black audience in a Georgia town in the heart of Jim Crow's cunning

universe to know that when the children of Israel assembled their memorial stones, they too had been obedient and reluctant in the face of God's commands, inspired and frightened by their faith, their heroism, and their history. He wanted them to find courage to look backward and forward.

But in any attempt to assert their past with pride in turn-of-the-century America, blacks faced a veritable cultural and political industry of aggressive forgetting and selective, if energetic, remembering. By 1900, and certainly as the fiftieth anniversary of the Civil War approached in 1910–11, Americans in the North and the South were being raised on a story of national reconciliation after the great conflict of the 1860s. On the one hand, the war was becoming a triumph of nationalism forged by the unsurpassable valor of soldiers on both sides, soldiers now memorialized in thousands of monuments on countless town greens and squares in both North and South. On the other hand, the war had become a story shrouded in white supremacist ideology and memory. Lost Cause writers and advocates in the South and some in the North had rehearsed for two to three decades a narrative that was no longer about loss at all. It was a story of victory—national and not merely sectional—over the racial and democratic experiments of Reconstruction. In the national memory that seeped into popular culture, textbooks, and the political culture, one might breathe a sigh of relief that slavery was gone; emancipation, however, slipped to the edges, to a vague sidelight in the narrative of what the war had been about. The subjugation of African Americans in law and society since Reconstruction was somehow history's necessary correction for too much revolution.

Most important for blacks, they now faced an aggressive counter-revolution in the South that used scurrilous laws, intimidation, torture, and ever more hideous modes of murder to rivet the freedmen's children in the status of laborer with no human rights. And in the realms of print and entertainment the culture was awash in images and stories of "faithful slaves," the loyal retainers and lasting embodiment of the way much of the white South and the nation preferred to remember slavery, as an essentially benevolent institution of noble, Christian masters and obedient, often essential black folk who served gratefully, even entertainingly, in their appointed places in God's hierarchy of man. The image of the faithful slave may be one of the most hackneyed clichés in American history, but no understanding of the place of race in Civil War memory is possible without knowing its ubiquitous uses in turn-of-the-century culture. Thousands of examples abound, but one will suffice.

Among all the creators of the faithful-slave imagery that permeated American culture by 1900, no one surpassed Thomas Nelson Page, of Virginia, for sheer scale and virtuosity. Page invented and sold a formula of racism in stories in popular dialect that became the most widely read "literature" of its time and provided a "literary reunion" of North and South that may have been easier than the political one. Page, who grew up on a small plantation in Hanover County, Virginia, was only twelve years old when the war ended in 1865. As a grand master of pathos, nostalgia, and stories in Negro dialect, Page created a world of prewar and wartime Virginia inhabited by the thoroughly stock characters of southern gentlemen ("Marse Chan"), gracious ladies ("Meh Lady" or "Mistis"), and the stars, the numerous Negro mammies and the un-waveringly loyal bondsmen ("Sam," "Unc Billy," "Unc Edinburgh," or "ole Stracted"). In every story loyal slaves reminisce about the era of slavery—"befo' de war"—before freedom left them lonely, bewildered, or ruined souls in a decaying landscape. Their function in the new order is to tell stories of the old days; they are the sacred remembrancers of the grace and harmony of the Old South. "Marse Chan: A Tale of Old Virginia" is Sam's reverent remembrance of his beloved master, whom he accompanied to war and whom he then carried home to his grave on a distant hill. "Ez 'tis, I remembers it jees' like 'twuz yistiddy," says Sam. "Yo' know Marse Chan an' me—we wuz boys togerr. I wuz older'n he wuz, yes' de same ez he wuz whiter'n me." As this widely popular story warms to its theme, Sam speaks his most famous lines:

> Dem wuz good ole times, marster—de bes' Sam ever see! . . . Niggers didn' hed nothin' t all to do—jes' hed to ten' to de feedin' an' cleanin' de hosses, an' doin' what de marster tell 'em to do; an' when dey wuz sick, dey had things sont 'em out de house, an' de same doctor come to see 'em whar ten' to de white folks when dey wuz po'ly. Dyar warn' no trouble nor nothin'.[9]

In this former Eden that Sam describes, swarms of northern readers of popular magazines, all of which competed for Page's stories, were introduced to a world they had all but destroyed in war.

Page's fiction, invariably told in a black voice, was one tale after another of sectional reunion, usually through love and marriage. In Page's story "Mey Lady," loyal slaves, Unc Billy and his wife Hannah, play matchmakers as faithful black Confederates for a former Yankee soldier, Wilton, and the young lady of their plantation. They even serve as body servants and lone witnesses as they conduct the wedding, "Ole Billy" giving Meh Lady away in a ceremony redolent with the "smell of wet clover blossoms," followed by a scene in which the two couples, one white and one black, sit on their respective porches watching the moon "meltin' over the yard." Thus national reunion was served up with the mesmerizing and reassuring music of black dialect.

Much of the emotional impact of this literature was due to the fact that a black voice narrated to white audiences the stories of courtship, of Blue-Gray fraternalism, of national reconciliation itself. A civil war among whites—the torn fabric of the nation—is mended by the wit, wisdom, and sacred memories of faithful blacks. What whites had torn asunder they might rediscover in the language of former slaves; they needed the freedmen, after all, to remind them of what *their* war had ruined. And the sensible freedman made no demands of their own; they did not even have real lives of their own to be remembered. Their "freedom" in the midst of the war became only a rarely mentioned disjuncture, a reality only as it was refused, a strange misfortune lost in the mists of reconciliation. How better to forget a war about slavery than by having faithful slaves play the mediators of a white folks' reunion.[10]

This onslaught against an emancipationist memory of the Civil War did not go unanswered. In season and out, Frederick Douglass spent the last third of his life, down to his death in 1895, trying to counter the Lost Cause tradition as well as the corrosive elements of reconciliationist memory. But all across the spectrum of black journalism and literary and community life, African Americans fought back against the viciousness of Page's fictions as well as the arguments of the Confederate legend more generally. They knew what they were up against, and they knew that among themselves no single kind of memory or legacy would ever be sufficient to counter the white supremacy at the heart of the national reunion. As early as 1890 the editors of the *Christian Recorder*, the national newspaper of the African Methodist Episcopal Church, named the problem. "We do not forget," they announced, "that even in the North much greater consideration is shown the white man who attempted the dissolution of this government than to the black man who saved it. The poetry of the 'Blue and the Gray' is much more acceptable than the song of the black and the white."[11] Here was the heart of the dilemma: how to bring about a racial reconciliation to somehow match the sectional reconciliation slowly taking hold in American culture. And how was it to be imagined in a society with ever-deteriorating race relations, with southern states moving to disenfranchise black voters and that now lynched in medieval rituals those blacks who dared to challenge the economic or political order?

In the 1890s Booker T. Washington, the brilliant founder and leader of Tuskegee Institute, a black college in Alabama, would rise to national prominence as the principal black spokesman of his people. He offered his own brand of reconciliation between southern whites and blacks, a bargain in which blacks would by and large postpone their demands for civil and political rights in exchange for a kind of social peace in which they would build schools and other economic institutions of their own. If segregation was necessary in order for blacks to become skilled industrial laborers and farmers in their own right, then perhaps time, patience, education, and goodwill would make the struggle over Civil War memory and over Jim Crow unnecessary. Washington's bargain was extremely difficult for many blacks to purchase, although thousands, especially in the South of sharecropping and the cunning dangers of the color line, became his loyal followers.

In Washington's view, the deepest legacy of the Civil War for blacks was the challenge to compete economically in the new age of industrialism, to "cast down their bucket" in the South of their roots and make independent lives of worthiness and prosperity. The past was to be largely a guide to present and future "progress," not a warrant on the nation to fulfill its promise of liberty and justice to the millions of blacks freed in the war. Washington believed that former Confederates and former slaves could ultimately sit at the same table of social progress, even if they had to get there by separate paths. It was a bold strategy with a logic rooted in the soil and the reality of the South's economy and in Washington's leadership style—he saw himself as the broker between African Americans and whites with power and money. It was also an argument about the legacies of emancipation that valued jobs above political liberty, and sometimes even racial peace above racial dignity.[12]

But many black writers and spokespersons challenged both the literary reunion and Washington's brand of reconciliation. They did so with an increasingly intricate combination of black patriotism, commemorative rituals, and celebrations and occasionally by giving America a strong dose of authentic tragedy in its national memory. Beginning especially about 1883, the twentieth anniversary of emancipation, and continuing for the next three decades, down to the fiftieth anniversary of the war in 1911–15, black communities large and small held exhibitions, celebrations, and other memorial events to mark the place of freedom in their story.[13]

Several strains of black Civil War memory, what might be called attitudes toward the past, competed during these years. One, the slave past as a dark void, a lost epoch, even a paralytic burden, was more frequently expressed by orators and writers than one might expect. Two, Booker Washington's philosophy of industrial education and his "progress of the race" rhetoric allowed large numbers to imagine a useable past through a celebratory-accommodationist mode of memory. Three, some saw the past and future through a view of black destiny that combined Pan-Africanism, millennialism, and Ethiopianism, the tradition—more a theory of history than a political movement—that anticipated the creation of an exemplary civilization, in Africa or in the New World, and saw American emancipation as one part of a long continuum of Christian development for black peoples. Four, certainly one of the dominant modes of black memory was rooted in an African American patriotism, characterized by an insistence that the black soldier, the Civil War constitutional amendments, and the story of emancipation ought to be at the center of the nation's collective remembrance. And five, some, especially intellectuals and writers, approached the past through a tragic vision of the war as the nation's fated but unfinished passage through a catastrophic transformation from an old order to a new one. At times, all of these strains of memory could virtually overlap and flow into one another.[14] Together they formed the conflicted determination of a people to forge new and free identities in a society committed to sectional reconciliation, even at the cost of forgetting the legacy and claims of its African American citizens.

At the turn of the century the ubiquitous discussion of the "Negro Problem" or the "Race Problem" put an emancipationist memory of the Civil War constantly under duress. Many blacks preferred to banish endless debate over the race problem in favor of going after its root causes—white supremacy, legal discrimination, and lynching. But American society dragged it into every consideration of black life and inherently forced every black commentator to confront it as a struggle over remembering and forgetting. In an address memorializing the hundredth anniversary of the birth of the abolitionist William Lloyd Garrison in Boston in 1905, the AME Church bishop Reverdy Ransom probed the intersection between the race problem and reunion. "We would see the wounds left by the War of the Rebellion healed," he announced, "but we would have them healed so effectually that they could not be trodden upon and made to bleed afresh by inhuman barbarities and unjust legislation." Ransom's indignation flowed with his poignant metaphors. "We would have the wounds of this nation bound up by the hands of those who are friendly to the patient," he declared, "so that they might not remain a political running sore." Ransom spoke for many when he said he would accept a national reunion, but not one that included "only white men North and South" and not one where an enduring "spirit of slavery walks."[15] In this appeal for healing with justice, Ransom defined the tragedy as well as a course not taken in Civil War memory.

By 1913, the fiftieth anniversary of emancipation, all forms of black Civil War memory were well rehearsed, at least within African American communities. Sometimes they reached whites as well. On 1 January 1913, on page one, the *New York Times* published the prominent black writer James Weldon Johnson's poem "Fifty Years." Reprinted in black newspapers and delivered as a reading at numerous commemorations to follow, Johnson's poem is a striking statement of the African American birthright. As though banishing the shame of slavery from memorial consciousness and transcending all the "progress"–versus–"race problem" rhetoric to move to a higher plane of tragic but true patriotism, Johnson insists on an honored place for blacks at the Civil War's semicentennial. Seven verses into the poem, he strikes his central theme:

> Then let us here erect a stone,
>   To mark the place, to mark the time;
> A witness to God's mercies shown,
>   A pledge to hold this day sublime.

> And let that stone an altar be,
>   Whereon thanksgivings we may lay,
> Where we in deep humility,
>   For faith and strength renewed may pray.
>
> . . . .
>
> For never let the thought arise
>   That we are here on sufferance bare;
> Outcasts, asylumed 'neath these skies,
>   And aliens without part or share.
>
> This land is ours by right of birth,
>   This land is ours by right of toil;
> We helped to turn its virgin earth,
>   Our sweat is in its fruitful soil.

Johnson claims the center of America's historical memory by right of birth and by right of labor. In the poem's middle he claims it by right of soldiering, of "blood" and devotion to the "flag": "we've bought a rightful sonship here, / And we have more than paid the price."[16] As the poem reaches its hopeful ending, Johnson celebrates the abolitionist tradition as America's national destiny and rejects any shame for blacks in the legacies of slavery. Johnson deftly converted emancipation into the Civil War's core memory. In so doing, however, he also demonstrated how divided Civil War memory was in America and how fifty years after the event, blacks remained alienated from the national community's remembrance of its most defining event.

If Johnson's invocation of memory was a tragic form of patriotism, it was left to W. E. B. Du Bois to lay the groundwork for a genuinely tragic sense of the meaning and legacy of the Civil War. The great scholar, involved in so many fields—including history, literature, sociology, philosophy, and even popular pageantry—never stopped probing the memory of emancipation and the Civil War during his long life (1868–1963). But in one stunning metaphor about passion and memory in chapter two of his masterpiece, *The Souls of Black Folk* (1903), Du Bois may have captured the meaning of the war's legacy better than anyone in the fifty years after the conflict. He describes "two figures" that typified the postwar era in the South:

The one a gray-haired gentleman, whose fathers had quit themselves like men, whose sons lay in nameless graves; who bowed
to the evil of slavery because its abolition threatened untold ill
to all; who stood at last, in the evening of life, a ... ruined form,
with hate in his eyes;—and the other a form hovering dark and
mother-like, her awful face black with the mists of centuries,
had aforetime quailed at that white master's command, had bent
in love over the cradles of his sons and daughters, and closed in
death the sunken eyes of his wife,—aye, too, at his behest had
laid herself low to his lust, and borne a tawny man-child to the
world, only to see her dark boy's limbs scattered to the winds by
midnight marauders riding after "damned niggers."

Without a pause, Du Bois presses the issue. "These were the saddest
sights of that woeful day," he concludes, "and no man clasped the hands
of these passing figures of the present-past; but hating, they went to
their long home, and hating their children's children live today."[17]

Past and present meet in this imagery with frightful intensity; the
picture Du Bois paints is an alternative vision of the meaning of the
Civil War. These are not the customary forms of old soldiers who had
met in battle and could now "clasp hands across the bloody chasm" in
the time-honored slogan of many Blue-Gray reunions. Here we have
a thoroughgoing opposition to the Lost Cause tradition and to any
semblance of faithful-slave imagery. Here sentiment is punctured with
the bluntness of genuine tragedy. Du Bois's "two figures" are veterans of
another conflict: an old male slaveholder, the broken symbol of wealth,
power, and sexual domination; and an old black woman, representing
"Mammy," mother, and survivor. The heritage of slavery lives on in these
"passing figures of the present-past," as though time past and time present or future can never be fully separated. Du Bois was arguing here
that racial reconciliation, unlike sectional reconciliation, demanded a
confrontation with the hostility rooted in rape, lynching, and racism.
Bridging this chasm remained the unfinished work in the legacies of
the Civil War.

But all was not so bleak by 1913 if the story of emancipation could
be kept alive in national memory. That task would forever be one of

recovery and constant competition for the nation's narrative of what the Civil war had been about. One story that had been lost but nevertheless shows what was yet to be found occurred in Charleston, South Carolina, just after the war ended in May 1865. In the power of this story we can see the hope embedded in James Weldon Johnson's poem "Fifty Years," as well as in countless other expressions of black Civil War memory over time.

Americans understand that Memorial Day, or "Decoration Day," as generations have called it, has something to do with honoring the nation's war dead. It is also a day devoted to picnics, road races, commencements, and baseball double-headers. But where did it begin, who created it, and why?

At the end of the Civil War the dead were everywhere, some in half-buried coffins and some visible only as unidentified bones strewn over the killing fields of Virginia or Georgia. Americans in both North and South faced an enormous spiritual and logistical challenge of memorialization. The dead were visible by their massive absence. Approximately 620,000 soldiers died in the war. American deaths in all other wars combined through the Korean conflict totaled 606,000. If the same number of Americans per capita had died in Vietnam as died in the Civil War, there would be 4 million names on the Vietnam Memorial. The most immediate legacy of the Civil War was its slaughter and the question how to remember it.

War kills people and destroys human creation, but as though mocking war's devastation, flowers inevitably bloom among its ruins. After a long siege, a prolonged bombardment from all around the harbor, and numerous fires, the beautiful port city of Charleston, South Carolina, where the war had begun in April 1861, lay in ruin by the spring of 1865. The city had been largely abandoned by white residents by late February. Among the first troops to enter and march up Meeting Street singing liberation songs were those of the Twenty-first U.S. Colored Infantry; their commander accepted the formal surrender of the city.

Thousands of black Charlestonians, most former slaves, remained in the city and conducted a series of commemorations to declare their sense of the meaning of the war. The largest of these events, unknown until some extraordinary luck in my research, took place on 1 May 1865. During the final year of the war, the Confederates had converted the planters' horse track, the Washington Race Course and Jockey Club, into an outdoor prison. Union soldiers were kept in horrible conditions in the interior of the track; at least 257 died of exposure and disease and were hastily buried in a mass grave behind the grandstand. Some twenty-eight black workmen went to the site, reburied the Union dead properly, and built a high fence around the cemetery. They whitewashed the fence and built an archway over an entrance on which they inscribed the words "Martyrs of the Race Course."[18]

Then black Charlestonians in cooperation with white missionaries and teachers staged an unforgettable parade of ten thousand people on the slaveholders' racecourse. The symbolic power of the low-country planter aristocracy's racetrack (where they had displayed their wealth, leisure, and influence) was not lost on the freedpeople. A *New York Tribune* correspondent who witnessed the event described "a procession of friends and mourners as South Carolina and the United States never saw before."

At 9:00 A.M. on the first of May the procession began, led by three thousand black schoolchildren carrying armloads of roses and singing "John Brown's Body." The children were followed by several hundred black women with baskets of flowers, wreaths, and crosses. Then came black men marching in cadence, followed by contingents of Union infantry and other black and white citizens. As many as possible gathered in the cemetery enclosure; a children's choir sang "We'll Rally around the Flag," "The Star-Spangled Banner," and several spirituals before several black ministers read from scripture. No record survives of which biblical passages rung out in the warm spring air, but surely present at those burial rites was the spirit of Leviticus 25: "for it *is* the jubilee; it shall be holy unto you . . . in the year of this jubilee he shall return every man unto his own possession."

Following the solemn dedication, the crowd dispersed into the infield and did what many of us do on Memorial Day: they enjoyed picnics, listened to speeches, and watched soldiers drill. Among the full brigade of Union infantry participating were the famous Fifty-fourth Massachusetts and the Thirty-fourth and 104th U.S. Colored Troops, who performed a special double-columned march around the gravesite. The war was over, and Decoration Day had been founded by African Americans in a ritual of remembrance and consecration. The war, they had boldly announced, had been all about the triumph of their emancipation over a slaveholders' republic, and not about states' rights, defense of home, nor merely soldiers' valor and sacrifice.

According to a reminiscence written long after the fact, "several slight disturbances" occurred during the ceremonies on this first Decoration Day, as well as "much harsh talk about the event locally afterward." But a measure of how white Charlestonians suppressed the memory of this founding in favor of their own creation of the practice came a half-century later, in 1917, when the president of the Ladies Memorial Association of Charleston received an inquiry about the parade of 1 May 1865. A United Daughters of the Confederacy official from New Orleans wanted to know if it was true that blacks had engaged in such a burial rite. Mrs. S. C. Beckwith responded tersely: "I regret that I was unable to gather any official information in answer to this." In the struggle over memory and meaning in any society, some stories get lost, while others attain mainstream dominance.

Officially, Memorial Day emerged as a national holiday in 1868, when General John A. Logan, commander in chief of the Grand Army of the Republic, the Union veterans' organization, called on all former northern soldiers and their communities to conduct ceremonies and decorate the graves of their dead comrades. On 30 May 1868, when flowers were plentiful, funereal ceremonies were attended by thousands of people in 183 cemeteries in twenty-seven states. The following year, some 336 cities and towns in thirty-one states, including southern states, arranged parades and orations. The observance grew manifold with time. In the South, Confederate Memorial Day took shape on three different dates: in many Deep South states on 26 April, the anniversary of General Joseph Johnston's final surrender to General William T. Sherman; in South and North Carolina on 10 May, the birthday of Stonewall Jackson; and in Virginia on 3 June, the birthday of Jefferson Davis.

Over time several American towns in the North and in the South claimed to be the birthplace of Memorial Day. But all of them commemorate cemetery-decoration events from 1866. Pride of place as the first to hold a large-scale Decoration Day ritual, therefore, goes to African Americans in Charleston. By their labor, their words, their songs, and their solemn parade of flowers and marching feet on their former owners' racecourse, they created for themselves and for others the Independence Day of the Second American Revolution.

The old racetrack is still there—an oval roadway in Charleston's Hampton Park, named for Wade Hampton, a former Confederate general and the white supremacist Redeemer governor of South Carolina after the end of Reconstruction. The lovely park sits adjacent to the Citadel, the military academy of South Carolina, and cadets can be seen jogging on the old track any day of the week. The old gravesite dedicated to the "Martyrs of the Race Course" is gone; those Union dead were reinterred in the 1880s to a national cemetery in Beaufort, South Carolina. Some stories endure, some disappear, some are rediscovered in dusty archives, in the pages of old newspapers, and in oral history. Stories such as that of the first Decoration Day are but prelude to future reckonings. If we keep our eyes and minds open, the past will never cease to surprise us.

Concluding Thoughts

JOHN M. McCARDELL, JR.

"If you at last must have a word to say, say neither in their way, 'it is a deadly magic and accursed,' nor 'it is blest,' but only 'it is here.'" These words of the poet Stephen Vincent Benét resonate especially in the mind of one asked, as I have been, to offer concluding thoughts. And perhaps those lines say it all.

These essays remind us of why the Civil War continues to absorb us, as scholars and also as citizens. It is all about memory, and we know that memory, especially historical memory, matters. From shared experience a culture defines itself.

Memory is also selective and personal. No two of us may remember the conference at which these essays were presented, or parts of it, in the same way. And yet what we remember, and how we remember it, shapes our own, and others', understanding of its meaning, its significance.

And so it is challenging at least, if not an act of utter presumption, to try to reduce what is said in the preceding essays to a handful of salient points and preserve them in memory. But that is my charge, which I undertake with considerable humility.

And summoning muses for inspiration—

First, Robert Frost, the quintessential Yankee. "The land *was* ours before we were the land's. . . . The deed of gift *was* many deeds of war. . . . Such as she was, such as she would become." As Professor McPherson reminds us, Lincoln's rhetorical shift bespoke fundamental changes—a broadening and a deepening to the point of transformation—in what this country was becoming, a nation, and it bespoke competing definitions of nationhood, emerging in sections of the country for whose inhabitants the term *antebellum* would have been nonsensically meaningless—competing, evolving, clarifying definitions, on a collision course. Where a Nathaniel Hawthorne could write, earlier in the century, that "New England is as large a lump of earth as my mind can comprehend," where a William Gilmore Simms could exclaim that "to be national in literature one must needs be sectional," and where subject-verb agreement was always in the plural, by 1865 there could clearly be discerned the outlines, at least, of a modern nation-state.

Which leads, naturally, to our second muse, Stephen Vincent Benét, who writes not only of the America we have become but also, as he describes the Old South, of the "America we have not been." Yet the poet, however lyrical, oversimplifies. There is indeed both a Confederate experience to be studied and a Confederate legacy that endures, and it is not entirely accurate to think "this destiny unmanifest." We are beginning to understand more fully that this experience and legacy have been multiple, not singular. And we are being prompted anew to decide as a culture what parts of that memory we retain as part of our cultural glue and what parts, if any and without peril, we must either revisit or reconsider, keeping in mind that each generation frames its own questions and someday will itself be challenged by those who may claim, and may or may not possess, a clearer eye. Because the challenging and complicated Confederate experience and legacy persist, and as we encourage its study we are mindful of Benét's closing words: let others "applaud the image or condemn; but keep your distance and your soul from them."

Modern nation-state. America we have not been. And finally a reminder from a third muse, Lincoln, who spoke compellingly not of self-evident truth—history and experience said otherwise—but of a fragile proposition, never secure, always at risk, now wholly reliant upon the last best hope of earth. A republican *experiment*. A nation dedicated to a *proposition*. Maybe or maybe not a destiny unmanifest. Maybe or maybe not the America we have not been. The years 1861–65 would not constitute the final test of a fragile proposition that all men are created equal. Indeed it would be tested over and over in the years to come.

It is being tested still.

Notes

1. The Civil War and the Transformation of America

1. J. Mills Thornton III, *Politics and Power in a Slave Society: Alabama, 1800–1860* (Baton Rouge: Louisiana State University Press, 1978), 216; Michael P. Johnson, *Toward a Patriarchal Republic: The Secession of Georgia* (Baton Rouge: Louisiana State University Press, 1977), 36; *Jefferson Davis, Constitutionalist: His Letters, Papers, and Speeches*, ed. Dunbar Rowland, 10 vols. (Jackson: Mississippi Department of Archives and History, 1923), 5:43, 202.

2. Henry Orr to his sister, 31 Oct. 1860, in *Campaigning with Parsons' Texas Cavalry Brigade, CSA: The War Journals and Letters of the Four Orr Brothers*, ed. John Q. Anderson (Hillsboro, TX: Hillsboro Junior College Press, 1967), 10; *Yankee Rebel: The Civil War Journal of Edmund DeWitt Patterson*, ed. John G. Barrett (Chapel Hill: University of North Carolina Press, 1966), 119.

3. James J. Womack Diary, entry of 18 Feb. 1862, privately printed, copy in Museum of the Confederacy, Richmond, VA.

4. William Cullen Bryant, in *New York Evening Post*, 18 Feb. 1861; *The Collected Works of Abraham Lincoln*, ed. Roy P. Basler, 9 vols. (New Brunswick, NJ: Rutgers University Press, 1953–55), 4:434n.

5. Lincoln, *Collected Works*, 4:439; John Hay, diary entry of 7 May 1861, in *Inside Lincoln's White House: The Complete Civil War Diary of John Hay*, ed. Michael Burlingame and John R. Turner Ettlinger (Carbondale: Southern Illinois University Press, 1997), 20.

6. Lincoln, *Collected Works*, 4:268; Walter Q. Gresham to Tillie Gresham, 28 Apr. 1861, Walter Gresham Papers, Library of Congress; Thomas T. Taylor to Antoinette Taylor, 23 May 1861, Taylor Papers, Ohio Historical Society, Columbus; James M. Goff to his brother, 29 Jan. 1862, Goff-Williams Collection, Huntington Library, San Marino, CA.

7. Lincoln, *Collected Works*, 2:255, 3:92, 4:250, 439.

158 NOTES TO PAGES 9–13

2. Slaveholding Nation, Slaveholding Civilization

1. Robert Barnwell Rhett, 4 Dec. 1860, quoted in C. Vann Woodward, *The Burden of Southern History* (Baton Rouge: Louisiana State University Press, 1968), 139.

2. James Henry Hammond, "Letters on Slavery," in *The Pro-Slavery Argument; as Maintained by the Most Distinguished Writers of the Southern States* (Charleston, SC: Walker, Richards, 1852), 151.

3. Ibid., 111.

4. See Robert R. Palmer, *The Age of the Democratic Revolution*, 2 vols. (Princeton, NJ: Princeton University Press, 1959–64).

5. Thomas Jefferson (hereafter TJ), first inaugural address, 4 Mar. 1801, in *Thomas Jefferson Writings*, ed. Merrill D. Peterson (New York: Viking, 1984), 494.

6. Nicholas Onuf and Peter Onuf, *Nations, Markets, and War: Modern History and the American Civil War* (Charlottesville: University of Virginia Press, 2006).

7. April Lee Hatfield, *Atlantic Virginia: Intercolonial Relations in the Seventeenth Century* (Philadelphia: University of Pennsylvania Press, 2004); Anthony Parent, *Foul Means: The Formation of a Slave Society in Virginia, 1660–1740* (Chapel Hill: University of North Carolina Press, 2003).

8. TJ to Edward Coles, 25 Aug. 1814, in *Thomas Jefferson Writings*, 1344–46; Ari Helo and Peter Onuf, "Thomas Jefferson and the Problem of Slavery," in *The Mind of Thomas Jefferson*, by Peter Onuf (Charlottesville: University of Virginia Press, 2007), 236–70.

9. Quoted in William S. Jenkins, *Pro-Slavery Thought in the Old South* (Chapel Hill: University of North Carolina Press, 1935), 31.

10. St. George Tucker, *A Dissertation on Slavery: With a Proposal for the Gradual Abolition of It, in the State of Virginia* (Philadelphia: Matthew Carey, 1796), 4–5.

11. [TJ], *A Summary View of the Rights of British America*, in *The Papers of Thomas Jefferson*, ed. Julian Boyd et al., 33 vols. to date (Princeton, NJ: Princeton University Press, 1950–), 1:130.

12. Eliga H. Gould, "Zones of Law, Zones of Violence: The Legal Geography of the British Atlantic, circa 1772," *William and Mary Quarterly* 60 (2003): 471–510.

13. TJ, Declaration of Independence [original rough draft], in *Papers of Thomas Jefferson*, 1:426.

14. Istvan Hont, *Jealousy of Trade: International Competition and the Nation-State in Historical Perspective* (Cambridge, MA: Harvard University Press, 2006); idem, *Wealth and Virtue: The Shaping of Political Economy in the Scottish Enlightenment* (Cambridge: Cambridge University Press, 1983); Joyce E. Chaplin, *An Anxious Pursuit: Agricultural Innovation and Modernity in the Lower South, 1730–1815* (Chapel Hill: University of North Carolina Press, 1993), chap. 1; Onuf and Onuf, *Nations, Markets, and War.*

15. TJ, *Notes on the State of Virginia*, query 6, in *Thomas Jefferson Writings*, 190–91.

16. Noah Webster, *Effects of Slavery on Morals and Industry* (Hartford, CT: Hudson & Goodwin, 1793), 5, 37.

17. Henry Laurens to Richard Oswald & Co., 29 June 1756, in *Documents Illustrative of the History of the Slave Trade to America*, ed. Elizabeth Donnan, 4 vols. (Washington, DC: Carnegie Institution, 1930–35), 4:354–55; Adam Hochschild, *Bury the Chains: Prophets and Rebels in the Fight to Free an Empire's Slaves* (Boston: Houghton Mifflin, 2005), 100–101.

18. Laurens to John Lewis Gervais, 5 Feb. 1774, in *The Papers of Henry Laurens,* ed. Philip M. Hamer et al., 16 vols. to date (Columbia: University of South Carolina Press, 1968–), 9:263–64.

19. Henry Laurens to John Laurens, 26 Oct. 1776, ibid., 11:276.

20. James Dana, *The African Slave Trade: a Discourse Delivered Before the Connecticut Society for the Promotion of Freedom by the Pastor of the First Congregational Church in Said City* (New Haven, CT: Thomas and Samuel Green, 1790), 32.

21. James Swan, *A Dissuasion to Great-Britain and the Colonies, from the Slave-Trade to Africa* (Boston: E. Russell, 1773), 30–32.

22. Samuel Hopkins, *A Discourse upon the Slave-trade, and the Slavery of the Africans: Delivered in the Baptist Meeting-house at Providence, before the Providence Society for Abolishing the Slave Trade, &c At their annual meeting, on May 17, 1793* (Providence, RI: J. Carter, 1793), 1, 18–19, 20–21.

23. Ferdinando Fairfax, "Plan for Liberating the Negroes within the United States," *American Museum,* Dec. 1790, 3, 5–6.

24. Tucker, *Dissertation on Slavery,* 5; [John Taylor of Caroline], *Arator: Being a Series of Agricultural Essays, Practical and Political . . .* (Petersburg, VA: Whitworth & Yancey, 1813), 74.

25. Francis Kinloch to TJ, 26 Apr. 1789, in *Papers of Thomas Jefferson,* 15:71–72.

26. TJ, *Notes on the State of Virginia,* query 14, in *Thomas Jefferson Writings,* 264.

27. TJ to John Dickinson, 6 Mar. 1801, in ibid., 1084–85. On the theme of amelioration, see Christa Dierksheide, "'The great improvement and civilization of that race': Jefferson and the Amelioration of Slavery, ca. 1770–1826," *Early American Studies* 6.1 (2008): 165–97.

28. Arthur Young, *Political Essays Concerning the Present State of the British Empire* (London, 1772), 19–20.

29. TJ to Dickinson, 6 Mar. 1801.

30. Patrick Henry, speech to the Virginia House of Burgesses, 18 Jan. 1773, Granville Sharp Papers, New-York Historical Society, New York, reel 1.

31. TJ to Coles, 25 Aug. 1814.

32. Peter Onuf, "Domesticating the Captive Nation: Thomas Jefferson and the Problem of Slavery," unpublished conference paper in author's possession.

33. Henry Laurens to Dr. [Richard] Price, 1 Feb. 1785, Henry Laurens Papers (George Bancroft Transcripts), New York Public Library.

34. Ralph Izard to Edward Rutledge, 28 Sept. 1792, Ralph Izard Papers, South Carolina Library, University of South Carolina, Columbia.

35. William Moultrie, undated fragment [1800?], William Moultrie Papers, ibid.

36. TJ to Thomas Cooper, 10 Sept. 1814, Papers of Thomas Jefferson, Library of Congress.

37. Ibid.

38. TJ, *Notes on the State of Virginia,* query 14, in *Thomas Jefferson Writings,* 264–67.

39. James Oakes, "'Whom Have I Oppressed?': The Pursuit of Happiness and the Happy Slave," in *The Revolution of 1800: Democracy, Race, and the New Republic,* ed. James P. Horn, Jan Lewis, and Peter S. Onuf (Charlottesville: University of Virginia Press, 2002), 220–39.

40. Historians have exaggerated the early development of proslavery thought. See, e.g., Jeffrey Robert Young, *Proslavery and Sectional Thought in the Early South, 1740–1829* (Chapel Hill: University of North Carolina Press, 2006); William W. Freehling, "The Founding Fathers and Slavery," *American Historical Review* 77 (Feb. 1972): 81–93; James Oakes, *The Ruling Race: A History of American Slaveholders* (New York: Garland, 1982); and Paul Finkleman, ed., *Slavery, Revolutionary America, and the New Nation* (New York, 1989). An exception is Michael O'Brien, *Conjectures of Order: Intellectual Life and the American South, 1810–1860*, 2 vols. (Chapel Hill: University of North Carolina Press, 2004), 2:938–92.

41. Spencer Roane to James Monroe, 16 Feb. 1820, in "Letters of Spencer Roane, 1788–1822," *Bulletin of the New York Public Library* 10 (1906): 174–75.

42. Adam Rothman, *Slave Country: American Expansion and the Origins of the Deep South* (Cambridge, MA: Harvard University Press, 2005), 22–27; William Giles, speech in the House, Mar. 1798, *Annals of Congress*, 5th Cong., 2nd sess., 1306–10.

43. TJ to Albert Gallatin, 26 Dec. 1820, in *Thomas Jefferson Writings*, 1447–50.

44. Marquis de Lafayette to TJ, 1 July 1821, 1 June 1822, in *Letters of Lafayette and Jefferson*, ed. Gilbert Chinard (Baltimore: Johns Hopkins Press, 1929), 407–9.

45. TJ to James Heaton, 20 May 1826, in *Thomas Jefferson Writings*, 1516.

46. Joyce E. Chaplin, *An Anxious Pursuit: Agricultural Innovation and Modernity in the Lower South, 1730–1815* (Chapel Hill: University of North Carolina Press, 1993).

47. For further discussion, see Peter Onuf, "The Problem of Nationhood in American and World History," in Beijing Forum, *Evolution of Civilizations: Historical Experiences in the Modern Times of the East and the West; Collection of Papers and Abstracts*, 3 vols. (New Brunswick, NJ: Transaction, 2006), 2:585–602.

48. Seymour Martin Lipset, *The First New Nation: The United States in Historical and Comparative Perspective* (New York: Doubleday, 1963); Onuf and Onuf, *Nations, Markets, and War*, 162–66, 225–39, 263–64.

49. TJ, *Notes on the State of Virginia*, query 6, in *Thomas Jefferson Writings*, 191.

50. Peter S. Onuf, "Nations, Revolutions, and the End of History," in *Revolutionary Currents: Nation Building in the Transatlantic World*, ed. Michael A. Morrison and Melinda Zook (Lanham, MD: Rowman & Littlefield, 2004), 173–88; Ernest Gellner, *Nations and Nationalism* (Ithaca, NY: Cornell University Press, 1983).

51. On this debate, see the exchange in 1814 between Jefferson and Thomas Cooper, Jefferson Papers, Library of Congress.

52. David Brion Davis, *Challenging the Boundaries of Slavery* (Cambridge, MA: Harvard University Press, 2003), 80–86; Joe Bassette Wilkins Jr., "Window on Freedom: The South's Response to the Emancipation of the Slaves in the British West Indies, 1833–1861" (PhD diss., University of South Carolina, 1977). We are particularly indebted to Brian Schoen, "The Fragile Fabric of Union: The Cotton South, Federal Politics, and the Atlantic World, 1783–1861" (PhD diss., University of Virginia, 2003).

53. Hugh Swinton Legaré to sister, 13 Oct. 1832, Hugh Swinton Legaré Papers, South Carolina Library. See also Palmer, *Age of the Democratic Revolution*.

54. William Harper, "Memoirs of Slavery," in *Pro-Slavery Argument*, 6. On southerners' rejection of natural-rights thinking, see Mark Hulliung, *The Social Contract of America: From the Revolution to the Present Age* (Lawrence: University Press of Kansas, 2007).

55. Thomas R. Dew, "Review of the Debate in the Virginia Legislature 1831–2," in *The Pro-Slavery Argument,* 455, 461.

56. Harper, "Memoirs of Slavery," 13.

57. Ibid., 55.

58. Hammond, "Letters on Slavery," 169–70.

59. Ibid., 132–33.

60. Ibid., 147.

61. Harper, "Memoirs of Slavery," 4.

62. Dew, "Review of the Debate," 461–62.

63. Ibid., 463.

3. Why Did Southerners Secede?

1. *Charleston Mercury,* 8 Nov. 1860; Charles Francis Adams Diary, 7 Nov. 1860, Adams Family Papers, Massachusetts Historical Society, Boston; Henry Adams, *The Education of Henry Adams,* ed. Ernest Samuels (1918; reprint, Boston: Houghton Mifflin, 1973), 99. Many of the events and interpretations developed in this essay, as well as some of the sources, are treated in Sean Wilentz, *The Rise of American Democracy: Jefferson to Lincoln* (New York: W. W. Norton, 2005), to which the reader is referred for fuller elaboration and documentation.

2. Abraham Lincoln, "Passage Written for Lyman Trumbull's Speech at Springfield, November 20, 1860," in *The Collected Works of Abraham Lincoln,* ed. Roy P. Basler, 9 vols. (New Brunswick, NJ: Rutgers University Press, 1953), 4:141 (hereafter cited as *CWAL*); Lincoln, "First Inaugural Address, March 4, 1861," ibid., 4:271.

3. Two of the more recent examples of this line of reasoning, from the libertarian Right, appear in Charles Adams, *When in the Course of Human Events: Arguing the Case for Southern Secession* (Latham, MD: Rowman & Littlefield, 2000); and Thomas J. DiLorenzo, *The Real Lincoln: A New Look at Abraham Lincoln, His Agenda, and An Unnecessary War* (Roseville, CA: Prima, 2002). Both books have gained a popular following despite their repeated use of bogus evidence and their faulty logic. For devastating reviews, see Daniel Feller, "Libertarians in the Attic, or a Tale of Two Narratives," *Reviews in American History* 32 (2004): 184–95; and Herman Belz, "Review Essay," *Journal of the Abraham Lincoln Association* 24 (2003): 57–65. The most distinguished variation on this argument—which crankily likens Lincoln to Bismarck and Lenin—arose from a very different part of the political and literary forest, in Edmund Wilson's introduction to his *Patriotic Gore: Studies in the Literature of the American Civil War* (New York: Oxford University Press, 1962). Wilson's interpretation of Lincoln later in the volume allows that Lincoln perceived and presented slavery as a moral issue and praises Lincoln's literary gifts but remains attached to the idea that the war was essentially a contest over brute power and material interests that Lincoln helped turn into a mythic "Holy War led by God" (113).

4. Lincoln, "Speech at Peoria, October 16, 1854," *CWAL,* 2:270. Lincoln offered his formula about "the course of ultimate extinction" on several occasions, most famously in his "House Divided" speech in Springfield, Illinois, on 16 June 1858, but the phrase first turns up in a fragment of a speech he wrote late in December 1857. See *CWAL,* 2:453, 461.

5. See esp. *CWAL*, 2:461–69.

6. "Republican Party Platform of 1860, May 17, 1860," http://www.presidency.ucsb. edu/ws/?pid=29620. Lincoln's position on slavery, the territories, and the Constitution evolved after 1854 to resemble those of the political abolitionists' Liberty Party, of the 1840s, and the Free Soil Party (later the Free Democratic Party), of the late 1840s and early 1850s. It was also in line with the basic idea behind the famous Wilmot Proviso of 1846, which Lincoln supported during his single term in Congress. Historians have had no difficulty describing these parties and initiatives as decidedly antislavery on various moral, economic, and political grounds; thus it seems odd to argue that the same cannot be said about Lincoln after 1854. Of course, for pragmatic reasons Lincoln chose to stick with the Whig Party until its demise in 1854 instead of joining one of the sectional antislavery parties. But if this reveals something about Lincoln's political calculations, it in no way contradicts his antislavery beliefs. Certainly, through the early 1850s antislavery sentiment was stronger among northern Whigs than it was among northern Democrats. And by 1856, with the Whig Party in ruins, Lincoln had enlisted in a sectional antislavery party, the Republicans, a step that some among the more conservative Whigs, especially in New England, found repellent.

As historians have constantly noted, Lincoln opposed, on constitutional grounds, the abolition of slavery by the federal government in those states where it already existed (until the Civil War opened the possibility of the Emancipation Proclamation). Before the war, by these lights, the government could not abolish slavery everywhere without a constitutional amendment permitting it to do so, an amendment that it would have been impossible to ratify in 1860. To attempt a peremptory full emancipation without an amendment, Lincoln believed, would violate the Constitution's unfortunate, tacit but undeniable protections of slavery where it existed and thereby shatter the nation's constitutional order. But Lincoln also believed, along with other Republicans, that slavery could be put on the road to eventual doom—in accord with the Constitution and while keeping the Union intact—by restricting slavery's expansion. According to this view, slavery, lacking room to expand, would eventually exhaust itself economically; and politically, the balance of free states versus slave states would grow so advantageous to the free states that slavery would be doomed. When pressed by Stephen A. Douglas, during their famous Senate campaign debates in 1858, to provide details about how this gradual emancipation would proceed, Lincoln became vague. But there is no question that Lincoln believed restriction would hasten eventual full emancipation or that he refused in 1860 and after to back down from his prorestriction views. Lincoln offered his formula about "the course of ultimate extinction" on numerous occasions, most famously in his "House Divided" speech in Springfield, Illinois, on 16 June 1858. See *CWAL*, 2:398–410. For a fuller explication of his logic that halting slavery's spread into the territories ensured its ultimate elimination everywhere, see Lincoln to John L. Scripps, 23 June 1858, in ibid., 2:471. For additional background, see Wilentz, *Rise of American Democracy*, 479, 547–59, 622–28.

7. Timothy Pickering to George Cabot, 29 Jan. 1804, in *Documents Relating to New England Federalism, 1800–1815*, ed. Henry Adams (Boston: Little, Brown, 1877), 341. On the New Englanders' plotting within the broader context of disunionism in the early republic, see Kevin M. Gannon, "Escaping 'Mr. Jefferson's Plan of Destruction': New

England Federalists and the Idea of a Northern Confederacy, 1803–1804," *Journal of the Early Republic* 21 (2001): 413–43.

8. On the Burr Conspiracy, the War of 1812, and the Hartford Convention, see Wilentz, *Rise of American Democracy,* 128–30, 141–78.

9. John C. Calhoun to Virgil Maxcy, 11 Sept. 1830, in *The Papers of John C. Calhoun,* ed. Robert L. Meriwether et al., 28 vols. (Columbia: University of South Carolina Press, 1959–2003), 11:2291; Robert Barnwell Rhett, quoted in Wilentz, *Rise of American Democracy,* 388.

10. Andrew Jackson, "Proclamation," in *A Compilation of the Messages and Papers of the Presidents,* ed. James D. Richardson, 10 vols. (1897; reprint, Washington DC: National Bureau of Literature, 1910), 2:1211, also available at http://www.presidency.ucsb.edu/ws/index.php?pid=67078&st=&st1=.

11. John Wyly and James Petigru, quoted in Wilentz, *Rise of American Democracy,* 383, 769.

12. Lincoln, "First Inaugural Address—Final Version, March 4, 1861," *CWAL,* 4:268, 270; David Gavin, quoted in Manisha Sinha, *The Counterrevolution of Slavery: Politics and Ideology in Antebellum South Carolina* (Chapel Hill: University of North Carolina Press, 2000), 225; Albert Gallatin Brown, quoted in John Ashworth, *Slavery, Capitalism, and the Politics of the Antebellum Republic,* vol. 1, *Commerce and Compromise, 1820–1850* (Cambridge: Cambridge University Press, 1995), 216.

13. Marc Egnal, "Rethinking the Secession of the Lower South: The Clash of Two Groups," *Civil War History* 50 (2004): 261–90; M. Shannon Mallard, "'I Had No Comfort to Give the People': Opposition to the Confederacy in Civil War Mississippi," *North & South* 6 (2003): 78–86; Margaret M. Storey, "Civil War Unionists and the Political Culture of Loyalty in Alabama, 1860–1861," *Journal of Southern History* 69 (2003): 71–106; Paul Horton, "Submitting to the 'Shadow of Slavery': The Secession Crisis and Civil War in Alabama's Lawrence County," *Civil War History* 44 (1998): 111–36.

14. William R. Smith, *The History and Debates of the Convention of the People of Alabama* (Montgomery: White, Pfister, 1861), 74; Thomas M. Peters to Andrew Johnson, 15 Jan. 1861, quoted in Allan Nevins, *The Emergence of Lincoln,* vol. 2, *Prologue to Civil War* (New York: Scribner, 1950), 424; Charles B. Dew, "Who Won the Secession Election in Louisiana?" *Journal of Southern History* 36 (1970): 18–32.

15. *Augusta Constitutionalist,* 16 Nov. 1860.

16. J. D. B. DeBow, "The Non-Slaveholders of the South: Their Interest in the Present Sectional Controversy Identical with That of the Slaveholders," *DeBow's Review* 30 (1861): 67–77; Stephen A. West, "Minute Men, Yeomen, and the Mobilization for Secession in the South Carolina Upcountry," *Journal of Southern History* 71 (2005): 75–104.

17. See Wilentz, *Rise of American Democracy,* 772.

18. Robert Tracy McKenzie, "Contesting Secession: Parson Brownlow and the Rhetoric of Proslavery Unionism, 1860–1861," *Civil War History* 48 (2002): 294–312, quotation on 306. On secessionism in the upper South, see, in addition to Wilentz, *Rise of American Democracy,* 769–70, Daniel W. Crofts, *Reluctant Confederates: Upper South Unionists in the Secession Crisis* (Chapel Hill: University of North Carolina Press, 1989); and William A. Link, *Roots of Secession: Slavery and Politics in Antebellum Virginia* (Chapel Hill: University of North Carolina Press, 2003).

19. Quoted in Wilentz, *Rise of American Democracy*, 770.

20. Jefferson Davis, quoted in ibid., 774.

21. R. N. Hemphill to William R. Hemphill, 14 Dec. 1860, quoted in Stephen A. Channing, *Crisis of Fear: Secession in South Carolina* (New York: Simon & Schuster, 1970), 289; Smith, *History and Debates*, 81; *An Ordinance to Repeal the Ratification of the Constitution of the United States of America* (Richmond, VA, 1861), 4–5. For a fuller discussion, see Wilentz, *Rise of American Democracy*, 769–79. Ordinary Confederate soldiers appear to have strongly agreed that secession, and then the Civil War, chiefly involved defending slavery. See Chandra Manning, *What This Cruel War Was Over: Soldiers, Slavery, and the Civil War* (New York: Knopf, 2007).

22. The quotations are from Charles Adams, *When in the Course of Human Events*, 3, 64, 73. Lincoln offered his formula about "the course of ultimate extinction" on numerous occasions, most famously in his "House Divided" speech in Springfield, Illinois, on 16 June 1858. See *CWAL*, 2:398–410. For a fuller explication of his logic that halting slavery's spread into the territories ensured its ultimate elimination everywhere, see Lincoln to Scripps, 23 June 1858, in ibid., 2:471.

23. *Louisville Daily Courier*, 26 May 1860; *New Orleans Daily Crescent*, 12 Nov. 1860; *Richmond Semi-weekly Examiner*, 9 Nov. 1860; *Wilmington (NC) Daily Herald*, 9 Nov. 1860. For a typical moderate view, between immediate secessionist and Unionist, see the *New Orleans Bee*, 8 Nov. 1860, which urged caution and insisted that "we have no right to judge Lincoln by anything but his acts."

24. Lincoln, "Address Delivered at the Dedication of the Cemetery at Gettysburg, November 19, 1963, Final Text," *CWAL*, 7:23.

4. "A party man who did not believe in any man who was not": Abraham Lincoln, the Republican Party, and the Union

Epigraph: George S. Boutwell, quoted in *Reminiscences of Abraham Lincoln by Distinguished Men of His Time*, ed. Allen Thorndike Rice (New York: North American, 1886), 134–36. Boutwell served three terms in the U.S. House of Representatives, from 1863 to 1869.

1. Alexander H. Stephens to unnamed recipient, 25 Nov. 1860, in *The Correspondence of Robert Toombs, Alexander H. Stephens, and Howell Cobb*, ed. Ulrich B. Phillips, in *Annual Report of the American Historical Association for the Year 1911*, vol. 2 (Washington, DC: American Historical Association, 1913), 504–5.

2. *The Collected Works of Abraham Lincoln*, ed. Roy P. Basler, 9 vols. (New Brunswick, NJ: Rutgers University Press, 1953–55), 5:318, 7:282 (hereafter cited as *CWAL*).

3. For a fuller exposition, see Richard Carwardine, *Lincoln: A Life of Purpose and Power* (New York: Knopf, 2006), esp. 14–32, 144–50, 198–221.

4. *CWAL*, 3:462–63, 471–82; 7:281.

5. Ibid., 2:266.

6. Ibid., 2:546, 3:362; Ward H. Lamon, *The Life of Abraham Lincoln; from his birth to his inauguration as president* (Boston: James R. Osgood, 1872), 347; James Gillespie, in *Herndon's Informants: Letters, Interviews, and Statements about Abraham Lincoln*, ed. Douglas L. Wilson and Rodney O. Davis (Urbana: University of Illinois Press, 1998), 183–84.

7. *CWAL*, 2:126, 222.

8. Ibid., 4:426, 439.

9. Ibid., 4:232–33.

10. Lerone Bennett, *Forced into Glory: Abraham Lincoln's White Dream* (Chicago: Johnson, 2000), 468–508, presents this interpretation in its most forceful and sustained form. Cf. Richard N. Current, *The Lincoln Nobody Knows* (New York: McGraw-Hill, 1958), 226–28.

11. *CWAL*, 5:388–89.

12. Ibid., 4:440; 5:49, 145, 222–23; 7:281.

13. This case is made most effectively in Phillip Shaw Paludan, *The Presidency of Abraham Lincoln* (Lawrence: University Press of Kansas, 1994).

14. *CWAL*, 8:403; Carwardine, *Lincoln*, 198–248. In the light of Lincoln's wartime statements rejecting federal imposition, it is probable that he would have left the definition and enforcement of postwar voting qualifications to state governments.

15. *Diary of Gideon Welles*, 3 vols. (Boston: Houghton Mifflin, 1911), 1:143. See also *The Salmon P. Chase Papers*, vol. 1, *Journals, 1829–1872*, ed. John Niven (Kent, OH: Kent State University Press, 1993), 394.

16. Carwardine, *Lincoln*, 249–309.

17. Essential to an understanding of party organization and mobilization in the wartime Union and the relationship between local, state, and national agencies are the following: Kenneth M. Stampp, *Indiana Politics during the Civil War* (1945; reprint, Bloomington: Indiana University Press, 1978); William B. Hesseltine, *Lincoln and the War Governors* (New York: Knopf, 1955); Joel H. Silbey, *A Respectable Minority: The Democratic Party in the Civil War Era, 1860–1869* (New York: W. W. Norton, 1977); Dale Baum, *The Civil War Party System: The Case of Massachusetts, 1848–1876* (Chapel Hill: University of North Carolina Press, 1984); Robert J. Cook, *Baptism of Fire: The Republican Party in Iowa, 1838–1878* (Ames: Iowa State University Press, 1994); Lex Renda, *Running on the Record: Civil War Era Politics in New Hampshire* (Charlottesville: University of Virginia Press, 1998); and Adam I. P. Smith, *No Party Now: Politics in the Civil War North* (New York: Oxford University Press, 2006). There is no modern study of Lincoln's relations with his party in Congress, which, despite an early period of positive collaboration, were rarely easy and were blighted by a sense among moderates and radicals that the administration lacked energy and focus. Michael F. Holt, "An Elusive Synthesis: Northern Politics during the Civil War," in *Writing the Civil War: The Quest to Understand*, ed. James M. McPherson and William J. Cooper Jr. (Columbia: University of South Carolina Press, 1998), 4. See also Robert J. Cook, "Stiffening Abe: William Pitt Fessenden and the Role of the Broker Politician in the Civil War Congress," *American Nineteenth Century History* 8:2 (2007): 145–67.

18. The foundational secondary work for this interpretation is Harry J. Carman and Reinhard H. Luthin, *Lincoln and the Patronage* (New York: Columbia University Press, 1943), esp. 331–36. See also Christopher Dell, *Lincoln and the War Democrats: The Grand Erosion of Conservative Tradition* (Rutherford, NJ: Fairleigh Dickinson University Press, 1975). For recent examples, see Paludan, *Presidency of Abraham Lincoln*, 167–81 (for Lincoln's determinedly inclusive resolution of the cabinet crisis of December 1862); and William E. Gienapp, *Abraham Lincoln and Civil War America* (New York: Oxford University Press, 2002), 189–93.

19. *Recollected Words of Abraham Lincoln,* ed. Don E. Fehrenbacher and Virginia Fehrenbacher (Stanford, CA: Stanford University Press, 1996), 288 (hereafter cited as *RWAL*).

20. *Congressional Globe,* 37th Cong., 3rd sess., 1862, 70.

21. Lincoln's early drafts had included defensive remarks about the Republican Party and the Philadelphia and Chicago national conventions, but encouraged by Henry Seward, he removed them. As delivered, the address alluded only to a "Republican Administration." *CWAL,* 4:249–71. See also Douglas L. Wilson, *Lincoln's Sword: The Presidency and the Power of Words* (New York: Knopf, 2006), 46–55.

22. *CWAL,* 4:341, 6:268–69; *Lincoln's Journalist: John Hay's Anonymous Writings for the Press, 1860–1864,* ed. Michael Burlingame (Carbondale: Southern Illinois University Press, 1999), 33.

23. *CWAL,* 6:260–69.

24. See, e.g., Edward Haight to John G. Nicolay, 17 June 1863, and Daniel S. Dickinson to Abraham Lincoln (hereafter AL), 19 June 1863, Abraham Lincoln Papers, Library of Congress (hereafter ALP).

25. AL to Carl Schurz, 10 Nov. 1862, ibid.

26. John W. Forney to AL, 24 Oct. 1864, ibid. Shortly after appointing Stanton, Lincoln told Congressman Henry L. Dawes, of Massachusetts, "that whenever a Union man was willing to break away from party affiliations and stand by the government in this great struggle, he was resolved to give him an opportunity and welcome him to the service." *RWAL,* 235–36. Lincoln turned to the life-long Democrat turned Unionist, Ohio governor David L. Tod, to replace Salmon P. Chase as secretary of the treasury in 1864, but Tod declined. Hesseltine, *Lincoln and the War Governors,* 226–27, 359. Lincoln appointed James Speed, a Douglas Democrat, to replace Edward Bates as attorney general in 1864. Dell, *Lincoln and the War Democrats,* 89, 293.

27. Forney to AL, 25 Mar. 1861, 24 Oct. 1864, ALP. Orville H. Browning wrote Lincoln that Senator James W. Grimes, of Ohio, was "*dead set* against Forney, but I think we can elect him. Have not yet acted upon the matter in caucus." [July 1861], ibid.

28. Samuel Galloway to AL, 22 Aug. 1863, ibid.

29. *RWAL,* 187.

30. Bruce Tap, *Over Lincoln's Shoulder: The Committee on the Conduct of the War* (Lawrence: University Press of Kansas, 1998), 6, 257–58. For General Ben Butler's account of his conversation with Lincoln about the need to balance the partisan appointments made by Republican governors, see Rice, *Reminiscences of Abraham Lincoln,* 140–42.

31. Schurz to AL, 8, 20 Nov. 1862, ALP.

32. AL to Schurz, 10, 24 Nov. 1862, ibid. The men mentioned by Lincoln were Edward A. Baker, Nathaniel Lyon, Henry Bohlen, Israel B. Richardson, Philip Kearney, Isaac I. Stevens, Jesse L. Reno, and Joseph K. F. Mansfield. For Lincoln's judicious handling of a military case in which partisanship, not disloyalty, was the issue—the case of Major Alexander Montgomery—see Edgar Cowan to AL, 22 Sept. 1863, ibid. See also *CWAL,* 6:385.

33. *RWAL,* 400.

34. Richard Carwardine, "Abraham Lincoln and the Fourth Estate: The White House and the Press during the American Civil War," *American Nineteenth Century History* 7:1 (2006): 1–27.

35. *RWAL*, 427. Cf. A. K. McClure, *Abraham Lincoln and Men of War Times* (Philadelphia: Times Publishing, 1892), 105–18, 425–49; and James A. Rawley, introduction to Ward Hill Lamon, *Recollections of Abraham Lincoln, 1847–1865*, ed. Dorothy Lamon Teillard, rev. ed. (1911; reprint, Lincoln: University of Nebraska Press, Bison Books, 1994), xx.

36. Forney to AL, 24 Oct. 1864, ALP.

37. William C. Jewett to AL, 29 Aug. 1863, ibid.

38. John Brough, *The Defenders of the Country and Its Enemies: The Chicago Platform Dissected* (Cincinnati, OH: Gazette, 1864); James C. Wetmore to AL [with endorsement by Lincoln, "Gov Brough's Speech"], 23 Sept. 1864, ALP; *CWAL*, 7:451; Hesseltine, *Lincoln and the War Governors*, 331–36.

39. Francis Lieber to AL, 16 June 1863, ALP.

40. *RWAL*, 400.

41. Smith, *No Party Now*, offers the richest and most penetrating analysis of how the evolving Union Party fused patriotism and partisanship to construct a dynamic antiparty nationalism.

42. Rice, *Reminiscences of Abraham Lincoln*, 134–36. The audience Boutwell addressed in the 1880s was not dissimilar to today's in its distrust of politicians and parties.

43. Ibid., 261–62.

44. Lincoln's continuing practice of appointing Republicans to civil positions led to protests even from his constant admirer Forney that the circumstances threatened to alienate War Democrats: *"I think it is your bounden duty to take the earliest opportunity to recognize and to distinguish leading Union Democrats in every part of the country,"* Forney wrote to him. "In this city [Philadelphia], . . . your political friends seem to have no recollection of these Democrats. I begged of you to appoint Dan Dougherty your District Attorney, at the death of Coffey, but you appointed Charles Gilpin, and after that act, save here and there a school director, and in one or two cases a member of the Legislature, the old Whig party, and the old Bell & Everett party consumed all the offices and this spirit exhibited in the principal officers of the party, has run all through its subordinate branches." Forney to AL, 24 Oct. 1864, ALP.

45. Carman and Luthin, *Lincoln and the Patronage*, 228–60.

46. Ibid., 282–84. AL, memorandum on meeting with Cornelius A. Walborn, 20 June 1864; William D. Kelley to AL, 3 Aug. 1864; AL to Morton McMichael, 5 Aug. 1864; Walborn to AL, 9 Aug. 1864; and John L. Scripps to AL, 15 July 1864, all in ALP. AL to Scripps, 4 July 1864, *CWAL*, 7:423–24. See also Isaac N. Arnold to AL, 2, 18 July 1864, ALP; and AL to Scripps, 20 July 1864, *CWAL*, 7:453.

47. Rice, *Reminiscences of Abraham Lincoln*, 51–52.

48. Wilson, *Lincoln's Sword*. See also Ronald C. White Jr.'s subtle and astute study of Lincoln's rhetoric, *The Eloquent President: A Portrait of Lincoln through His Words* (New York: Random House, 2005).

49. Chicago Tribune Company to Nicolay, 16 June 1863, ALP.

50. Horace Greeley to Nicolay, 14 June 1863, ibid.

51. Roscoe Conkling to AL, 16 June 1863, ibid.

52. C. W. Hebard to AL, 18 June 1863, and Nicolay to Hebard, 20 June 1863, ibid.

53. Hesseltine, *Lincoln and the War Governors*, 273–307.

54. *CWAL*, 6:406.

55. See, e.g., *Inside Lincoln's White House: The Complete Civil War Diary of John Hay*, ed. Michael Burlingame and John R. Turner Ettlinger (Carbondale: Southern Illinois University Press, 1997), 217–42; and Henry J. Raymond to AL, 30 Aug. 1864, Raymond to Nicolay, 11 September 1864, Forney to AL, 14 Sept. 1864, and AL to William S. Rosecrans, 26 Sept. 1864, all in ALP.

56. Mark E. Neely Jr., *The Union Divided: Party Conflict in the Civil War North* (Cambridge, MA: Harvard University Press, 2002), esp. 173–201.

57. John M. Read to AL, 14 Oct. 1863 ("Forney . . . has stumped the state, . . . and he has brought over numbers of the loyal democrats to our support"), and Forney to AL, 20 Aug. 1863, 24 Sept., and 22 Oct. 1864, all in ALP. For a broader statement of the political benefits that party competition brought Lincoln, see Eric L. McKitrick, "Party Politics and the Union and Confederate War Efforts," in *The American Party Systems: Stages of Political Development*, ed. William Nisbet Chambers and Walter Dean Burnham, 2nd ed. (New York: Oxford University Press, 1967), 117–51.

58. Cowan to William H. Seward, 8 Aug. 1862, and Cowan to AL, 17 June 1863, ALP.

59. Henry Wilson to AL, l5 Sept. 1864, ibid. Cf. Wilson to AL, 25 Oct. 1863, ibid.

60. Hans L. Trefousse, *The Radical Republicans: Lincoln's Vanguard for Racial Justice* (New York: Knopf, 1969), 295–96. For the 1864 campaign, see David E. Long, *The Jewel of Liberty: Abraham Lincoln's Re-election and the End of Slavery* (Mechanicsburg, PA: Stackpole Books, 1994); and Michael Vorenberg, *Final Freedom: The Civil War, the Abolition of Slavery, and the Thirteenth Amendment* (New York: Cambridge University Press, 2001).

61. Rice, *Reminiscences of Abraham Lincoln*, 540.

62. Zachariah Chandler to AL, 15 Nov. 1863, ALP. The exception was New Jersey, which went for McClellan.

63. Lincoln here referred to the Missouri radicals in particular. Hay, *Inside Lincoln's White House*, 101, 125.

64. AL to John H. Bryant, 30 May 1864, ALP.

65. Quoted in Adam I. P. Smith, "The Presidential Election of 1864: Party Politics and Political Mobilisation during the American Civil War" (PhD thesis, University of Cambridge, 1999), 109.

66. *RWAL*, 394.

67. See, e.g., Owen Lovejoy's request for Lincoln's support in his bid for reelection to Congress in 1862. Forney to AL, 21 Oct. 1862, ALP. For the administration's role in the key electoral successes of fall 1863, see Hesseltine, *Lincoln and the War Governors*, 308–39.

68. Benjamin H. Brewster to AL, [Feb.] and 29 Aug. 1864, ALP.

69. Forney to AL, 14 Feb. 1864, ibid.

70. Jesse Fell, quoted in Trefousse, *Radical Republicans*, 289.

71. *CWAL*, 7:23–24.

5. Rebels and Patriots in the Confederate "Revolution"

1. Images from Confederate States of America, Archives Papers, Miscellany Section, box 35, Rare Book, Manuscript, and Special Collections Library, Duke University (hereafter cited as Duke). Such images could become powerful symbols that helped citizens

deal with complex information and troubling times. For a general discussion, see Murray Edelman, *Politics as Symbolic Action* (Chicago: Markham, 1971), 31–44, 76–81. For a helpful treatment of how Confederates used the iconography of the American Revolution, see Anne Sarah Rubin, *A Shattered Nation: The Rise and Fall of the Confederacy, 1861–1868* (Chapel Hill: University of North Carolina Press, 2005), 14–23.

2. Herman Hattaway and Richard E. Beringer, *Jefferson Davis, Confederate President* (Lawrence: University Press of Kansas, 2002), 24.

3. *The Secret Eye: The Journal of Ella Gertrude Clanton Thomas, 1848–1889*, ed. Virginia Ingraham Burr (Chapel Hill: University of North Carolina Press, 1990), 184; *Charleston Mercury*, 7 June 1861, 12 Jan. 1864.

4. *Richmond Daily Dispatch*, 10 July, 15 Aug. 1861, 4 Oct. 1864.

5. Ibid., 6 May 1861; William N. Bilbo, *The Past, Present and Future of the Southern Confederacy: An Oration Delivered by Col. W. N. Bilbo in . . . Nashville, October 12, 1861* (Nashville: J. D. W. Green, 1861), 5–12; J. W. Easterby, ed., *The South Carolina Rice Plantation as Revealed in the Papers of Robert F. W. Allston* (Chicago: University of Chicago Press, 1945), 175–76.

6. *The Papers of Jefferson Davis*, ed. Lynda Lasswell Crist et al., 12 vols. to date (Baton Rouge: Louisiana State University Press, 1971–), 7:46 (hereafter cited as *PJD*); James D. Richardson, ed., *A Compilation of the Messages and Papers of Jefferson Davis and the Confederacy, Including Diplomatic Correspondence, 1861–1865*, 2 vols. (Nashville: United States Publishing, 1905), 1:187–88.

7. John W. DuBose, *Life and Times of William Lowndes Yancey*, 2 vols. (New York: Peter Smith, 1942), 1:376.

8. *New Orleans Daily Picayune*, 4 July 1861; *Richmond Daily Dispatch*, 5 July 1861; A. W. Terrell, *Oration Delivered on the Fourth Day of July, 1861 at the Capitol, Austin, Texas* (Austin: John Marshall, 1861), 14; *Richmond Enquirer*, 23 Apr., 28 May 1861; *Charleston Mercury*, 12 Apr. 1861; *PJD*, 9:11.

9. George C. Rable, *Civil Wars: Women and the Crisis of Southern Nationalism* (Urbana: University of Illinois Press, 1989), 137; *Richmond Daily Dispatch*, 27 Apr., 13 May 1861; *Richmond Enquirer*, 28 May, 23 July 1861; *PJD*, 7:413; *Charleston Mercury*, 10 Aug. 1864.

10. On these themes, see Charles Royster, *A Revolutionary People at War: The Continental Army and American Character, 1775–1783* (Chapel Hill: University of North Carolina Press, 1979).

11. Sarah Wadley Diary, entry of 28 July 1861, Southern Historical Collection, University of North Carolina, Chapel Hill; *PJD*, 7:213.

12. *Richmond Daily Dispatch*, 4 June, 11 July 1861, 19 Feb., 13 Oct., 27 Dec. 1862; *Charleston Mercury*, 27 Nov. 1861, 3 Mar. 1864.

13. *The Papers of Zebulon Baird Vance*, ed. Frontis W. Johnston and Joe A. Mobley, 2 vols. (Raleigh: North Carolina Division of Archives and History, 1963–95), 2:245–46; *Richmond Daily Dispatch*, 12, 25 Feb. 1862; *Augusta Constitutionalist*, n.d., 10 Jan. 1865; *Charleston Mercury*, 5 Dec. 1863, 1 Nov. 1864.

14. J. William Jones, *Life and Letters of Robert Edward Lee, Soldier and Man* (New York: Neale, 1908), 121; Susan Cornwall Book, entry of 31 Jan. 1861, Southern Historical Collection, University of North Carolina, Chapel Hill.

15. Robert P. Dick, *To the Freemen of the Sixth Congressional District. . . . Speech of*

Robert P. Dick, of Guilford, in Convention, June 5th, 1861 (Greensboro, [NC?], 1861); Henry Cleveland, *Alexander H. Stephens, in Public and Private* (Philadelphia: National, 1866), 136–37. South Carolina secessionists seemed especially wary of "revolution." William W. Freehling, *The Road to Disunion*, vol. 2, *Secessionists Triumphant, 1854–1861* (New York: Oxford University Press, 2007), 352.

16. Dwight Lowell Dummond, ed., *Southern Editorials on Secession* (New York: Appleton-Century-Crofts, 1931), 515–16; James Henry Hammond to John D. Ashmore, 2 Apr. 1861, James H. Hammond Papers, Manuscripts Division, Library of Congress; John H. Reagan, *Memoirs, with Special Reference to Secession and the Civil War*, ed. Walter F. McCaleb (New York: Neale, 1906), 109.

17. *Journal of the Congress of the Confederate States of America, 1861–1865*, 7 vols. (Washington, DC: GPO, 1904), 1:845: *PJD*, 7:47; George H. Reese, ed., *Proceedings of the Virginia State Convention of 1861*, 4 vols. (Richmond: Virginia State Library, 1965), 4:382; *Address of the Atlanta Register, to the People of the Confederate States* (Atlanta: J. A. Sperry, 1864), 12–16; Robert Hardy Smith, *Address to the Citizens of Alabama on the Constitution and Laws of the Confederate States of America* (Mobile: Mobile Daily Register Print, 1861), 6; *New Orleans Daily Picayune*, 5 Feb. 1861. Even in Emory Thomas's classic work, the emphasis is on the "revolutionary" policies adopted by the Confederates and the "revolutionary" impact of the war rather than on how Confederates embraced the idea of revolution. Emory M. Thomas, *The Confederacy as a Revolutionary Experience* (Englewood Cliffs, NJ: Prentice-Hall, 1971).

18. When delegates from the seceding states assembled in Montgomery, Alabama, in February 1861, they created the Provisional Congress, which would draft a constitution and serves as the Confederacy's legislative branch for a year, until elections could be held and the so-called Permanent Congress could convene.

19. *Journal of the Congress of the Confederate States*, 1:845–46; J. H. Thornwell, "Our Danger and Our Duty," *DeBow's Review* 33 (May–Aug. 1862): 43–51; *Daily Richmond Examiner*, 6 Mar. 1861; George Fitzhugh, "The Revolutions of 1776 and 1861 Contrasted," *Southern Literary Messenger* 37 (Nov.–Dec. 1863): 718–26. Adopting the terminology of Arno Mayer, James McPherson described southern secession as a "preemptive counterrevolution." James M. McPherson, *Battle Cry of Freedom: The Civil War Era* (New York: Oxford University Press, 1988), 245. For a somewhat different but perceptive take on this question of revolution, see Drew Gilpin Faust, *The Creation of Confederate Nationalism: Ideology and Identity in the Civil War South* (Baton Rouge: Louisiana State University Press, 1988), 21, 29–33.

20. *Rome (GA) Weekly Courier*, 8 Feb. 1861; "Address of Congress to the People of the Confederate States," *Southern Historical Society Papers* 1 (Jan. 1876): 25.

21. *The War of the Rebellion: A Compilation of the Official Records of the Union and Confederate Armies*, 128 vols. (Washington, DC: GPO, 1880–1901), ser. 4, 1:9, 772; Thomas Jefferson Chambers, *To the People of Texas* (announcing his candidacy for governor) (Austin, 1861); "Thoughts Suggested by the War," *DeBow's Review* 31 (Sept. 1861): 302.

22. Benjamin Morgan Palmer, *A Discourse before the General Assembly of South Carolina, on December 10, 1863* (Columbia: Charles P. Pelham, 1864), 11; J. Henly Smith to Alexander H. Stephens, 15 July 1861, Alexander H. Stephens Papers, Manuscripts Di-

vision, Library of Congress; An Alabamian, "The One Great Cause of the Failure of the Federal Government," *Southern Literary Messenger* 32 (May 1861): 329–34; Thomas J. Devine, *Speeches Delivered on the 17th January 1862 in the Representative Hall, Austin, Texas by Thos. J. Devine and A. We. Terrill* (Austin: John Marshall, 1862), 22.

23. Stephen Elliott, *New Wine Not to be Put into Old Bottles: A Sermon Preached in Christ Church, Savannah, on Friday, February 28th, 1862, Being the Day of Humiliation, Fasting, and Prayer, Appointed by the President of the Confederate States* (Savannah, GA: John M. Cooper, 1862), 8–18; "The True Question: A Contest for the Supremacy of the Race, As Between the Saxon of the North and the Norman of the South," *Southern Literary Messenger* 33 (July 1861): 19–27; Frank H. Alfriend, "A Southern Republic and a Northern Democracy," ibid. 37 (May 1863): 283–90; *Richmond Daily Whig*, 19 Dec. 1861.

24. Reese, *Proceedings of the Virginia State Convention*, 1:368–69, 2:315–16, 3:631; John K. Bettersworth and James W. Silver, eds., *Mississippi in the Confederacy*, 2 vols. (Baton Rouge: Louisiana State University Press, 1961), 1:41; John K. Bettersworth, *Confederate Mississippi: The People and Policies of a Cotton State* (Baton Rouge: Louisiana State University Press, 1943), 19–21; William R. Smith, *The History and Debates of the Convention of the People of Alabama* (Montgomery: White, Pfister, 1861), 156–57.

25. *Richmond Daily Dispatch*, 18 June 1861; *Journal of the Senate of South Carolina: Being the Sessions of 1861* (Columbia: Charles P. Pelham, 1861), 23–25; "Past and Present," *DeBow's Review* 30 (Feb. 1861): 189–90.

26. *Richmond Daily Whig*, 8 July, 4, 7, 14, 30 Dec. 1861, 10 Jan. 1862; *The Diary of Edmund Ruffin*, ed. William Kauffman Scarborough, 3 vols. (Baton Rouge: Louisiana State University Press, 1972–89), 2:184–85. For broader discussions of state constitutional questions, see Faust, *Creation of Confederate Nationalism*, 36–40; and George C. Rable, *The Confederate Republic: A Revolution against Politics* (Chapel Hill: University of North Carolina Press, 1994), 39–43.

27. *Jefferson Davis: The Essential Writings*, ed. William J. Cooper Jr. (New York: Modern Library, 2003), 197; *Journal of the Second Called Session, 1861, and the First Regular Annual Session of the Senate of the State of Alabama* (Montgomery: Advertiser Book and Job Office, 1861), 28–29; *The American Annual Cyclopedia and Register of Important Events of the Year 1862* (New York: D. Appleton, 1872), 240; *Richmond Daily Dispatch*, 4 July 1863; *Address of the Atlanta Register*, 1.

28. *War of the Rebellion*, ser. 4, 3:129; *Atlanta Southern Confederacy*, 25 Oct. 1862.

29. "Past and Present," 198; *Journal of the Congress of the Confederate States*, 1:846; *Shreveport (LA) Southwestern*, 18 Sept. 1861; *Washington (AR) Telegraph*, 14 May 1862; *Richmond Daily Dispatch*, 13 Oct. 1862. For a more extended discussion of antiparty ideology in the Confederacy, see Rable, *Confederate Republic*.

30. Edward Mayes, *Lucius Q. C. Lamar: His Life, Times and Speeches, 1825–1893* (Nashville: Methodist Episcopal Church, South, 1896), 637; "What of the Confederacy?—The Present and Future," *DeBow's Review* 31 (Dec. 1861): 519–21; William B. McCash, *Thomas R. R. Cobb, 1823–1862: The Making of a Southern Nationalist* (Macon, GA: Mercer University Press, 1983), 219–23; *Richmond Daily Dispatch*, 4 Dec. 1861.

31. "Future Revolution in Southern School Books," *DeBow's Review* 30 (May–June 1861): 606–14; Adolphus Spalding Worrell, *The Principles of English Grammar* (Nashville:

Graves, Marks, 1861), iii; *Charleston Mercury*, 16 Feb. 1864; Calvin Henderson Wiley et al., *Address to the People of North Carolina* [Raleigh?, 1861?]; *Papers of Zebulon Vance*, 1:234.

32. Richardson, *Messages and Papers of Davis and the Confederacy*, 1:277, 395–400; David Eicher, *Dixie Betrayed: How the South Really Lost the Civil War* (New York: Little, Brown, 2006), 213.

33. *Charleston Mercury*, 25 Jan. 1862; "The Correspondence of Thomas Read Rootes Cobb, 1860–1862," ed. Augustus Longstreet Hull, *Southern Historical Association Publications* 11 (July 1907): 257–58; W. Gordon McCabe, "Political Corruption," *Southern Literary Messenger* 34 (Feb.–Mar. 1862): 81–89; Virginius, "Treating at Election-Time," ibid., 154–56; *Nashville Christian Advocate*, n.d., quoted in *Southern Cultivator* 19 (Nov. 1861): 293.

34. Augustus Baldwin Longstreet, *Fast-day Sermon Delivered in the Washington Street Methodist Episcopal Church, Columbia, S.C., June 13, 1861* (Columbia: Townsend & North, 1861), 4–12; Benjamin Morgan Palmer, *National Responsibility before God: A Discourse Delivered on the Day of Fasting, Humiliation and Prayer . . . June 13, 1861* (New Orleans: Price-Current Steam Book and Job Printing Office, 1861), 16–19; *Charleston Mercury*, 4 Feb. 1861.

35. *Mobile Daily Advertiser*, 15 Feb. 1861; *Atlanta Southern Confederacy*, 6 Mar. 1861; *Southern Historical Society Papers* 44 (1923): 91–92; *Speeches of William L. Yancey, Senator from the State of Alabama; Made in the Senate of the Confederate States* (Montgomery: Advertiser Book and Job Office, 1862), 10–16; Mary S. Estill, ed., "Diary of a Confederate Congressman, 1862–1863," pt. 1, *Southwestern Historical Quarterly* 28 (Apr. 1935): 276; *Charleston Mercury*, 13 June 1862.

36. *Charleston Mercury*, 31 Jan. 1862; *Memphis Daily Appeal* (Atlanta, GA), 21 Apr. 1864; Allen D. Candler, ed., *The Confederate Records of Georgia*, 5 vols. (Atlanta: Charles P. Byrd, 1909–11), 2:596–97; E. Merton Coulter, *The Confederate States of America, 1861–1865* (Baton Rouge: Louisiana State University Press, 1950), 394.

37. *Charleston Mercury*, 4 Mar. 1862, 18 Apr. 1863, 30 Mar. 1864.

38. Herschel Johnson to A. E. Cochran, 8 Oct. 1862, Herschel V. Johnson Papers, Rare Book, Manuscript, and Special Collections Library, Duke University; *The Correspondence of Jonathan Worth*, ed. James G. de Roulhac Hamilton, 2 vols. (Raleigh, NC: State Department of Archives and History, 1909), 1:141–42; Candler, *Confederate Records of Georgia*, 1:65; John Beauchamp Jones, *A Rebel War Clerk's Diary at the Confederate States Capital*, 2 vols. (Philadelphia: J. B. Lippincott, 1866), 1:24; *Memphis Daily Appeal* (Atlanta, GA), 22 Jan. 1864; Frank H. Alfriend, "The Great Danger of the Confederacy," *Southern Literary Messenger* 37 (Jan. 1863): 39–43; "Confederate Republicanism or Monarchy," *DeBow's Review* 32 (Jan.–Feb. 1862): 113–19.

39. *Richmond Enquirer*, 20 Mar. 1862; *War of the Rebellion*, ser. 1, 7:820; DuBose, *Yancey*, 2:682–83, 704; William L. Yancey to C. W. Jones et al., 8 Oct. 1862, William L. Yancey Papers, Alabama Department of Archives and History, Montgomery; *The Correspondence of Robert Toombs, Alexander H. Stephens, and Howell Cobb*, ed. Ulrich B. Phillips (Washington, DC: American Historical Association, 1913), 605–6; *Atlanta Southern Confederacy*, 25 Mar. 1864; *A Southern Woman of Letters: The Correspondence of Augusta Jane Evans Wilson*, ed. Rebecca Grant Sexton (Columbia: University of South Carolina Press, 2002), 92.

40. Lewis M. Ayer to Hammond, 29 Dec. 1863, Hammond Papers; Robert Fleming, *The Revised Elementary Spelling Book, Revised and Adapted to the Youth of the South-*

ern Confederacy, Interspersed with Bible Readings on Domestic Slavery (Atlanta: J. J. Toon, 1863), 97; DuBose, *Yancey*, 2:677–79; John Beauchamp Jones, *Rebel War Clerk's Diary*, 2:89–90; *Atlanta Southern Confederacy*, 2 Feb. 1864.

41. J. Barrett Cohen to Stephens, 1 Apr. 1864, Stephens Papers, Library of Congress; Stephens to Howell Cobb, 29 Aug. 1863, Alexander H. Stephens Papers, Robert W. Woodruff Library, Emory University, Atlanta; *Correspondence of Toombs, Stephens, and Cobb*, 636–37; *Milledgeville (GA) Confederate Union*, 28 Feb., 14, 21 Mar. 1865.

42. *Savannah Republican*, 13 Feb. 1864; *Daily Richmond Enquirer*, 20 Mar., 10 Aug. 1863; Henry St. Paul, *Our Home and Foreign Policy* (Mobile, AL: Office of the Daily Register and Advertiser, 1862), 12–13; Richard Hooker Wilmer, *Future Good—The Explanation of Present Reverses: A Sermon Preached at Mobile and Sundry Other Points in the State of Alabama during the Spring of 1864* (Charlotte, NC: Protestant Episcopal Church Publishing Association, 1864), 17–18.

43. *Senator Benjamin H. Hill of Georgia: His Life, Speeches and Writings* (Atlanta: H. C. Hudgins, 1891), 268–72, 288; *Milledgeville (GA) Southern Recorder*, 15 Sept. 1863; *Richmond Daily Dispatch*, 30 Sept. 1863, 13 Jan. 1864.

44. John J. D. Renfroe, *"The Battle is God's": A Sermon Preached before Wilcox's Brigade, on Fast Day, The 21st August, 1863, near Orange Court-House, Va.* (Richmond: Macfarlane & Fergusson, 1863), 26.

45. *New Orleans Daily Picayune*, 12 Mar. 1862; Frank A. Moore, ed., *The Rebellion Record: A Diary of American Events*, 12 vols. (New York: Arno, 1977), 8:341–45; Coulter, *Confederate States of America*, 394; *Correspondence of Toombs, Stephens, and Cobb*, 629.

46. *Charleston Mercury*, 25 Jan. 1862; Leroy M. Lee, *Our Country—Our Dangers—Our Duty: A Discourse Preached in Centenary Church, Lynchburg, Va., on the National Fast Day, August 21, 1863* (Richmond: Soldiers' Tract Association, [1863]), 20–21; Albert Gallatin Brown, *State of the Country: Speech of Hon. A. G. Brown of Mississippi in the Confederate Senate, December 24, 1863* ([Richmond?], 1863), 2; Wilson, *Southern Woman of Letters*, 77; *Richmond Enquirer*, 19 Feb. 1864; Moses D. Hoge et al., *Appeal to the People of Virginia, Richmond, February 22, 1865* (Richmond, 1865), 1–4. For a fine discussion of the sins of extortion and materialism in Confederate thought, see Faust, *Creation of Confederate Nationalism*, 41–57.

47. *Baton Rouge Advocate*, n.d., quoted in *Shreveport (LA) Southwestern*, 1 May 1861; *War of the Rebellion*, ser. 4, 1:318–19; *Atlanta Southern Confederacy*, 30 Oct. 1862; State of Virginia, *Documents. Called Session, 1863, and Session of 1863–64* (Richmond, 1863–64), no. 1, iii–viii; John Paris, *A Sermon Preached before Brig. Gen. Hoke's Brigade, at Kinston, N.C., on the 28th of February, 1864, by Rev. John Paris, Chaplain Fifty-Fourth Regiment N.C. Troops, upon the Death of Twenty-Two Men, Who Had Been Executed in the Presence of the Brigade for the Crime of Desertion* (Greensboro, NC: A. W. Ingold, 1864), 8–15.

48. John Beauchamp Jones, *Rebel War Clerk's Diary*, 2:271; *Tuskegee (AL) South Western Baptist*, 6 Nov. 1862; Stephen Elliott, *Gideon's Water-Lappers: A Sermon Preached in Christ Church, Savannah, on Friday, the 8th Day of April 1864. The Day Set Apart by the Congress of the Confederate States as a Day of Humiliation, Fasting and Prayer* (Macon, GA: Burke, Boykin, 1864), 15–20; *PJD*, 11:84.

49. The most cogent critique of Jefferson Davis as a revolutionary leader remains David M. Potter, "Jefferson Davis and the Political Factors in Confederate Defeat," in

Why the North Won the Civil War, ed. David Donald (Baton Rouge: Louisiana State University Press, 1960), 91–112.

50. *PJD*, 11:79; Stephen Elliott, *Ezra's Dilemma: A Sermon Preached in Christ Church, Savannah, on Friday, August 21st, 1863, Being the Day of Humiliation, Fasting and Prayer, Appointed by the President of the Confederate States* (Savannah, GA: Power Press of George N. Nichols, 1863), 8–12.

51. St. Paul, *Our Home and Foreign Policy*, 8–12; Mary Chesnut, *Mary Chesnut's Civil War*, ed. C. Vann Woodward (New Haven, CT: Yale University Press, 1981), 352; entry of 13 Aug. 1863, David Schenck Books, Southern Historical Collection, University of North Carolina, Chapel Hill; *Richmond Daily Dispatch*, 20 Jan. 1865.

52. *Richmond Daily Dispatch*, 10 Mar. 1864.

6. Wartime Nationalism and Race: Comparing the Visions of Confederate, Black Union, and White Union Soldiers

1. Captain Robert Snead, 50 VA, Greenbrier Courthouse, VA, to his wife, 18 Oct. 1861, Robert Winn Snead Papers, Confederate Military Manuscripts, ser. A, reel 40, Virginia Historical Society, Richmond.

2. *Missouri Army Argus* (Osceola), 30 Nov. 1861, 4, Missouri Historical Society, St. Louis. The *Argus* was the camp paper of the Missouri (Confederate) State Guard.

3. Josiah Patterson, Manassas, VA, to his sons, 13 Dec. 1861, in *Dear Mother: Don't Grieve About Me. If I Get Killed I'll Only be Dead; Letters from Georgia Soldiers in the Civil War*, ed. Mills Lane (Savannah, GA: Beehive, 1977), 89.

4. Private Thomas Taylor, 6 AL, Fairfax Station, VA, to his wife, 15 Oct. 1861, Thomas S. Taylor Letters, Alabama Department of Archives and History, Montgomery. See also Private Ivy Duggan, 15 GA, Manassas Junction, VA, to *Central Georgian*, 7 Sept. 1861, Ivy W. Duggan Letters, Georgia Department of Archives and History, Atlanta.

5. Confederates were not wholly unique, of course, in connecting nationalism to self-interest and to the best interests of their families. David Potter famously discussed such a dynamic within the phenomenon of nationalism more generally in his essay "The Historian's Use of Nationalism and Vice Versa," *American Historical Review* 67 (July 1962): 924–50. But Confederates' understanding of the relationship between personal and national interests differed from that of Union soldiers and civilians. See the discussion below, as well as Nina Silber, *Gender and the Sectional Conflict* (Chapel Hill: University of North Carolina Press, 2009), esp. chap. 1.

6. Private James Zimmerman, 57 NC, Orange Court House, VA, to his wife, 16 Aug. 1863, James Zimmerman Papers, Special Collections, Perkins Library, Duke University, Durham, NC. See also Private J. Marcus Hefner, 57 NC, Goldsboro, NC, to his wife, 4 Mar. 1864, Marcus Hefner Papers, North Carolina Department of Archives and History, Raleigh.

7. Sergeant John French White, 32 VA, Fredericksburg, VA, to Martha White, 30 Nov. 1862, John French White Papers, Confederate Military Manuscripts, ser. A, reel 42, Virginia Historical Society. White did not desert; as was true for many soldiers, White's allegiance to the Confederacy was taxed but not broken.

8. Lieutenant Frank Peak, Byrne's Infantry Battery (AR), Alleghany City, PA, diary, Dec. 1863, Frank P. Peak narrative, Confederate Military Manuscripts, ser B, reel 5, Louisiana and Lower Mississippi Valley Collection, Hill Memorial Library, Louisiana State University, Baton Rouge.

9. See esp. Mark A. Noll, "The Bible and Slavery," in *Religion and the American Civil War,* ed. Randall M. Miller, Harry S. Stout, and Charles Reagan Wilson (New York: Oxford University Press, 1998), 43–73. For a collection of antebellum and wartime sermons emphasizing the relationship between slavery and moral orthodoxy, see the sermons of Charles Colcock Jones, James H. Thornwell, Benjamin Morgan Palmer, and J. W. Tucker in *God Ordained This War: Sermons on the Sectional Crisis,* ed. David Chesebrough (Columbia: University of South Carolina Press, 1991). For recent emphasis on a particular group of Confederate soldiers' religious certainty, see Jason Phillips, *Diehard Rebels: The Confederate Culture of Invincibility* (Athens: University of Georgia Press, 2007), chap. 1.

10. See Stephanie McCurry, *Masters of Small Worlds: Yeoman Households, Gender Relations, and the Political Culture of the Antebellum South Carolina Low Country* (New York: Oxford University Press, 1995); Silber, *Gender and the Sectional Conflict;* and LeeAnn Whites, *The Civil War as a Crisis in Gender: Augusta, Georgia, 1860–1890* (Athens: University of Georgia Press, 1995). I would like to thank James Oakes, whose critique of this point pushed me to sharpen and clarify my meaning.

11. "The Irrepressible Conflict," *Richmond Enquirer,* 2 Oct. 1860, 1.

12. Private John Washington Calton, 56 NC, Weldon, NC, to his brother and sister-in-law, 27 Mar. 1864, John Washington Calton Letters, North Carolina Department of Archives and History. Although such rumors were almost certainly false, they were no less potent, because men like Calton fervently believed they were true and saw them as reason to fight. For another soldier's remarks on the dangers of black men seducing white women if the Yankees won, see Private Thomas Kelley, Henrico County, VA, to his cousin, 6 June 1864, Thomas F. Kelley Papers, Special Collections, Perkins Library, Duke University.

13. Private John Street, 8 TX, Tishomingo County, MS, to Melinda Street, 25 Feb. 1862, John K. and Melinda East Street Papers, Southern Historical Collection, University of North Carolina, Chapel Hill.

14. See Bertram Wyatt-Brown, *Southern Honor: Ethics and Behavior in the Old South* (New York: Oxford University Press, 1982); idem, *Yankee Saints and Southern Sinners* (Baton Rouge: Louisiana State University Press, 1985); Edward L. Ayers, *Vengeance and Justice* (New York: Oxford University Press, 1984), esp. chap. 1; Kenneth Greenberg, *Masters and Statesmen: The Political Culture of American Slavery* (Baltimore: Johns Hopkins University Press, 1985); and idem, *Honor and Slavery* (Princeton, NJ: Princeton University Press, 1996).

15. "The Fight," a popular antebellum story by the Georgian writer Augustus Baldwin Longstreet, illustrates important points about the concepts of honor and insult. "The Fight" is about friends named Billy Stallings and Bob Durham. When Billy insults Bob's wife without knowing who she is, both men quickly recognize that the insult questions Bob's right and ability to control his wife and protect her reputation and therefore can not be allowed to pass. The two men pitch into a brawl that costs Bob his left ear and

one of his fingers and costs Bill the tip of his nose. See Augustus Baldwin Longstreet, "The Fight," in *Georgia Scenes, Characters, Incidents &c in the First half Century of the Republic, By a Native Georgian* (New York, 1851), 53–64. This work of fiction commented on a well-documented historical reality: rates of personal violence among white southern men exceeded national rates, and fights did arise from perceived insults or slights. See Ayers, *Vengeance and Justice,* 9–33; Elliott J. Gorn, "'Gouge and Bite, Pull Hair and Scratch': The Social Significance of Fighting in the Southern Backcountry," *American Historical Review* 90 (Feb. 1985): 18–43; and Christopher J. Olsen, *Political Culture and Secession in Mississippi: Masculinity, Honor, and the Antiparty Tradition, 1830–1860* (New York: Oxford University Press, 2000).

16. Charles Trueheart, Charlottesville, VA, to his sister, 1 Mar. 1861 (misdated), in *Rebel Brothers: The Civil War Letters of the Truehearts,* ed. Edward B. Williams (College Station: Texas A & M University Press, 1995), 21–22.

17. Private William Bellamy, 18 NC, near Richmond, VA, diary, July 1862, William James Bellamy Papers, Southern Historical Collection, University of North Carolina, Chapel Hill.

18. "Irrepressible Conflict," 1.

19. Petition signed by "North Carolinians in prison at Johnson's Island, 231 in all," Johnson's Island, OH, 30 Mar. 1864, Thomas Jefferson Green Papers, Southern Historical Collection, University of North Carolina, Chapel Hill.

20. Duggan Camp Taylor, Centreville, VA, to *Central Georgian,* 13 Sept. 1861, Duggan Letters.

21. Lieutenant Christopher Winsmith, 1 SC, Sullivan's Island, SC, to his mother, 24 Apr. 1861, John Christopher Winsmith Papers, Museum of the Confederacy, Richmond, VA.

22. Private Joseph Bruckmuller, 7 TX, address delivered to other prisoners at Ft. Douglas Prison, Chicago, June 1862, Joseph Bruckmuller Notebook, Center for American History, University of Texas, Austin.

23. Chaplain Robert Bunting, 8 TX Cavalry, Auburn, AL, to *Houston Telegraph,* 17 Feb. 1865, Robert Franklin Bunting Papers, Tennessee State Library and Archives, Nashville.

24. Private Grant Taylor, 40 AL, Spanish Fort, AL, to Malinda Taylor, 11 Jan. 1865, in *This Cruel War: The Civil War Letters of Grant and Malinda Taylor, 1862–1865,* ed. Ann K. Blomquist and Robert A. Taylor (Macon, GA: Mercer University Press, 2000), 322–23.

25. Desertion rates soared to 40% and beyond in some units; once the Army evacuated Richmond, the rate became impossible to estimate, even as the number continued to dwindle to the approximately 28,000 who remained on 9 April 1865 (down from approximately 56,000 on 1 March). See William Marvel, *Lee's Last Retreat: The Flight to Appomattox* (Chapel Hill: University of North Carolina Press, 2002); J. Tracy Power, *Lee's Miserables: Life in the Army of Northern Virginia from the Wilderness to Appomattox* (Chapel Hill: University of North Carolina Press, 2002); and Mark A. Weitz, *More Damning Than Slaughter: Desertion in the Confederate Army* (Lincoln: University of Nebraska Press, 2005). By the spring of 1865, soldiers had many reasons for deserting besides black enlistment of course, the suffering of their families at home most likely topping the list, but that suffering was not new in March, whereas black enlistment was, meaning that for

men who had been torn between home needs and the continued fight, black enlistment proved a final straw.

26. *Liberator*, 30 Aug. 1861, quoted in James M. McPherson, *The Negro's Civil War: How American Negroes Felt and Acted during the War for the Union* (New York: Pantheon Books, 1965), 40.

27. *Anglo-African*, 11 May 1861, 1.

28. Alfred Green, "The Colored Philadelphians Forming Regiments," *Philadelphia Press*, 22 Apr. 1861; idem, *Letters and Discussions on the Formation of Colored Regiments* (Philadelphia, 1862).

29. J. H. Hall, 54 MA, Morris Island, SC, to editor of *Christian Recorder* (Philadelphia), 3 Aug. 1864, printed 27 Aug. 1864, 1.

30. For a discussion of white soldiers' view of the relationship between soldiering and manhood, see Reid Mitchell, *Civil War Soldiers* (New York: Touchstone Books, 1988), esp. chap. 3 and pp. 17–18, 42. See also Stephen Berry, *All That Makes a Man: Love and Ambition in the Civil War South* (New York: Oxford University Press, 2003). On black men's view of the relationship between manhood and the Civil War, including, though not exclusively, soldiering, see Kathleen Ann Clark, *Defining Moments: African American Commemoration and Political Culture in the South, 1863–1913* (Chapel Hill: University of North Carolina Press, 2005), 13–24, 56–60.

31. Sergeant Isaiah Welch, 55 MA, Folly Island, SC, to editor of *Christian Recorder* (Philadelphia), 15 Oct. 1863, printed 24 Oct. 1863, 2.

32. Private Spotswood Rice, 67 United States Colored Infantry, Benton Barracks, MO, to Miss Kitty Diggs, 3 Sept. 1864, quoted in *Freedom: A Documentary History of Emancipation, 1861–1867*, vol. 1, *The Destruction of Slavery*, ed. Ira Berlin et al. (New York: Cambridge University Press, 1982), 689–90.

33. Welch to editor of *Christian Recorder* (Philadelphia), 2 Dec. 1863, printed 19 Dec. 1863, 2.

34. Private Daniel Walker, 54 MA, Morris Island, SC, to editor of *Christian Recorder* (Philadelphia), 15 Jan. 1864, printed 30 Jan. 1864, 1.

35. David Williamson, 11 United States Heavy Artillery, Fort Banks, LA, to editor of *Anglo-African*, Mar. 1865, printed 8 Apr. 1865, 2.

36. For further discussion of the millennial idea among white northerners that the United States had special responsibilities to serve as a worldwide example, see Robert Bellah, *The Broken Covenant: American Civil Religion in Time of Trial* (New York: Seabury, 1975); Samuel S. Hill Jr., *The South and the North in American Religion* (Athens: University of Georgia Press, 1981); Richard T. Hughes and C. Leonard Allen, *Illusions of Innocence: Protestant Primitivism in America, 1630–1875* (Chicago: University of Chicago Press, 1988); Stuart McConnell, *Glorious Contentment: The Grand Army of the Republic, 1865–1900* (Chapel Hill: University of North Carolina Press, 1992); Randall M. Miller, Harry S. Stout, and Charles Reagan Wilson, introduction to Miller, Stout, and Wilson, *Religion and the American Civil War;* James H. Moorhead, *American Apocalypse: Yankee Protestants and the Civil War, 1860–1869* (New Haven, CT: Yale University Press, 1978); and Philip Shaw Paludan, "Religion and the American Civil War," in Miller, Stout, and Wilson, *Religion and the American Civil War.*

37. Captain Alphonso Barto, 52 IL, near Corinth, MS, to his father, 27 May 1862, Al-

phonso Barto Letters, Illinois State Historical Library, Springfield; *Illinois Fifty-Second* (Stewartsville, MO), 1 (15 Jan. 1862), 3, Illinois State Historical Library.

38. Private Leigh Webber, 1 KS, Tipton, MO, to the John S. Brown family, 24 Apr. 1862, John S. Brown Family Papers, reel 2, Kansas State Historical Society, Topeka.

39. Sergeant E. C. Hubbard, 13 IL, Rolla, MO, to his brother, 9 Aug. 1861, E. C. Hubbard Letters, Special Collections, University of Arkansas, Fayetteville.

40. See, e.g., Hubbard, Rolla, MO, to his sister, 3 Dec. 1861, ibid., in which he complained that policies that were not aimed at slavery were prolonging the war.

41. M., 8 WI, Pilot Knob, MO, to *Wisconsin State Journal,* 15 Nov. 1861, E. B. Quiner Correspondence of Wisconsin Volunteers, reel 1, 2:22, State Historical Society of Wisconsin, Madison. In "Slavery and the Slave Power: A Crucial Distinction," *Civil War History* 15 (1969): 5–18, Larry Gara differentiates between northern hostility to slaveholders' power and northerners' feelings about slavery, an institution, he argues, about which they were largely indifferent. That distinction may very well have applied before the war, but during the war Union troops did not merely talk about punishing or chastening slaveholders or curtailing the power of an oligarchy that just happened to own slaves. Instead, they clearly and repeatedly identified the institution of slavery itself as the source of the country's problems. To take just a few examples, it was the "stigma" of slavery, not the actions or attitudes of slaveholders, as Private Jerome Cutler, of Vermont, saw it, that brought "animosities and wranglings" down on the nation. Private Jerome Cutler, 2 VT, Camp Griffin, VA, to his fiancée, 11 Nov. 1861, Jerome Cutler Letters, Vermont Historical Society, Barre. When two slave women about to be sold as concubines ran to the Seventh Wisconsin, "every private in the ranks" cursed, not the individual who owned the women or the wealth and power that the sale of them would generate, but rather the actual "system" of slavery, because it "tramples on the honor of man, and makes merchandise of the virtue of women." W.D.W., 7 WI, Arlington Heights, VA, to his hometown newspaper, 16 Dec. 1861, E. B. Quiner Correspondence of Wisconsin Volunteers, reel 1, 2:4–5. For similar points, see also, among many others, Sgt. C. Frank Shepard, 1st MI Cavalry, Washington, DC, to his wife, 14 Oct. 1861, C. Frank Shepard Papers, Schoff Collection, Clements Library, University of Michigan; Private George Baxter, 24 MA, near Annapolis, MD, to Jim Baxter, 14 Dec. 1861, George H. Baxter Correspondence, Massachusetts Historical Society, Boston; and Webber, Trenton, TN, to Brown family, 27 June 1862, Brown Family Papers, reel 2.

42. "Enlisted soldier," 3 WI, near Harper's Ferry, VA, to *Wisconsin State Journal,* Oct. 1861, E. B. Quiner Correspondence of Wisconsin Volunteers, reel 1, 1:176.

43. Private John Boucher, 10 MO, Camp Holmes, MO, to his wife, 7 Dec. 1861, Boucher Family Papers, Civil War Miscellany Collection, 2nd ser., United States Army Military History Institute, Carlisle, PA.

44. Quartermaster Sergeant Thomas Low, 23 NY Artillery, Washington, DC, diary, 29 Mar. 1862, Thomas Low Papers and Diary, Special Collections, Perkins Library, Duke University.

45. Webber, Gibson County, TN, to Brown family, 24 July 1862, Brown Family Papers, reel 2.

46. Private Adelbert Bly, 32 WI, Memphis, TN, to Anna, 9 Nov. 1862, Adelbert M. Bly Correspondence, State Historical Society of Wisconsin.

47. Lieutenant J. Q. A. Campbell, 5 IA, near Winchester, TN, diary, 12 Nov. 1863, quoted in *The Union Must Stand: The Civil War Diary of John Quincy Adams Campbell, Fifth Iowa Volunteer Infantry,* ed. Mark Grimsley and Todd D. Miller (Knoxville: University of Tennessee Press, 2000), 131.

48. Campbell, near Vicksburg, MS, diary, 4 July 1863, quoted in ibid., 110.

49. Sgt. James Jessee, 8 IL, Helena, AR, diary, 31 Dec. 1863, James W. Jessee Diaries, Special Collections, University of Kansas. A New Hampshire soldier agreed that God had sent a "durstructive war" as a rebuke to all who, through sins of commission or omission, allowed slavery to woo them away from "the side of truth and rite." See Private Roswell Holbrook, 14 NH, Washington, DC, to his cousin, 11 Jan. 1864, Roswell Holbrook Letters, Vermont Historical Society.

50. Private Ransom Bedell, 39 IL, "American Slavery," original essay written for his cousin, summer 1863, Ransom Bedell Papers, Illinois State Historical Library.

51. Private Wilbur Fisk, 2 VT, near Warrenton, VA, to *Green Mountain Freeman,* 13 Aug. 1863, in *Hard Marching Every Day: The Civil War Letters of Private Wilbur Fisk, 1861–1865,* ed. Emil Rosenblatt and Ruth Rosenblatt (Lawrence: University of Kansas Press, 1992), 135. That Fisk wrote this letter to a public forum, his hometown newspaper, suggests that he may have hoped to help change the attitudes he wrote about.

52. Captain Carlos Lyman, 100 United States Colored Troops, Camp Foster, TN, to his sister, 12 Feb. 1865, Carlos Parsons Lyman Papers, Western Reserve Historical Society, Cleveland, OH.

53. Jessee, Helena, AR, diary, 31 Dec. 1863.

54. Private Constant Hanks, 20 NY Militia, near Brandy Station, VA, to his mother and sister, 1 Apr. 1864, Constant Hanks Papers, Special Collections, Perkins Library, Duke University.

55. Captain William Dunham, 36 OH, Meadow Bluffs, VA, to his wife, 3 June 1862, William Dunham Letters, Civil War Miscellany Collection, United States Army Military History Institute.

56. Captain M. M. Miller, 9 LA Volunteers of African Descent, above Vicksburg, MS, to his aunt, 10 June 1863, published in *Galena (IL) Advertiser,* reprinted in *Anglo-African,* 11 July 1863, 1.

57. Sergeant William Stevens, 4 VT, "Camp Parole," Annapolis, MD, to his sister, 26 Mar. 1864, quoted in *A War of the People: Vermont Civil War Letters,* ed. Jeffrey D. Marshall (Hanover, NH: University Press of New England, 1999), 219. When he wrote this letter, Stevens had just been released from a Richmond prison and was waiting to go home.

58. Private George Hudson, 100 IL, Blue Springs, TN, to folks at home, 10 Apr. 1865, George A. Hudson Collection, People at War, collection 138, reel 54, Library of Congress.

59. Hanks to his mother and sister, 1 Apr. 1864; Lieutenant Joseph Scroggs, 5 United States Colored Troops, near Norfolk, VA, diary, 30 Mar. 1864, Joseph Scroggs Diary, *Civil War Times Illustrated* Collection, United States Army Military History Institute.

60. The camp paper of the Second Colorado Cavalry, for example, embraced black suffrage, desegregation of public facilities, and the news that a John Rock had been accepted to argue before the Supreme Court. See *Soldier's Letter* (Fort Riley, KS), 17 June, 13 Feb. 1865, Kansas State Historical Society.

61. Hubbard, Woodville, AL, to his brother, 12 Apr. 1864, Hubbard Letters.

62. "Now and in time to be / Wherever green is worn / Are changed, changed utterly: / A terrible beauty is born." William Butler Yeats, "Easter 1916," first published in *Michael Robartes and the Dancer* (1921), reprinted in *W. B. Yeats: The Poems*, ed. Richard J. Finneran (New York: Macmillan, 1989), 180–82.

7. Emancipation without Slavery: Remembering the Union Victory

1. Nina Silber, *The Romance of Reunion: Northerners and the South, 1865–1900* (Chapel Hill: University of North Carolina Press, 1993), 3. On the new orientation in the historical profession, see Peter Novick, *That Noble Dream: The "Objectivity Question" and the American Historical Profession* (Cambridge: Cambridge University Press, 1988), 72–80; on historians' acceptance of Confederate history, see Jim Cullen, *The Civil War in Popular Culture: A Reusable Past* (Washington, DC: Smithsonian Institution Press, 1995), 20–23.

2. Tony Horwitz, *Confederates in the Attic: Dispatches from the Unfinished Civil War* (New York: Pantheon Books, 1998), 135.

3. C. Vann Woodward, *The Strange Career of Jim Crow* (New York: Oxford University Press, 1955), 17–21; Novick, *That Noble Dream*, 76–77; Silber, *Romance of Reunion*, 93–123; David Blight, *Race and Reunion: The Civil War in American Memory* (Cambridge, MA: Harvard University Press, 2001), 171–210.

4. Blight, *Race and Reunion*, 4.

5. Eric Foner, *Reconstruction: America's Unfinished Revolution* (New York: Harper & Row, 1988), 255; idem, *The Story of American Freedom* (New York: W. W. Norton, 1998), 100; David Brion Davis, *Slavery and Human Progress* (New York: Oxford University Press, 1984), 270–71.

6. Thomas J. Brown, *The Public Art of Civil War Commemoration: A Brief History with Documents* (New York: Bedford/St. Martin's, 2004), 142; Foner, *Story of American Freedom*, 15–16; idem, *Reconstruction*, 66.

7. Elizabeth Cady Stanton, Susan B. Anthony, and Matilda Joslyn Gage, eds., *A History of Woman Suffrage*, vols. 1–3 (New York: Fowler & Wells, 1881–89), 2:3, 790.

8. Ibid., 2:88, 3:226. On the emergence of an independent women's suffrage movement in the Reconstruction era, see Ellen DuBois, *Feminism and Suffrage: The Emergence of an Independent Women's Movement in America, 1848–1869* (Ithaca, NY: Cornell University Press, 1978).

9. Amy Dru Stanley, *From Bondage to Contract: Wage Labor, Marriage, and the Market in the Age of Slave Emancipation* (Cambridge: Cambridge University Press, 1998), 60–97, quotations from 87 and 86.

10. Ibid., 75.

11. Brian Donovan, *White Slave Crusades: Race, Gender, and Anti-Vice Activism, 1887–1917* (Urbana: University of Illinois Press, 2006), 17–36. On antebellum abolitionists' linkage of slavery and prostitution, see Stanley, *From Bondage to Contract*, 240–43.

12. Clifford Roe, quoted in Donovan, *White Slave Crusades*, 32–33.

13. Quotations from ibid., 33–34. Donovan also observes how the narratives regarding the urban white slave trade were racialized in stories suggesting that African Ameri-

cans worked as the procurers of young white women, deemed sexually innocent because of their race. See ibid., 93–107.

14. Ellen Henrotin, quoted in ibid., 35.

15. Anti-imperialist speaker, quoted in Michael Salman, *The Embarrassment of Slavery: Controversies over Bondage and Nationalism in the American Colonial Philippines* (Berkeley and Los Angeles: University of California Press, 2001), 34.

16. Eric Love, *Race over Empire: Racism and U.S. Imperialism, 1865–1900* (Chapel Hill: University of North Carolina Press, 2004), 183–84.

17. David Starr Jordan, quoted in Salman, *Embarrassment of Slavery*, 32–33. For a fascinating discussion of German imperialist attitudes regarding the need to impose coercive labor practices on nonwhite colonial subjects, see Andrew Zimmerman, "A German Alabama in Africa: The Tuskegee Expedition to German Togo and the Transnational Origins of West African Cotton Growers," *American Historical Review* 110 (Dec. 2005): 1362–98.

18. James McPherson, *The Abolitionist Legacy: From Reconstruction to the NAACP* (Princeton, NJ: Princeton University Press, 1975), 327; Edward Atkinson, quoted in Salman, *Embarrassment of Slavery*, 37.

19. Salman, *Embarrassment of Slavery; Davis, Slavery and Human Progress*, 236–37. The tendency among European powers to draw on a legacy of emancipation is analyzed in Frederick Cooper, "Conditions Analogous to Slavery: Imperialism and Free Labor Ideology in Africa," in *Beyond Slavery: Explorations of Race, Labor, and Citizenship in Postemancipation Societies*, ed. Frederick Cooper, Thomas Holt, and Rebecca Scott (Chapel Hill: University of North Carolina Press, 2000), 107–49.

20. Love, *Race over Empire*, 45.

21. Quotations from ibid., 169; Willard Gatewood, *Black Americans and the White Man's Burden, 1898–1903* (Urbana: University of Illinois Press, 1975), 194; and Salman, *Embarrassment of Slavery*, 208.

22. Lloyd George, quoted in Merrill Peterson, *Lincoln in American Memory* (New York: Oxford University Press, 1994), 199.

23. Gatewood, *Black Americans and the White Man's Burden*, 282; James Weldon Johnson, quoted in Mary Renda, *Taking Haiti: Military Occupation and the Culture of U.S. Imperialism, 1915–1940* (Chapel Hill: University of North Carolina Press, 2001), 191, 193.

24. Penny Von Eschen, *Race against Empire: Black Americans and Anti-Colonialism, 1937–1957* (Ithaca, NY: Cornell University Press, 1997), 40–43; *Chicago Defender*, quoted in ibid., 41.

25. McPherson, *Abolitionist Legacy*, 327–28; Renda, *Taking Haiti*, 149.

26. NSC 68, quoted in Foner, *Story of American Freedom*, 253.

27. For more on the international context that shaped the United States' discussion of its history of racism and civil rights, see Mary Dudziak, *Cold War Civil Rights: Race and the Image of American Democracy* (Princeton, NJ: Princeton University Press, 2000). On the antislavery and anticolonial message of Hollywood films of the 1950s, see Melani McAlister, *Epic Encounters: Culture, Media, and U.S. Interests in the Middle East since 1945* (Berkeley and Los Angeles: University of California Press, 2005), 43–83.

28. For the full transcript of Condoleeza Rice's interview with *Essence* magazine, see http://www.scoop.co.nz/stories/WO0609/S00094.htm (accessed 3 November 2008).

8. Redeeming a Failed Revolution: Confederate Memory

1. For a succinct discussion of wartime casualties, see James M. McPherson, *Battle Cry of Freedom: The Civil War Era* (New York: Oxford University Press, 1988), 471–77, 854. In *General Lee's Army: From Victory to Collapse* (New York: Free Press, 2008), Joseph Glatthaar concludes that nearly one in eight men in Lee's army (11.8%) was killed in action. Almost precisely the same number (11.6%) died from disease. Along with those who were killed in accidents, executions, or other noncombat violence, nearly one in four men (23.9%) died while in military service. Almost three in ten additional soldiers (28%) were wounded at least once. Another quarter (26.7) were captured before the final surrender. In total, nearly half of all soldiers (48.1%) were killed, wounded, or died of disease, and more than two of every three were killed, wounded, captured, or died of disease. See esp. the prologue to Glatthaar's book.

2. Eric T. Dean, *Shook over Hell: Post-Traumatic Stress, Vietnam, and the Civil War* (Cambridge, MA: Harvard University Press, 1997), 100–114; Judith Pizzaro, Roxane Cohen Silver, and JoAnn Prose, "Physical and Mental Costs of Traumatic War Experience among Civil War Veterans," *Archives of General Psychiatry* 63 (2006): 193–200; David Andrew Silkenat, "Suicide, Divorce, and Debt in Civil War Era North Carolina" (PhD diss., University of North Carolina at Chapel Hill, 2007), chap. 4. For dissenting views, see Gaines M. Foster, "Coming to Terms with Defeat: Post-Vietnam America and the Post–Civil War South," *Virginia Quarterly Review* 66 (1990): 20–22; and Wiley Sword, *Southern Invincibility: A History of the Confederate Heart* (New York: St. Martin's, 1999).

3. Silkenat, "Suicide, Divorce, and Debt," 79–80.

4. Mitchell Snay, *Gospel of Disunion: Religion and Separatism in the Antebellum South* (Chapel Hill: University of North Carolina Press, 1997); Christopher H. Owen, *The Sacred Flame of Love: Methodism and Society in Nineteenth-Century Georgia* (Athens: University of Georgia Press, 1998), 93–113; W. Scott Poole, *Never Surrender: Confederate Memory and Conservatism in the South Carolina Upcountry* (Athens: University of Georgia Press, 2004), 37–56; Charles Reagan Wilson, *Baptized in Blood: The Religion of the Lost Cause, 1865–1920* (Athens: University of Georgia Press, 1980); Edward Blum, *Reforging the White Republic: Race, Religion, and American Nationalism, 1865–1898* (Baton Rouge: Louisiana State University Press, 2005); Mark A. Noll, *The Civil War as a Theological Crisis* (Chapel Hill: University of North Carolina Press, 2006).

5. Rev. J. L. Gilbert, quoted in Wilson, *Baptized in Blood*, 74.

6. Wallace Evan Davies, *Patriotism on Parade: The Story of Veterans' and Hereditary Organizations in America, 1783–1900* (Cambridge, MA: Harvard University Press, 1955); Gaines M. Foster, *Ghosts of the Confederacy: Defeat, the Lost Cause, and the Emergence of the New South* (New York: Oxford University Press, 1987), esp. chaps. 7–8.

7. Kathleen Lynn Gorman, "When Johnny Came Marching Home Again: Confederate Veterans in the New South" (PhD diss., University of California, Riverside, 1994), chap. 2; idem, "Confederate Pensions as Southern Social Welfare," in *Before the New Deal: Social Welfare in the South, 1830–1930*, ed. Elna C. Green (Chapel Hill: University of North Carolina Press, 1999), 24–39.

8. *Confederate Veteran* 1 (May 1893): 353; Herman Hattaway, "Clio's Southern Soldiers: The United Confederate Veterans and History," *Louisiana History* 12 (Summer 1971):

214–16. On the Sons of the Confederacy, see Foster, *Ghosts of the Confederacy*, 178–79.

9. Mrs. George T. Fry, "Memorial Day—Its Origin," *Confederate Veteran* 1 (May 1893): 149; *A History of the Origins of Memorial Day as Adopted by the Ladies' Memorial Association of Columbus, Georgia* (Columbus: Lizzie Rutherford Chapter of the Daughters of the Confederacy, 1898), 24–25; Ellen M. Litwicki, *America's Public Holidays, 1865–1920* (Washington, DC: Smithsonian Institution Press, 2000), chap. 1.

10. *Ceremonies in Augusta, Georgia, Laying the Cornerstone of the Confederate Monument with an Oration by Clement A. Evans* (Augusta, GA, 1875), 9. On women, memorialization, and gender tensions, see Drew Gilpin Faust, *Mothers of Invention: Women of the Slaveholding South in the American Civil War* (Chapel Hill: University of North Carolina Press, 2004), 234–54; Foster, *Ghosts of the Confederacy*, 36–46; and LeeAnn Whites, *The Civil War as a Crisis in Gender: Augusta, Georgia, 1860–1890* (Athens: University of Georgia Press, 1995), 160–224.

11. Patricia R. Loughridge and Edward D. C. Campbell Jr., *Women in Mourning* (Richmond, VA: Museum of the Confederacy, 1985), 25.

12. On white women and the romanticized fiction of the southern past, see David Blight, *Race and Reunion: The Civil War in American Memory* (Cambridge, MA: Harvard University Press, 2001), esp. chap. 7; Jane Turner Censer, *The Reconstruction of White Southern Womanhood, 1865–1895* (Baton Rouge: Louisiana State University Press, 2003); and Sarah Gardner, *Blood and Irony* (Chapel Hill: University of North Carolina Press, 2003).

13. Mildred L. Rutherford Scrapbook VII, 67, Museum of the Confederacy, Richmond, VA; Cordelia Powell Oldenheimer to Janet Randolph, 11 Feb., 14 Mar. 1923, box 15, Randolph Papers, Museum of the Confederacy; Catherine Clinton, *Tara Revisited: Women, War, and the Plantation Legend* (New York: Abbeville, 1995), 191–204; Grace Elizabeth Hale, *Making Whiteness: The Culture of Segregation in the South, 1890–1940* (New York: Pantheon, 1998), 85–120; Micki McElya, "Commemorating the Color Line: The National Mammy Monument Controversy of the 1920s," in *Monuments to the Lost Cause: Women, Art, and the Landscapes of Southern Memory*, ed. Cynthia Mills and Pamela H. Simpson (Knoxville: University of Tennessee Press, 2003), 203–18; Cheryl Thurber, "The Development of the Mammy Image and Mythology," in *Southern Women: Histories and Identities*, ed. Virginia Bernhard et al. (Columbia: University of Missouri Press, 1992), 87–108.

14. On women and Confederate monuments, see W. Fitzhugh Brundage, *The Southern Past: The Clash of Race and Memory* (Cambridge, MA: Harvard University Press, Belknap Press, 2005), esp. chap. 1; and Foster, *Ghosts of the Confederacy*. The best discussion of the enduring impact of Confederate memory is Karen L. Cox, *Dixie's Daughters: The United Daughters of the Confederacy and the Preservation of Confederate Culture* (Gainesville: University Press of Florida, 2003).

9. Traced by Blood: African Americans and the Legacies of the Civil War

1. William Faulkner, *The Hamlet: A Novel of the Snopes Family* (New York: Random House, 1931), 84.

2. Booker T. Washington, *Up From Slavery*, ed. W. Fitzhugh Brundage (Boston: Bedford Books, 2004), 47; Frederick Douglass, *Narrative of the Life of Frederick Douglass, an American Slave*, ed. David W. Blight (Boston: Bedford Books, 2003), 89.

3. Frederick Douglass, "Speech at the Thirty-Third Anniversary of the Jerry Rescue," Syracuse, NY, 1884, in Frederick Douglass Papers, reel 15, Library of Congress; idem, "Address Delivered on the Twenty-sixth Anniversary of Abolition in the District of Columbia," 16 Apr. 1888, ibid., reel 16.

4. Joseph C. Price, "The Race Problem Stated," in *Negro Orators and Their Orations*, ed. Carter G. Woodson (1925; reprint, New York: Russell & Russell, 1969), 490.

5. Mrs. A. W. Garber, ed., *In Memoriam Sempiternam*, commemorative book produced by the Confederate Memorial Literary Society (Richmond, VA: Confederate Museum, 1896), copy in Museum of the Confederacy, Richmond, 37–38. I thank John Coski for introducing me to this volume.

6. Ibid., 50–52, 54–56.

7. On Floyd's speech and the Augusta event, see *Atlanta Constitution*, 2 Jan. 1909.

8. Ibid.

9. Thomas Nelson Page, "Marse Chan," in *In Ole Virginia, or Marse Chan and Other Stories* (1887; reprint, New York: Scribner's, 1920), 4, 10. "Marse Chan" first appeared in *Century* 27 (Apr. 1884): 932–42.

10. Thomas Nelson Page, "Meh Lady," in *In Ole Virginia*, 80, 84–85. On Page's sentimentalism and influence over Civil War memory, see David W. Blight, *Race and Reunion: The Civil War in American Memory* (Cambridge, MA: Harvard University Press, 2001), 222–27.

11. *Christian Recorder* (Philadelphia), 13 July 1890.

12. On Booker T. Washington's efforts to forge a black reconciliationist memory, see Blight, *Race and Reunion*, 324–34.

13. On emancipation exhibitions, see ibid., 301–7, 372–75.

14. See ibid., chaps. 9–10.

15. Reverdy C. Ransom, "William Lloyd Garrison: A Centennial Oration," in Woodson, *Negro Orators and Their Orations*, 535–36.

16. James Weldon Johnson, "Fifty Years," *New York Times*, 1 Jan. 1913, reprinted in Johnson, *"Fifty Years" and Other Poems* (Boston: Cornhill, 1917), 1–5.

17. W. E. B. Du Bois, *The Souls of Black Folk* (1903; reprint, Boston: Bedford Books, 1997), 54–55.

18. For the story of Decoration Day at the Charleston racecourse, see Blight, *Race and Reunion*, 64–71. I first encountered the story in a file titled "First Decoration Day," in the Military Order of the Loyal Legion Collection, Houghton Library, Harvard University, which in turn led me to two newspapers accounts, *New York Tribune*, 13 May 1865, and *Charleston Daily Courier*, 2 May 1865. The account of the first Decoration Day in the paragraphs that follow is from these three sources.

Contributors

DAVID W. BLIGHT is Class of 1954 Professor of American History at Yale University. His publications include *A Slave No More: Two Men Who Escaped to Freedom, Including Their Narratives of Emancipation* and *Race and Reunion: The Civil War in American Memory*.

W. FITZHUGH BRUNDAGE is William B. Umstead Professor of History at the University of North Carolina, Chapel Hill. His publications include *The Southern Past: A Clash of Race and Memory* and *Lynching in the New South: Georgia and Virginia, 1880–1930*.

RICHARD CARWARDINE is Rhodes Professor of American History at St. Catherine's College, Oxford University. His publications include *Lincoln: A Life of Purpose and Power* and *Evangelicals and Politics in Antebellum America*.

WILLIAM J. COOPER, JR. is a Boyd Professor at Louisiana State University. His publications include *Jefferson Davis and the Civil War Era* and *Jefferson Davis, American*.

CHRISTA DIERKSHEIDE is a graduate student in history at the University of Virginia.

JOHN M. MCCARDELL, JR., is President Emeritus and College Professor of History at Middlebury College. His publications include *The Idea of a Southern Nation: Southern Nationalists and Southern Nationalism* and numerous articles.

JAMES M. MCPHERSON is George Henry Davis 1886 Professor of American History emeritus at Princeton University. His publications include *This Mighty Scourge: Perspectives on the Civil War* and *Battle Cry for Freedom: The Civil War Era.*

CHANDRA MANNING is an associate professor of history at Georgetown University. Her publications include *What This Cruel War Was Over: Soldiers, Slavery, and the Civil War* and numerous articles.

PETER S. ONUF is Thomas Jefferson Memorial Foundation Professor of History at the University of Virginia. His publications include *Jefferson's Empire: The Language of American Nationhood* and *Statehood and Union: A History of the Northwest Ordinance.*

GEORGE C. RABLE is Charles E. Summersell Professor of Southern History at the University of Alabama. His publications include *Fredericksburg! Fredericksburg!* and *The Confederate Republic: A Revolution against Politics.*

NINA SILBER is a professor of history at Boston University. Her publications include *Daughters of the Union: Northern Women Fight the Civil War* and *The Romance of Reunion: Northerners and the South, 1865–1900.*

SEAN WILENTZ is Sidney and Ruth Lapidus Professor in the American Revolutionary Era at Princeton University. His publications include *The Age of Reagan: A History, 1974–2008* and *The Rise of American Democracy: Jefferson to Lincoln.*

Index